COLLECTOR'S GUIDE TO
AMERICAN PRESSED GLASS
1825–1915

Wallace-Homestead Collector's Guide™ Series

Harry L. Rinker, Series Editor

Collector's Guide to American Pressed Glass, 1825–1915, by Kyle Husfloen
Collector's Guide to American Toy Trains, by Al and Susan Bagdade
Collector's Guide to Autographs, by Helen Sanders, George Sanders, and Ralph Roberts
Collector's Guide to Baseball Cards, by Troy Kirk
Collector's Guide to Comic Books, by John Hegenberger
Collector's Guide to Early Photographs, by O. Henry Mace
Collector's Guide to Quilts, by Suzy McLennan Anderson
Collector's Guide to Toys, Games, and Puzzles, by Harry L. Rinker
Collector's Guide to Treasures from the Silver Screen, by John Hegenberger
Collector's Guide to Victoriana, by O. Henry Mace

Contents

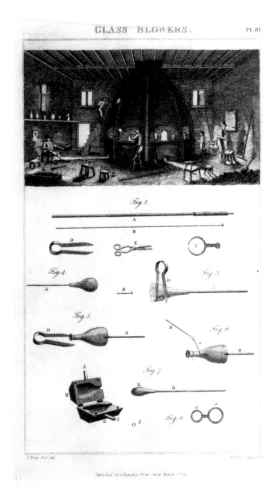

Fig. 2.

Fig. 4.   *Fig. 3.*

Fig. 5.

Fig. 6.

Fig. 7.

Fig. 8.

Fig. 1-2 An early English engraving showing glass blowers at work and their various tools, ca. 1810. Courtesy of the Corning Museum of Glass.

inside the mold and expand the gather slightly so that its sides pressed into the ribbing of the mold. The glass then could be raised carefully out of the mold and, now embossed with the ribbing design, blown even larger and shaped into a final form. This sort of pattern-molding had been used for generations as a simple way to dress up plain glass objects like bottles and small flasks, and it was used widely for this purpose in the eighteenth and into the nineteenth century. As technology improved these simple molds were produced in metal with hinges that made removing an object from them much easier. In the early nineteenth century, the larger hinged molds were carved with more complex geometric, figural, and scrolling designs. These full-sized molds, about the same size as the finished glass object they molded, were used extensively. From roughly 1820 to 1870 such molds produced decorative whiskey flasks that are highly collectible today. Versions of such molds also were used in the production of a special form of glass now called *blown-three-mold* by most collectors. Blown-three-mold glass, which includes pieces made in two-part and four-part molds, was more complex in design and more decorative than simple bottles and flasks. Pieces such as decanters, bowls, pitchers, tumblers, and a variety of simple tableware were produced widely using this technique. Anyone collecting early American glass should keep in mind that pattern-molded and blown-three-molded glassware continued in produuction even after the first true pressed glass was being made in this country. Being fairly simple and inexpensive to produce, this glassware competed well with early pressed glass and remained on the market until more sophisticated and efficient glass-pressing machines came into general use by the 1840s.

CHAPTER 2

Glassmaking after Jamestown:
The German Connection

After the failure of the glassmaking venture at Jamestown, it was many decades before the manufacture of glass was again attempted in the American colonies. Reportedly, glasshouses were set up during the mid–seventeenth century at scattered sites in Massachusetts and New York and near Philadelphia, but they did not prosper and probably supplied only a limited local market with the cheapest, poorest-quality glass for bottles and window panes. The best-quality glass had to be imported from abroad—and in British America that generally meant England. Any piece of glass would have been rare in seventeenth-century America, and only prosperous city dwellers had access to even crude glass for windows and common objects such as wine bottles and demijohns. Not until well into the eighteenth century did some Americans have enough money or status to worry about owning glass pieces, especially tableware.

As the English colonies grew and prospered in the eighteenth century, they provided a ready market for English-made textiles, metalware, ceramics, and glassware, and it became the policy of the English government to discourage any local production of luxury items in the colonies. As every student of American colonial history knows, the burgeoning factories established during the Industrial Revolution in eighteenth-century England used America as a dumping ground for their ever-growing output. In spite of controls from abroad, a few noteworthy entrepreneurs founded successful glass factories in colonial America and, using the production methods described earlier, began making glass for the American market. However, the most successful and famous of the early glassmakers were not English but German immigrants.

For centuries before America was settled, glassmaking had been a prosperous industry in regions of Germany. The production of cheap tableware in common greenish bottle glass as well as expensive colored wares predated Medieval Germany, and these wares found a ready market throughout Europe. No wonder the founders of Jamestown brought over Germans to help initiate their first feeble attempt at glassmaking. Thousands of German immigrants settled in "English" America in the late seventeenth and early eighteenth centuries, and three of these arrivals were responsible for the most notable glassworks set up in eighteenth-century America.

The first of these German glassmakers was Caspar Wistar, a Philadelphia brass buttonmaker by trade, who founded a glass factory in southern New Jersey in 1739. New Jersey was rich in high-quality sand to produce glass and forests to fire the furnace. Wistar brought fellow Germans from Europe to operate his glassworks, and they produced bottles and window glass as well as some tableware such as pitchers, bowls, and similar simple dishes. Although these wares would not have had a tremendous impact on a marketplace where imported English glass was most in demand, there apparently was a large enough local demand, especially in nearby Philadelphia, to keep the factory operating until 1780. All of the factory's output would have been free-blown pieces made from an everyday grade of dark green or amber glass, colors common in unrefined glass batches made with cheap, local ingredients. The style of the items made, particularly bottles and tableware, most likely would have followed the corresponding styles of peasant glassware made in Germany and central Europe during the same period. This makes sense when one considers where the glassmakers had been trained.

Fig. 2-1 These are among the few pieces that can be attributed to Caspar Wistar's glassworks. All descended in his family. The wine bottle carries the seal of Richard Wistar. Courtesy of the Corning Museum of Glass.

Not long after the Wistar factory was sold off by Caspar's son, Richard, former employee Jacob Stanger (Stenger) and his brothers started another factory in nearby Glassboro, New Jersey. Other of Wistar's workers probably found work there, and they and their glassmaking descendants continued to produce the traditional forms of early American free-blown glass that have long been referred to as the South Jersey style. In the last decades of the eighteenth century and into the early nineteenth century, glassworkers trained in the tradition of South Jersey carried their talents north and west. As the country grew and the demand for cheap glassware increased, their talents were used in glass factories popping up across the young United States. Until the art of glassblowing declined with the introduction of mechanical glass pressing, glassmakers practiced the South Jersey tradition.

Second of the noteworthy German-American glass manufacturers was Henry William Stiegel (Stēe′-gal), an immigrant from Cologne, Germany, which had long been a glassmaking center. A very ambitious young man, Stiegel married the daughter of the owner and operator of a well-established iron furnace in Lancaster County, Pennsylvania, within a few years of his arrival. This was quite a social coup for a man without any recorded assets or important family ties. Soon Stiegel was running the iron furnace where cast-iron stoveplates and firebacks (shields for the backs of fireplaces) were produced for the local German-American population. He must have been very good at this work since the locals soon referred to him as "Baron," even though he had no noble lineage. After his first wife died and he remarried, the Baron continued to run the successful iron furnace and even expanded operations to another ironworks not far away. These prospering iron furnaces were used by Stiegel to bankroll his expansion into glassmaking in the early 1760s. It was in 1763 that the first glassworks, known as the Elizabeth Furnace (named after his first wife), began operating near the site of Stiegel's first ironworks. A couple of years later he opened a second factory in Manheim, Pennsylvania. Having been successful with his first two ventures, in Manheim in 1768 he began to construct his third and largest glassworks, which was completed in 1769.

Adding to the interest and appeal of Baron Stiegel is not just that he was an intriguing and romantic figure, but that he also was the first glass-

maker in America who carefully documented his business endeavors. Many of these early records, which include daybooks, factory ledgers, and letters, were written by Stiegel himself. He also advertised his glassware widely in newspapers throughout colonial America and actually had agents selling his wares as far away as New York City, Boston, and Baltimore.

Also adding to the unique status of Stiegel and his glass is that his glasshouses went well beyond the production of everyday, cheap wares such as bottles and window glass. They produced much higher quality wares that directly competed with expensive imported glass from England and continental Europe. Records indicate that Stiegel's factories produced not only glass in the Germanic (South Jersey) tradition, but also included fine enamel-decorated pieces and possibly engraved wares typical of glass from Germany. Further, he produced mold-blown wares to rival the finest English flint glass of that time.

Flintware was the most expensive glass of the period since it was produced using lead oxide instead of soda in the glass batch. The lead produced a heavy, more sparkling glass especially suitable for cutting and engraving (and later for pressing). The term *flint glass* derived from the fact that the lead originally was refined from ground and burnt flint stone. What all this means is that the Baron was going head-to-head with the "big boys," which eventually led to his downfall.

Apparently a wide selection of glass was produced at the Stiegel factories, especially small pocket flasks, tumblers, small jugs (pitchers), and footed salt dips (individual small bowls for salt). In the colonies just before the American Revolution, there was a growing resentment of English policies, and Americans began to turn away from imported items, most notably tea. Apparently Stiegel hoped Americans in the towns and cities neighboring Pennsylvania also would reject imported glassware in favor of his domestic wares. Unfortunately, this does not appear to have happened—at least to the extent hoped for—since imported wares were better known and more widely distributed. Hence, in 1774 the Manheim glasshouses closed. Soon afterward, Stiegel was shipped off to debtor's prison for a few months.

Although the Baron was only in prison a short time, he was, by modern standards, bankrupt, hav-

Fig. 2-2 This goblet was a wedding gift to Henry William Stiegel's daughter, Elizabeth, when she married William Old. It undoubtedly was made at Stiegel's glass factory. The bride and groom's initials were engraved by Lazarus Isaacs, ca. 1773–1774. Courtesy of the Corning Museum of Glass.

ing lost all his assets and income. His final years must have been a sad anticlimax to his glory years in the iron and glass businesses. When he died in 1785, he was buried in an unmarked grave.

The complex and romantic Stiegel story has appealed to generations of glass lovers. In fact, the first book devoted to Stiegel and his glass, Frederick William Hunter's *Stiegel Glass,* was published in 1914. From a collector's viewpoint today, Stiegel glass has a special mystique. Although the glassworks themselves were quite well documented, glass pieces directly attributable to the

Stiegel factories are very rare. Complicating the situation, Stiegel glass was made to imitate imported English and European glass closely, and it was made by English and German glassworkers using the same techniques their brethren were using across the Atlantic. Stiegel succeeded so well in copying imported wares that today only a few designs and a handful of pieces can be attributed definitely to his works. Any surviving eighteenth-century glass of the types Stiegel made therefore is referred to as Stiegel-type glass. Keep in mind, also, that since the early twentieth century, when Stiegel glass first attracted serious American collectors, reproductions of similar wares have been made in Europe (especially in Czechoslovakia) and the United States. Great care should be taken so that the charm of the Stiegel story does not cloud one's judgment if one comes across an ancient-looking little glass piece offered as "Stiegel."

Third in the triumvirate of early German-American glassmakers was John Frederick Amelung. Not nearly as dashing a figure as Baron Stiegel, Amelung was the only one of the three who was a trained glassmaker by trade. He arrived from Bremen, Germany, in 1784, not long after the American Revolution, and brought with him a group of trained glassworkers with the intent of starting a glass factory. This undertaking was backed by funds and support from a group of merchants in Bremen, and when the new factory was established near Frederick, Maryland, the company was named the New Bremen Glass Manufactory. The Germans must have realized there would be a strong market for quality glassware in the new United States. They relied on American patriotic pride in home industries to insure the success of their factory. With a staff of trained glass blowers and abundant raw materials, the Amelung glassworks must have been among the best run in early America.

A wealth of documentary evidence and records gives a complete picture of how the factory was organized and run and what sorts of wares were being produced. Quality was the keynote of Amelung's output, and the factory specialized in fine, clear, nonlead tableware often highlighted with fine, sophisticated engravings of floral wreaths and bands. Especially noteworthy is that, in an effort to promote his factory, Amelung produced a good number of specially engraved presentation pieces that still exist today. These are the only eighteenth-

Fig. 2-3 A clear glass tumbler made for the Repold family at the Amelung glass factory, ca. 1792. The engraving is typical of pieces attributed to Amelung. Courtesy of the Corning Museum of Glass.

century American glass pieces that can be attributed without question to a specific glass factory. This group of rare and unique presentation pieces, now mostly in museum collections, has helped glass historians analyze the quality and style of Amelung's production and has allowed glass authorities to ascribe closely related pieces to the Amelung factory. Again, remember that the Amelung glassmakers were making glass that looked a great deal like the English and German wares against which they were competing. Only a narrow range of non-presentation pieces definitely can be called Amelung.

As with the Wistars and Stiegel before him, Amelung ran into trouble competing with well-organized, long-established factories abroad that, after the Revolution, flooded this country with cheap exports of all types, including glass. Not unlike many of today's American industries, this early endeavor suffered from foreign competition. Amelung worked long and hard to promote his quality wares and petitioned the state and federal governments to enact protective tariffs to aid his and other fledgling industries, but even legislative assistance was not enough. By 1795 the Amelung factory was out of business, leaving historians to sort out the facts and fables surrounding America's third great glassworks.

The American glass industry did not die out completely with the failure of the Amelung works, of course. During the 1790s and early 1800s, a number of other glass factories started around the young United States, including sites in and around New York, Boston, Cape Cod, Philadelphia, and, most notably, Pittsburgh. This was the western frontier of the United States at that time. Western Pennsylvania was a rapidly growing region where plentiful resources, a good river transportation system, and an expanding market soon assured the success of the area's early glass factories. Before long glassmaking was a premier industry in what was then called the Midwest, a position of supremacy held throughout the nineteenth century.

Part II
The Lacy Period,
1825–1845

CHAPTER 3

Americans and the Development of Early Glass Pressing

Glassmaking in America had a long and checkered history by the time the nineteenth century opened. Many glass factories came and went, operating with varying degrees of success. Not until the early nineteenth century did a well-developed American market for glassware evolve. Finally, after the War of 1812, when the United States once again affirmed its independence from Great Britain, there was a period of social and economic stability called the Era of Good Feelings. At this time American industry in general and the glass industry in particular met with sustained success.

The first twenty-five years of the nineteenth century saw a strong growth of economic and political power. The fast-growing population was moving westward into the Old Northwest Territory, and towns and cities were springing up all along the Ohio River Valley and down the Mississippi River to New Orleans. Markets for all sorts of household necessities and some luxuries followed this burgeoning growth, and newly dug canals and the system of natural waterways made the transportation of such manufactured goods increasingly easy. More than ever, there was a demand for inexpensive, utilitarian glass for bottles, windows, and tableware. Glass was a step up from everyday hand-

turned woodenware and cheap pottery, but it still was not as expensive as some manufactured metalware or imported fine china or porcelain. The stage was set for the next big step in American glassmaking: the introduction of the glass-pressing machine.

As with many innovations in the history of industrial development, the machine for mechanically pressing glassware did not originate in the mind of one genius. It was the result of a gradual evolution in glassmaking technology and the efforts of a number of individuals.

Small-scale hand-pressing of glass was already being done by English and Dutch glasshouses in the late eighteenth century. Using a hand-held iron tool reminiscent of an old waffle iron or lemon squeezer, glassmakers stamped out small pieces such as feet or bases for attachment to free-blown or mold-blown pieces. With this primitive molding method they also turned out flattened, round disc- or wheel-form stoppers for decanters. The technique was slow and laborious, but it was a form of pressing glass and undoubtedly it inspired the major advances in glass pressing developed in the United States in the 1820s.

Although it is accepted generally that Ameri-

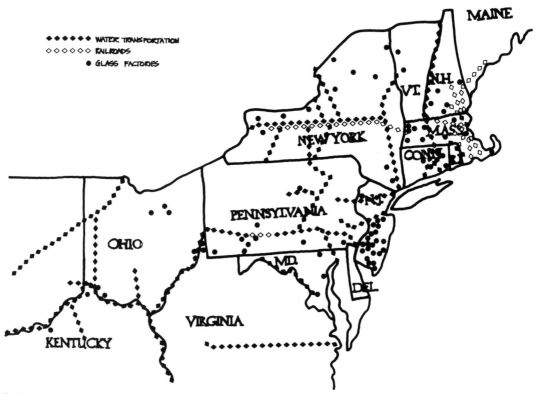

Fig. 3-1 A map showing the growth of the American glass industry in the second quarter of the nineteenth century. Indicated are the locations of glass factories, water routes, and railroad lines then in use. Courtesy of the Corning Museum of Glass.

cans were the first to develop a large, hand-operated glass-pressing machine capable of turning out, in one step, a complete (albeit small) glass object, exactly where and when this sort of machine was used first never has been discovered. Early glass researchers poured over early glass company records and written descriptions of inventions recorded at the U.S. Patent Office but came up with only a few facts. The earliest known patent for mechanically pressing a glass object was taken out by J. P. Bakewell of Bakewell and Company in Pittsburgh, Pennsylvania, for an "improvement in making glass furniture knobs." Other patents in the late 1820s were granted to glassmakers working on various refinements in the pressing technique. A number of people associated with different glass factories contributed to the refinements to the glass-pressing machines just coming into use.

As mentioned, the first recorded patent for a mechanically pressed object was for a glass furniture knob. During the next few years several patents for similar knobs were issued to various glassmakers, so these knobs were among the first—if not *the* first—widely produced and distributed pieces of American pressed glass. Most of these early knobs were cylindrical, resembling old wooden thread spools, or mushroom-shaped with a ribbed, rayed, or florette design in the top. Especially interesting to glass collectors is that they were produced in such large numbers, and many are still available on the collecting market and at quite reasonable prices. Matched sets, of course, are scarcer. Such knobs were produced for at least two or three decades after the first patents in the 1820s, so do not be fooled into thinking that every small glass knob you see dates from the 1820s. Adding to the interest of

Figs. 3-2 and 3-3 Typical early pressed lacy furniture knobs. Figure 3-2 shows a clear example attributed to the Boston and Sandwich Glass Company. Figure 3-3 shows an opaque blue piece attributed to some other New England factory. Both pieces ca. 1830–1840. Courtesy of the Corning Museum of Glass.

the search is that a number of companies that produced these early knobs had their molds marked so the word ''patent,'' or possibly the company's initials, was stamped on the base of each knob. Since the patents ran for a number of years, one can get an idea of the company that made such a knob and the period when it was made. The marked examples are the most sought by serious collectors. One may find an early piece of furniture that carries its original glass knobs or, with luck, a knob or set of knobs that can be retrofitted onto an early piece of furniture.

CHAPTER 4

The Glass Called "Lacy"

When the first glass in America began to be pressed, it was discovered that not just any glass mixture would work well in the simple, early pressing machines. The common type of soda-based glass used in free-blowing and mold-blowing glass was not pliable enough to work well when pressed in a mold. Glassmakers had to resort to the more expensive lead-based glass mixture that since the seventeenth century, had been called flint glass. The lead formula produced a heavy, pliable molten mixture more easily controlled in the early pressing machines. The first machines required that each individual piece be pressed separately, one at a time. It was basically a two-person operation. One had to take a gather of molten glass on the end of a punty rod. Carrying it to the machine, his more-skilled partner then snipped off a piece of this glob with shears and let it drop into the waiting open mold fitted on the machine. Immediately, with his other hand, he brought down a long lever handle that closed the mold and pressed the molten glass into shape. It took a great deal of experience to know how much glass to drop into the mold and how much pressure to exert so that the piece would be formed properly. The early machines could handle only very small molds, so the glassmakers produced simple wares such as furniture knobs, as well as small or flat tableware including small plates, bowls, and salt dips.

Many things might have gone wrong as each piece was pressed. Too much glass might be dropped into the mold, or the glass might cool too fast and crack before it could be carried to the cooling (annealing) oven. Even the plunger half of the two-part mold could come down slightly askew

Fig. 4-1 A drawing of a typical early glass-pressing machine. From Apsley Pellat's book *Curiosities of Glassmaking*, London, 1849. Courtesy of the Corning Museum of Glass.

and produce a crooked or underfilled piece. In order to overcome some of these problems and still produce attractive pieces, glass companies had molds made with ornate designs. Such designs featured leaves, flowers, hearts, scrolls, classical motifs, or overall crisscross and geometric designs, all on a finely stippled background. These busy and delicate designs reminded early glass collectors in the 1920s and 1930s of fine lace, and soon they referred to all early pressed glass with such designs as "lacy glass," a term still generally used today.

Production Centers: Dealing with the Sandwich Myth

For over sixty years it has been common for collectors and dealers to lump all examples of lacy glass under the generic heading *Sandwich*. Although today this is considered somewhat inaccurate, it does make sense when one looks at the sources of lacy glass and the information early researchers into American glass discovered in the 1920s and 1930s.

Sandwich, of course, relates to glassware produced by the Boston and Sandwich Glass Company of Sandwich, Massachusetts, a small Cape Cod town south of Boston. In my earliest days of collecting I had heard the term "Sandwich glass," but being on the West Coast, far removed from glassmaking centers and other collectors, I was not sure why it had that name. I assumed it had something to do with the fact that early glass was squeezed out in sandwich-style two-part molds resembling a waffle iron. Imagine my surprise and delight when I finally read that the name originated with the title of an actual glass company.

Since those innocent days I have learned a great deal more about early glass and glassmaking, but the appeal of the Sandwich glass story is still strong. The Boston and Sandwich Glass Company was not only one of the first glass firms to mass produce pressed glass, but it also became one of the largest and best known. Early glass researchers, most of them living in the Northeast, found a wealth of material relating to this factory and its colorful founder, Deming Jarves, and so a great deal was written about the company and its products. Much of what was written fifty or sixty years ago is still interesting and quite accurate, but certain conclusions they made, like the assumption that Sandwich produced most of the lacy glass, now have been refuted.

Jarves neither claimed to have invented glass pressing nor to have entered the first patents for pressing pieces, but he has become one of the most-studied and best-documented of early American glassmakers. This probably is due to his autobiographical recollections of his career in glassmaking entitled *Reminiscences of Glass Making,* published in 1854, near the end of his long career. Because Jarves was such as distinguished entrepreneur, his life and influence on the American glass industry have proven worthy of much study.

Jarves was born in 1790. As a young man he became a Boston merchant in glass and chinaware, and in 1818 he became the agent (general manager) of the newly formed New England Glass Company, a firm specializing in quality blown and cut glassware. Later this firm became a major glass-pressing rival of the Sandwich company. In 1825 Jarves and associates organized a new glass company in Sandwich, which, by 1826, was called the Boston and Sandwich Glass Company. A major producer of the pattern-molded blown-three-mold glass, the Sandwich firm was also one of the first glass companies to go into large-scale production of pressed glass. It was producing cup plates by 1827 and may have been one of the first factories to manufacture glass tableware. Jarves also is known to have patented several processes relating to mechanical glass pressing in the late 1820s and early 1830s, so he was a leading figure in the industry's early evolution and development.

Under Jarves's energetic guidance, the Sandwich company grew and prospered. It had a fine location with access to good-quality sand and other ingredients for mixing glass as well as sources of timber for firing the furnaces. Of special importance in that day, it also was near the coast, which meant the finished products easily could be loaded on ships for distribution to large merchandising centers in Boston, New York, and other cities along the Eastern Seaboard or overseas. Before good highways and railroads, waterways were the best and most efficient method of shipping all goods. Positioning on the coast or near a major river system was vitally important to all American industry.

In 1837, with the Sandwich plant in full operation, Jarves decided to establish another glassworks for his son, George D., obviously in hopes of perpetuating a glassmaking dynasty. The company, named the Mount Washington Glass Works, was set up in south Boston. Here the firm produced blown, cut, and pressed glass and later became famous for fine-quality art glass wares in the late nineteenth century. By 1866 the factory was owned by William L. Libbey, a former employee, who moved the business to New Bedford, Massachusetts, in 1869 and sold it in 1870. Mount Washington became part of the Pairpoint Manufacturing Company, famous makers of silver plate. Libbey went to work for the New England Glass Company and some years later took charge of that company. His son, Edward D., shut down this company in 1888 during labor troubles and moved it to Toledo, Ohio. He changed the name to the Libbey Glass Company, and it soon became a leader in the production of Brilliant Period cut glass of the 1890s. The Libbey company, referring to itself as America's oldest glass company, continues to operate in Toledo and produces a variety of glass products.

Jarves continued to head the Sandwich Company until 1858, when he ended his connection with the firm, probably because of disagreements with younger men then taking over the glass industry. He did not end his association with glassmaking, however, as he soon founded the Cape Cod Glass Company, also near Sandwich. It appears he started this factory for another son, John W. The Cape Cod firm also specialized in quality pressed glass, probably closely related to Sandwich ware. After his son died in 1863, Jarves apparently lost interest in the factory. After his own death in 1869, the works closed down, and so ended the colorful career of one of our great industrial impresarios, the man whose energy and drive helped inspire the still-intriguing Sandwich myth.

Glassmakers of the New Midwest

Although New England is famous as a center of early American glass production, from the 1820s onward it had a strong rival in the new Midwest. Remember that in the early nineteenth century the term "Midwest" referred to western Pennsylvania, around Pittsburgh, as well as what later became West Virginia and eastern Ohio. The Midwest of that time was an unsettled and largely unexplored wilderness.

There were glassworks in the Midwest as early as the late eighteenth century. The earliest known glass-pressing patent was issued in 1825 to John P. Bakewell of Bakewell and Company of Pittsburgh. The Bakewell firm had been founded in 1808 and early on specialized in the finest free-blown and mold-blown glass. It also became famous for quality cut glass on par with the finest Anglo-Irish cut ware, top-of-the-line glass in the late eighteenth and early nineteenth centuries. The Bakewell firm even made a glass service for President James Monroe, a unique honor at a time when American industry was struggling to compete with foreign imports.

Bakewell and Company became a leading producer of early pressed glass ware and, though going through numerous name changes, continued to operate under the direction of members of the Bakewell family until 1882, a period of seventy-four years.

Although this firm was one of the earliest and largest of the midwestern glassmakers, several others began operations in the region before the mid-nineteenth century. Most also became involved with the production of lacy and pressed pattern glass and operated with varying degrees of success. Among these other companies were R. B. Curling and Sons (later Curling, Robertson and Company, 1828–1857); John Robinson and Sons (1823–1845); and in nearby Wheeling, West Virginia, Ritchie and Wheat Company (1829–1836); M. and R. H. Sweeney (1831–1868); and Hobbs, Barnes and Company (1845–1863), which later became Hobbs, Brockunier and Company.

Although the New England and midwestern factories were the largest and today the most famous, other glassworks also were producing pressed wares in the 1825–1860 period. Competition was stiff among all these firms, and those with the best locations and access to raw materials, qualified workers, and a good transportation system were the most successful and long lived.

Forms and Designs

Most pieces of early pressed glass of the lacy era were quite small in size. The size restriction, however, did not limit the diversity of the designs produced in the years from the mid-1820s to the waning of the lacy era after the mid-1840s.

Among the most common pieces produced in lacy glass (pieces that still are abundant on the collecting market) were little round dishes called *cup plates* and rectangular, round, or boat- or sleigh-shaped dishes called *salt dips*.

Cup plates were common adjuncts to the dining table in the early nineteenth century and served a very specialized purpose. Readers who have ever studied early nineteenth-century china teaware are probably aware that a large percentage of the teacups were made *without* handles and had very wide

Fig. 4-2 An early American lacy cup plate with a simple, crude design and thick, scalloped rim formed without the benefit of a cap ring.

and deep saucers. It was socially acceptable, during that period, to pour hot tea from the cup into the deep saucer and "saucer" it, that is, drink it from the saucer. Strange as this sounds today, it was common practice among all levels of society at that time. The need for cup plates was a natural outgrowth of this practice, since it solved the question of what to do with the wet, dripping teacup. One did not want it to soil the table linens, hence, we have the little glass cup plate upon which to rest the empty cup. Cup plates, which also were widely produced in chinaware, seem to have been most common in pressed glass and apparently were sold in matching sets. A complete set would be rare today, but a multitude of individual plates are still around in hundreds of pattern variations.

Collecting cup plates became fashionable in the 1930s and 1940s. In 1948 noted early glass historian Ruth Webb Lee and James H. Rose coauthored, the now-standard reference *American Glass Cup Plates,* which illustrated and described hundreds of glass cup plate designs.

The little cup plates, generally three to four inches in diameter, are still the most abundant and inexpensive pieces of early pressed glass you can collect, but other similar plates also were produced in closely related designs. Two types are *toddy plates* (four to five inches in diameter), and *tea plates* (approximately six inches in diameter). These pieces also are quite common. Larger plates and shallow bowls also were made in lacy designs in sizes up to about ten inches across, and a few whoppers are known in the ten-to-twelve-inch range.

Salt dishes (or dips) in various shapes and in dozens of lacy designs also were heavily produced. After cup plates, salt dishes are among the most available of early pressed pieces. In the nineteenth century formal dining required that several open salt dishes be set around the table for the diners' use. This was long before salt could be refined so that it poured easily, so it was necessary to grind it up and serve it in little open vessels. Tiny salt spoons often were placed in the salt dishes for easier serving, or, if individual-sized salts were provided for each diner, foods like celery could be "dipped" directly into the dish. Early salt dishes were produced in varied shapes to appeal to many decorating tastes. Many were simple rectangles while others were round, footed dishes. Other more ornate examples were molded with scrolls and shells and resembled little miniature cradles or sleighs. One of the most famous salts (as they are also called) of the lacy era was produced at the Boston and Sandwich Glass Company in the late 1820s. It is a miniature model of a paddlewheel steamboat of the era. It is unique because it has the

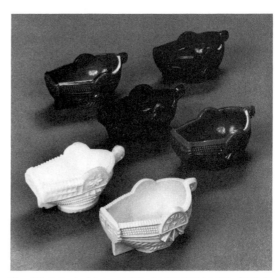

Fig. 4-3 A fleet of lacy paddlewheeler-shaped salt dishes in various colors. In the foreground is a Sandwich "La Fayet" marked example.

name "La Fayet" raised on the side of the paddle-wheels and is marked on the stern with "B. & S. Glass Co.," for Boston and Sandwich Glass Company. This is one of the very rare pieces of early American glass marked with the name of the company that made it. It was long assumed that the name on the boat was meant to honor the Marquis de Lafayette, the French nobleman who became famous for fighting alongside George Washington for independence during the American Revolution. He returned to tour the United States in 1825, and some glass researchers thought this piece might have commemorated that visit. This seems unlikely, since the piece could not have been produced for several years after the visit and thus would not have been a timely souvenir. More likely it was made to represent an early sidewheeler that operated along the East Coast in the late 1820s. However, no specific ship has ever been discovered that exactly matches the design of this little vessel. Although the Sandwich salt is the most famous, another one, a similar boat-shaped piece, was produced that also was marked on the stern by the maker. That salt carries the name "J. Robinson and Sons—Pittsburgh" or just "Pittsburgh" and was the product of one of the early glass-pressing firms in Pittsburgh.

After cup plates, salt dishes and small, round dishes, probably the most commonly found pieces of lacy glass are covered sugar bowls. These were most often a footed octagonal or round deep dish with a domed cover. They were produced in several lacy designs. A few creamers also were made in lacy designs, but these were not made to accompany the sugar bowls and their patterns do not match them. Collectors should keep in mind that lacy glass pieces were not made to match one another. Most lacy designs were unique to a particular piece, although they might closely resemble other lacy designs.

Much rarer than any of the previously mentioned pieces are objects such as footed open compotes, unusually shaped trays, casket-form deep dishes, rectangular panes of glass used in furniture doors, and toy-sized dishes. Lamps and candlesticks also were made but usually had pressed lacy glass bases and blow-glass fonts or sockets.

What makes certain forms so rare in lacy glass is that the earliest pressing machines were simple, hand-operated mechanisms that were hard to con-

Fig. 4-4 A rare lacy toy-sized covered compote is dark blue. It is only 3″ long.

Fig. 4-5 A lacy "butterfly" pattern 7″ l. tray. This is another design attributed to Sandwich.

trol. Small, shallow items such as cup plates were relatively easy to stamp out in the two-part molds. One could drop the gather of molten glass in the dished-out bottom of the mold, bring down the plunger arm with the top half of the mold, and squeeze the piece into shape. These early molds usually had the pattern carved on the mold's plunger half, and thus pieces were formed upside down with the lacy pattern molded into the bottom. The inside was smooth. More unusual pieces with complex shapes or molded handles were much harder to produce in this manner, and their production was quite limited. As the years passed, more refinements were made in the pressing machines, and methods of better controlling the amount of glass dropped into the mold and the pressure used to press the piece evolved. A key development along this line was the introduction, before 1830, of the *cap ring*, a ring of metal that fit around the mold plunger with its carved design. When the mold was closed, this ring helped control the distribution of the molten glass around the edge of the mold. Before this development early pressed pieces might be underfilled around the edges or might have excess glass squeezed out around the rim of the mold. The cap ring sealed the edges of the mold and also was cut with designs that formed the edges of the finished pieces of glass.

Even with refinements like the cap ring, it still was impossible for early glass presses to produce certain forms like large pitchers and large lamps. A number of rare pieces, like compotes, were pressed in two parts and the base and top joined together by a molten wafer of glass while the two sections still were hot. By a similar technique it was possible to press a lacy pattern foot (often an inverted cup plate) that could be attached to a free-blown or mold-blown lamp font or the socket of a candlestick. In these rare items we see the marriage of ancient glassblowing and the modern glass-pressing technology.

Fig. 4-6 A pair of graceful candlesticks combining pressed lacy bases in a hairpin design with free-blown stems and sockets. They probably were made at a Midwestern factory between 1830 and 1845. Courtesy of the Corning Museum of Glass.

Items Made in Early Lacy Glass

(Listed by relative rarity of form)

Relatively Common
Cup plates (three to four inches in diameter)
Salt dishes
Toddy plates
Small bowls (five to six inches in diameter)
Clear sugar bowls
Small rectangular dishes (five to six inches long)

Scarce
Creamers

Large bowls and plates (eight to twelve inches in diameter)
Toy-sized dishes

Rare
Compotes
Chambersticks (one piece)
Candlesticks with lacy bases
Lamps with lacy bases
Covered round and rectangular dishes
Oblong trays with open pressed handles
Panes of glass

Specific Design Motifs

There are probably hundreds of different lacy designs, but certain themes were commonly repeated and many patterns copied by competing glass companies. The most important of these are listed and described below as a guide to what to look for.

Gothic

There was a growing interest in this Romantic style of architecture in the early nineteenth century, and certain Gothic details often were used on lacy glass. These details included Gothic arches, rosettes, quatrefoils, lancets, and hairpins.

Fig. 4-7 The base of a *Gothic Arch* pattern lacy sugar bowl in scarce teal blue. This was probably made at a New England factory ca. 1840–1860.

Classical

Since the eighteenth century, when the Roman ruins of Pompeii and Heraculum were discovered and first excavated, there was an ongoing interest in the ancient Roman and Greek art, architecture, and interior decoration. In the late eighteenth and early nineteenth centuries, European and American designs, especially for furniture, mirrored this interest. In the young United States, the Founding Fathers stressed the budding nation's connection with the ancient Roman Republic, and all that related to the classical era became popular symbols of the young republic. Early lacy glass also picked up some of this Roman-inspired detailing with such motifs as acanthus leaf scrolls, palmettes, cornucopia, swords, oak leaves, and shells.

Romantic

This broad category includes designs based on motifs such as hearts and flowers and includes all sorts of floral bouquets, harps, and thistles, especially in the centers of pieces. Heart borders were common on the edges of lacy pieces, especially cup plates.

Geometric

Any overall design in a piece of glass that consists of diamonds, circles, and crosshatched bands would fall under this general heading. Such details

could be used in conjunction with the other designs. The early designers tended to mix and match motifs when designing a mold.

Historical

A very important development in pressed glass during the lacy era was the production of special commemorative designs relating to then-current events in the United States. Today any of these designs are referred to as "historical." Already mentioned was the La Fayet boat salt, but in lacy glass, especially cup plates, dozens of other designs relating to current events are known. Designs usually restricted to the center of a cup plate show sailing ships and early steamboats, sometimes with their names included in the design. Also shown are political figures, with portraits of George Washington, Henry Clay, or Major Ringold, a Mexican War hero. One especially interesting group relates to the presidential campaign of 1840, the famous "Log Cabin and Cider" campaign. Quite a number of cup plates were produced that illustrated a log cabin with a cider barrel beside it, which was the emblem of General William Henry Harrison, the winning candidate. His bust portrait also was put into the center of some cup plates.

Another very common design—probably the most common of the historical types—is the Bunker Hill Monument cup plate. This variety illustrates in its center an obelisk surrounded by circles of inscriptions and garland bands. The design commemorates the completion, in 1841, of the Bunker Hill Monument in Boston, site of the famous Revolutionary War battle.

Another historical design very popular on cup plates was the American eagle, basically patterned after the national emblem. The spread-winged eagle with a banner in its beak was popular and appeared on several design variations, all of which are highly collectible.

An interesting group of cup plate designs relates to the coronation of England's Queen Victoria in 1837 and her marriage in 1841 to Prince Albert. These pieces feature their bust portraits in the center. Although examples of these show up quite often on the American market, it has not been proven conclusively that they were made in this country. For many years some of these patterns have been attributed to Sandwich or other New England fac-

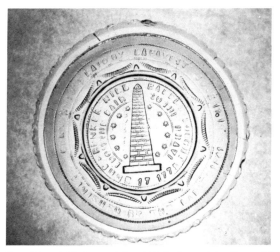 

Figs. 4-8 and 4-9 Two early lacy historical cup plates. Figure 4-8 shows the common "Bunker Hill Monument" example, while Figure 4-9 illustrates one version of the "Log Cabin" design, ca. 1840.

tories, but no actual documentation has surfaced yet. They remain collectible, however, and are much sought by modern Anglophiles.

With the charming variety of designs in early glass, it is easy to see why it is still so appealing today. Designs for almost any taste and pocketbook are available.

Regional Variations

As mentioned, for many years the terms lacy and Sandwich glass were used interchangeably. However, through the efforts of various glass researchers, most notably the late Lowell Innes, it has been firmly established that glass companies in and around Pittsburgh, Pennsylvania, produced as much if not more early pressed lacy glass than their New England competitors. For decades there has been debate about the relative merits of lacy ware from each region. Today there is still somewhat of a premium placed on products of the Sandwich factory, but the midwestern lacy deserves and is getting more recognition. In fact, some of the finest and rarest examples of lacy glass—which bring thousands of dollars—are from Pittsburgh firms.

It is not easy for the novice to differentiate between the products of New England and those of Pittsburgh. Innes, in an article on Pittsburgh pressed glass for the magazine *Antiques* (September 1949), made a few points that can be used to help decide from which region a piece may have come. In general, he noted, the Sandwich and other New

Fig. 4-10 A midwestern-made cup plate featuring a band of bull's eyes around the center, a typical design on midwestern cup plates. Note that it has cruder stippling than many eastern lacy pieces.

England examples used a finer-quality, clearer, and more brilliant glass. Also, the background stippling on the designs was finer and the designs themselves are more sophisticated. However, these are just generalizations that do not always hold true, and using them can be subjective at best.

Other more reliable factors can be used to identify a piece from a Pittsburgh factory. First, rims of lacy pieces from Pittsburgh often have a band of dots or buttons as part of the scalloped edge. These buttons seldom appear on the rims of New England pieces. Second, a similar band of small buttons was sometimes used around the center bottom rim of midwestern lacy plates and bowls. These buttons or knobs form small rounded feet on which the piece rests. New England and Sandwich lacy pieces nearly always rest on the bottom rim band of the item. There are no knobs to form tiny feet.

After decades of neglect and ill-repute, the lacy pieces from midwestern factories finally are taking their deserved position alongside the best of the Sandwich and New England wares.

Fig. 4-11 The bottom of the midwestern lacy cup plate showing the five little knob "feet," a feature typical of midwestern cup plates.

Foreign Lacy

As if the differences and similarities between New England and midwestern lacy glass were not enough to confuse the novice collector, there is another variety to touch upon: European lacy glassware.

Although research continues into the types of early pressed glass produced in England and on the European continent, it has been known for years that French companies in particular were producing a wide variety of what we call lacy glass at least as early as the 1840s. It does not appear that such products were widely exported to the United States at that time, but they can show up on the market today, so we need to be aware of their existence. One of the key references to French lacy glass available is the circa 1840 catalog of Launay, Hautin and Cie, a glass wholesale firm of Paris. This publication, now in the collection of the Corning Museum of Glass, clearly illustrates dozens of sophisticated pieces made by various French glass companies in careful line drawings. At first glance there may appear to be close similarities between these French pieces and American lacy pieces, but a little study shows the differences. For instance,

the French appear to have made more larger pieces, such as covered compotes, than American firms; their designs seem to be heavier looking than American ones. Also of interest is that the French produced a wide selection of lacy glass tumblers, which are practically unheard of in American lacy glass. The French also made a large variety of footed goblets with lacy designs; such goblets never were made by American companies.

The Launay catalog has proven invaluable to glass researchers, but it does not answer all questions. Little has been written about lacy wares produced in England and other European countries such as Belgium, Denmark, and Norway, although wares similar in type to the French products apparently also were being made in those locations. In fact, growing evidence shows that French and other European lacy glass designs may have remained in production for quite a while longer than American lacy wares—possibly into the 1860s or later. The weight and overall quality of the glass may have decreased, but the general lacy motifs were still in use. Since the English and Europeans have not taken much interest in this period of their glass

Fig. 4-12 A page from the Launay, Hautin and Cie catalog of French lacy, ca. 1840. Many of these forms are totally different from American-made lacy glass. Courtesy of the Corning Museum of Glass.

Fig. 4-13 Do not confuse this little toy compote with American-made lacy miniatures. It is a greenish glass of poor quality and was probably made in Europe ca. 1860–1890. It stands only 1½" high.

Fig. 4-14 This 4½" d. lacy-style plate has a crudely stippled design, ca. 1860–1890. The greenish color is similar to the toy compote in Figure 4-13, and they may have come from the same factory or region.

production, very little reference material has been written and published. American researchers and collectors seem to be most interested in investiga-ting foreign pressed glass and its relationship to our own much-studied glass heritage.

Desirability and Values

As with all antiques and collectibles, several factors help determine what any specific piece might sell for on the open market. In glassware a number of general factors hold true in determining what makes one piece rare and another common.

Important guidelines to keep in mind with glass

in general and lacy glass in particular are size, form, pattern, color, and condition.

The sizes and forms in lacy glass have been discussed previously. Basically, the larger an object, the rarer it is. Similarly, very small pieces, such as toy dishes, are also desirable.

There are so many pattern variations in lacy glass that they really do not play a major role in determining value. The exceptions are pieces that carry the name or initials of the glass company that made them and some rare historical designs or design variations. Excellent references are available that go into great detail about which pieces and patterns are rarest, and these are "must" reading if you want to specialize in lacy glass.

Color is another major factor that helps determine a piece's relative rarity and desirability. The chemical makeup of a glass batch determines the final color of the glass produced. Basically, common free-blown or mold-blown glass was produced in shades of green, brown, and aquamarine, each color determined by the chemical impurities in the batch. Since ancient times, however, it has been known that the addition of specific refined chemicals could change the color of the finished piece. Special chemical formulae were developed by glassmakers and often became trade secrets, guarded jealously and passed discriminately from generation to generation. By the time the American pressed glass industry was established, the general mechanics of mixing a glass batch were known to many trained glassmakers, and their services were always in demand at factories. Since the seventeenth century clear glass was the rarest and most desirable for quality glass production. By the early nineteenth century, clear flint glass was the norm, and the vast majority of early lacy glass was produced in clear flint glass. Although some glassworks did not get all the impurities (such as small pieces of sand or tiny pebbles) out of the batch, the glass they pressed still was generally bright and clear. Today these impurities add a certain charm and appeal to this old glass. When originally marketed these defects were accepted on the cheap, everyday wares because any form of glass was saleable to the general American consumer. To add to the eye appeal of glass, specific chemicals were used from time to time to make colored examples.

Various metallic oxides mixed in the molten glass batch produced varying hues. In small amounts, manganese helped produce a good, clear glass and could be added in larger amounts to produce a light purple color. Various shades of blue could be obtained by adding cobalt or copper. The yellow-green color today referred to as "vaseline," since it resembles the color of Vaseline petroleum jelly, was produced by adding uranium (long before its radioactive properties had been discovered). Red, one of the rarest colors in early American glass, was costly to produce since it required the addition of gold or copper. Contrary to popular myth, glassmakers did not toss gold rings into a molten batch to obtain the red. The gold had to be carefully refined and measured to produce the proper color. Randomly tossing jewelry into the furnace just would not have made sense.

A wide spectrum of color was available to early glassmakers, but the expense of the ingredients in the first half of the nineteenth century limited the production of colored lacy glass.

All colored lacy is scarce, but quite a number of dark blue and purple pieces, especially in smaller wares such as cup plates and salt dips, are available. Opaque white (now called "milk glass") and opalescent milky white (fiery opalescent) pieces also show up occasionally. Much rarer are dark green, yellow, or vaseline and amber items. A true red color is extremely rare. As far as collectors are concerned, any piece of colored lacy is good. Rare colors may bring more money, but generally speaking the blues are most appealing to today's collectors—just as they must have been to the original buyers of the 1830s—since blue seems to have been produced more than any other color except clear.

Condition is a final factor to consider when collecting. Generally speaking, badly chipped and cracked pieces are avoided by collectors unless they are extremely rare or unique. Common cup plates in clear with bad rim chips or cracks are a dime a dozen. A few small edge flakes or chipped scallops on a piece are acceptable, but don't pay too much just because you are told it is Sandwich glass. Interestingly, common pieces in clear lacy glass still can sell for a fraction of the price of much later pattern glass and even 1930s Depression glass. One just has to know what one is looking at.

Value Ranges

The following is a brief survey of current value ranges for lacy glass.

$15–$30 range: Common clear cup plates and small dishes.

$30–$75 range: Scarcer cup plates and some in color; larger clear lacy dishes (four to seven inches in diameter); more common salt dishes.

$75–$200 range: Rare cup plates and many colored salt dishes; small colored lacy sauce dishes and some more common clear miniatures.

$200–$1,000+ range: This is an open-ended category for rare forms such as covered sugar bowls, creamers, very large bowls and plates, candlesticks, trays, and compotes. Prices for similar objects will double or triple if in pristine condition or in a scarce color. For instance, a common lacy covered sugar bowl in clear might be found for $400–$600, but in color it would probably cost $1,500–$3,000 or more. Rare forms and colors can bring thousands of dollars. A colored lacy pane for furniture, marked with the name of the Pittsburgh company that produced it, brought over $10,000 a few years ago.

For the general collector lacy glass offers one of the best bargains in the glass collecting field today. A good, representative collection of small pieces could be gathered for a few hundred dollars.

Old Versus New

The bane of every collector is the worry about reproductions. Unfortunately, early lacy glass also fell victim to this scourge. Fortunately, reproductions in lacy glass are fewer and easier to identify than those of many other types of American pressed glass.

The key factor to keep in mind when trying to determine the age of a lacy piece is that it must be flint glass and should ring when tapped. All pressed glass from 1825 through the mid-1860s was produced with lead oxide, which made a heavy, clear glass that gives off a lovely metallic ring when gently tapped. If you come across a small piece of lacy glass, the simplest test is to pick it up between your thumb and forefinger, without letting it touch any other part of your hand, and tap the edge gently with a pencil or snap it softly with your other hand. The object should ring like a bell with a resounding "piinnggg." If it just goes "ping" without much resonance, it is most likely a later reproduction. Remember: only conduct this test with the permission of the owner; don't walk through a shop or show randomly "pinging" everything in sight. A reputable dealer should let one ring the piece oneself or offer to tap it for one. If the dealer will not allow this, it is probably best to pass on the piece until you develop more expertise at recognizing quality pieces.

The most abundant reproductions of lacy glassware were of historical cup plates. Very few other dishes, bowls, and larger pieces were ever reproduced convincingly because the time necessary and expense of making a new mold and producing the flint glass would make it unprofitable. Small cup plates, however, were much easier to copy, and reproductions of some of them date back to the 1920s. They may show signs of age and wear similar to the originals. Remember: no ring, no sale. Also, there are excellent references that discuss and illustrate the commonly reproduced cup plates.

When handling a lacy cup plate or other piece of lacy glass, there are a few clues one can look for in addition to the "ping."

Since these pieces basically were made one at a time in hand-operated presses, they often show some signs of this early manufacture. By carefully examining the surface of a piece, one may be able to recognize clues to early production.

First, look for signs of *underfilling* of the mold and *unevenness* in the thickness of a piece caused by uneven pressure during pressing. Underfills on a lacy piece are usually obvious on the scalloped rim.

Fig. 4-15 Authentic and reproduction lacy *Heart* cup plates, side by side. The real one, on the left, has finer stippling but cruder hearts than the reproduction on the right.

A scallop may be missing or partially missing. Such a gap in the design will be smooth and rounded and not easily disguised as a smoothed-over rim flake or chip, which should have sharp edges. Unevenness of the surface may be a little harder to notice, but in extreme examples one rim of a piece will be visibly thinner than that on the opposite edge.

Another clue that may help identify an early piece is the *shear mark* found near the center of most lacy pieces. This shear mark appears as a slightly indented swirl at the inside center and is the result of the shearing or cutting off of the gather of molten glass as it was dropped into the mold. The molten glass blob, like honey dropped from a spoon, formed a teardrop tapering to a thin tail. When this tail melted back into the surface of the glass in the mold, it often left the swirled indentation. Some modern reproductions of lacy glass do have this shear mark, so it is not an infallible sign of age, but taken into account with other guidelines it can be helpful.

Related to shear marks are *annealing marks* and *annealing cracks*. These marks originated dur-

Fig. 4-16 A close-up to illustrate the overfilling sometimes found on early lacy pieces. Note the little "fins" of glass between the three scallops on the far left side of this lacy dish.

ing the annealing (cooling) process of a piece as it passed through the lehr. During the annealing process, as the glass contracted and cooled, small fissures sometimes appeared in the surface of a piece. They could occur almost anywhere on a piece but most often showed up along the edges. Similar to

Fig. 4-17 A close-up of the swirled shear marks in the center of an early lacy cup plate.

these fissures are actual small cracks caused by the same tensions in the cooling glass. Sometimes these cracks appear at the spot where a blown handle is applied to the body of a creamer or pitcher. Because the two pieces of glass could cool at a slightly different rate, this crack occurred as the glass contracted. Small fissures and tiny cracks along rims generally are not considered serious damage since they happened "in the making." Cracks at the base of handles, however, are a more serious problem and probably will reduce somewhat the market value of that piece.

Over the years the annealing marks just described have sometimes been called "straw marks" in the mistaken belief that just after a piece of glass was pressed it was dropped onto a pile of straw to cool and, while the glass was still plastic, the straw left indentations on its surface. This was not done and would have been a messy and unnecessary

Fig. 4-18 This photograph illustrates how lacy patterns carried over into later flint-era designs. The *Peacock Feather* pattern lacy dish on the left, ca. 1840, has much the same design as the *Horn of Plenty* (M'Kee's *Comet*) spoon holder on the right, ca. 1860.

procedure. It was important to get the still-hot piece of glass to the lehr as soon as possible, before it cooled too quickly. Any piece allowed to cool on a bed of straw probably would have shattered during the annealing process. The straw mark is one of those myths of glass collecting that developed years ago. Today, with better understanding of early glass production techniques, this myth should be put to rest and the slight imperfections referred to more properly as annealing marks. They are one other indication to watch for in establishing a date for a piece of pressed glass.

Until one becomes better acquainted with early lacy glass, one may be confused by lacy-looking patterns that continued to be produced later in the nineteenth century and some that were revived in the twentieth century.

As mentioned in the discussion of European lacy pieces, foreign factories appear to have continued making lacy patterns later than their American counterparts. In the United States true lacy designs had nearly died out by the 1850s, but there were a few holdovers. The pattern that most readily comes to mind is the *Princess Feather* pattern (originally called *Rochelle* by its makers in the 1850s). This scrolling design with stippling continued to be made after flint glass died out in the 1870s and can be found in nonflint-quality glass. There are also new patterns of the 1870s and later that featured flowers against a stippled ground and which, at first glance, may resemble older lacy. Some of these patterns include *Rose in Snow, Ivy in Snow,* and various stippleds such as *Stippled Daisy, Stippled Cherry,* and *Stippled Forget-Me-Not.* Besides the fact that these were made in nonflint glass, the pieces in these lines are generally thinner and lighter in weight than comparable lacy objects. The later pressed glass patterns, as will be seen, also were produced in a wide range of forms unknown or rare in lacy glass such as goblets, tumblers, large compotes, and pitchers.

Beginning around the 1920s, when early Sandwich glass first attracted the attention of collectors and there was a general revival of interest in all things early American, many reproductions and adaptations of eighteenth- and early nineteenth-cen-

Fig. 4-19 A *Ray* pattern dish at right dates ca. 1860 but mimics in a cruder form the *Rayed Peacock Eye* lacy dish, ca. 1830, left.

tury designs were produced. Early furniture pieces and metalware, especially pewter, were copied widely. Early glass, both blown and pressed, also was reproduced or adapted to modern glass lines. Familiar to collectors of Depression-era glass of the 1930s and 1940s are the Sandwich patterns produced by the Hocking Glass Company and the very similar line produced by the Indiana Glass Company from the 1920s to the 1980s. A novice might be fooled by these and similar revivals of lacy designs at first, but after handling a piece or two, the differences become apparent. Color, weight, and forms of pieces are vastly different from their nineteenth-century ancestors.

Finally, there are the close copies of early glass being produced for some large American museums. These copies are very good, with outstanding quality and mold work. Sometimes the pieces are *too* perfect, and this can be one clue to dating them. Early lacy pieces almost invariably have some "dings" around the rim. The museum-made copies sometimes will feel as heavy as the originals and may have the ring of the old, but generally they show few signs of wear, especially around the rims. Their biggest saving grace is that they are carefully marked by the museums, marked, usually with tiny initials in the base design. It may take some looking, but one should be able to locate initials such as "MMA" (for the Metropolitan Museum of Art in New York), or "SM" (for the Sandwich Glass Museum in Sandwich, Massachusetts).

Fig. 4-20 A close-up showing the "SM" initials for the Sandwich Glass Museum in the bottom of a reproduction lacy tray. Can you see the markings? They are in the top two corner loops in the center band.

The Henry Ford Museum also had some copies made that carry the institution's initials. Some new cup plates are being produced in flint glass that ring quite well, but most of these are made in modern designs, often as commemoratives, with no counterpart in old glass. With a little care and study these and the museum releases should not be difficult to recognize, but until one has seen and handled the real thing, it is probably safest to buy from reputable dealers and experienced collectors.

Part III
The Colonial Era of Pressed Glass
1845–1865

CHAPTER 5

Flint Glass of the Mid-Nineteenth Century

Why, one might ask, is the period of American pressed glass production stretching from about 1845 to 1865 referred to here as the colonial era? The actual American colonial period ended with the Declaration of Independence in 1776. However, many years ago in glass collecting circles, a number of simple and elegant pressed glass patterns of the 1845 to 1865 era were first referred to as the "colonial group." Pioneering glass author and researcher Ruth Webb Lee, in her book *Early American Pressed Glass* (which was first published in 1931), noted that "perhaps the thickness of the ware and the simplicity of the design suggesting primitive times" was responsible for the designation "colonial." Lee then went on to list and describe seventeen patterns of heavy and brilliant pressed flint glass that are included under the colonial heading.

Although Lee and her contemporaries may have considered these patterns primitive, my personal feelings and those of many pressed glass lovers is that these patterns, and others of the era, are among the loveliest and most elegant ever developed. Many of the patterns continued in production after the flint glass period following the Civil War and, as will be seen, were copied and revived right through the twentieth century. Some, with variations, may be seen in production today.

Historically speaking, the period of the 1840s

through the 1860s hardly can be called primitive. This time was one of tremendous social and industrial growth in the United States. American heavy industry, including the glass industry, really took hold, and old centers of production in New England and the Midwest continued to prosper as new western frontiers opened up and markets enlarged. Millions of foreign immigrants arrived on American shores to seek work in industrial centers, and new cities and towns mushroomed throughout the Midwest and West. Travel and communication systems were expanding with the arrival of the telegraph, railroads, canal systems, and steamboat traffic on major river systems such as the Ohio, Mississippi, and Missouri. Whereas pressed glass production in the 1820s was restricted somewhat because factories had to locate near sources of raw materials and retail markets, by the mid–nineteenth century it was much easier to obtain materials needed for production and to ship the finished products to the far corners of the country and overseas.

This was also the era when Americans took up the call of Manifest Destiny and decided to take control of the entire continent from coast to coast. The nation thrashed its poor neighbor, Mexico, in a war in the late 1840s, took over California and the Southwest, and eventually pushed the British out of the Pacific Northwest and north of the forty-ninth parallel. Some people even dreamed of annexing parts of Central America and the Caribbean. This mood of expansionism extended to every segment of American society, and American industry looked forward to serving an ever-growing marketplace.

Glassware of any type had been quite rare in colonial America and through the first quarter of the nineteenth century. The average American household probably only had a few bottles, flasks, and utilitarian pieces. By the time the lacy period died out, nearly every American could afford to own at least a few small plates and bowls of glass for a tea service or to present a special dessert. Pressed glass was no longer a luxury item by the end of the American Civil War. A good selection of serviceable pieces was to be had nearly anywhere in the country. Although there were no huge retail outlets, almost any town with one or more general mercantile stores had a supply of pressed glass available. Even on the edge of the western frontier, pioneers recently arrived from the East cherished a few pieces of chinaware and pressed glass.

As American consumers became more sophisticated and discriminating, American manufacturers strove to produce a better quality and range of wares in the latest styles. Patterns and designs in pressed glass, as well as other realms, reflected this growing sophistication. Even the most mundane of pressed glassware tried to imitate and emulate the high-priced cut- and blown-glass pieces coming from England and Europe. There was still a huge gap between the rich and the poor, but an ever-expanding middle class demanded all sorts of products, including glass, which would give at least an impression of taste.

Improvements in glass-pressing technology meant that a larger range of pieces was being manufactured. This is when specific patterns first evolved and diverse objects such as bowls, plates, pitchers, creamers, and sugar bowls were made in matching lines to be used as part of a unified table setting.

By the end of the Civil War, many American households undoubtedly could boast of at least a four-piece table setting featuring a covered butter dish, covered sugar bowl, creamer, and spoon holder (or "spooner") to grace their sideboards or serving tables. Handsome, heavy bell-toned flint glass sparkled on dining tables all across the burgeoning United States.

Forms and Designs

Although records from early glass factories are scarce (especially regarding pressed glass patterns), by the late 1840s and early 1850s some nonlacy patterns apparently were being produced on a fairly large scale. This marked the beginning of the true pattern glass era in American glassmaking. In this sense *pattern glass* refers to a line of pressed glass with an easily recognized design produced in a number of matching pieces. As mentioned, lacy glass, although pressed, was not made in a wide selection of matching items. People sometimes will ask about the difference between pressed glass and pattern glass. Actually, there is no difference, since a majority of the glass now referred to as pattern glass was produced by means of a pressing machine and is, therefore, pressed glass. Most glass produced today for everyday use is pressed and often appears in specific patterns with a variety of pieces. Technically, it is pressed pattern glass. However, in glass collecting circles pattern glass is the term used to refer to those pressed designs made from the 1840s through the turn of the twentieth century that were made in a range of items for table use. A longer title sometimes used for this glassware is *Early American pattern (pressed) glass,* often abbreviated in advertisements offering antique glass as *EAPG.* Early in this case means anything before World War I or thereabouts.

The Colonials

As mentioned at the beginning of this section, the earliest patterns of pressed glass from this period have been referred to for many years as the colonial group. These seventeen patterns are quite varied but have certain design characteristics in common. They were bold and simple patterns featuring large indented circles (often called "bull's eyes" or "thumbprints"), arching and rounded loops and panels or square panels or blocks. The manufacturer selected these motifs to copy or emulate the then-popular designs of expensive cut-glass ware. Unlike the fancy and fussy cut-glass designs of the Brilliant Period of the late nineteenth and early twentieth centuries, fine cut glass of the late eighteenth and early nineteenth centuries featured deeply cut, bold, and simple design elements. These sorts of patterns could be adapted readily to molds for pressing glass and so were popular beginning in the 1840s and 1850s. Not many people in America could afford the expensive cut glass imported from England or Europe (and made on a limited scale in New England and Pittsburgh), but the pressed imitations were affordable to nearly everyone.

Studying these early patterns is made easier because, for the first time, some of them are illustrated in advertisements and original company catalogs dating from the 1850s and 1860s. With the help

of such printed materials and other records, glass researchers over the years have been able to put together a very complete listing of the patterns and pieces made.

As far as the colonial group of patterns is concerned, it is important to know that they were made in a smaller range of pieces than the slightly later flint glass patterns and in a much smaller range than later nineteenth-century nonflint pressed wares. Most common in these early patterns are drinking vessels such as goblets. Some of the pattern lines had half a dozen different vessels to serve liquid refreshment, including a goblet; wine, champagne, and cordial glasses, a mug, and perhaps a few sizes of tumblers. Not all the patterns were made with all these pieces, but all of them included at least some of them. Bowls and footed compotes, both with and without covers, also were abundant and show up on the market quite often today. Common pieces such as spoon holders (usually low-footed, small vases), sugar bowls, creamers, decanters, eggcups (for

Fig. 5-1 A variety of stemware sizes in the flint *Huber* pattern. From left to right: a goblet, a wine glass, and a cordial glass. The champagne glass, sized between the goblet and wine glass, is not shown.

serving soft-boiled eggs), sauce dishes (four to six inches in diameter), and usually one or two sizes of pitchers also are available. The pitchers are today referred to as milk pitchers or water pitchers, although originally they could have been used for any liquid refreshment.

One fairly common piece of pressed flint glass popular with collectors is the *spill holder*. The "spill" was a piece of paper that would be placed under an oil lamp while it was being filled in order to soak up any spilled fuel. This paper then was rolled up tightly to form a punk for later use in lighting the lamp. The spill holder was meant to hold these rolled rods of fuel-soaked paper for easy access. Spill holders usually are cylindrical, flat-bottomed vases raised on a short, thick pedestal foot. Many were produced in patterns that do not match any tableware line of the period, although a few did. Recent research indicates, however, that the term "spill" was not used to describe this vessel until the 1870s at the earliest. The original glass catalogs of the 1850s and 1860s that show these pieces refer to them as "spoon holders." Spoon holders, of course, are part of the four-piece table set common in pattern glass from the 1860s onward. Most people think of spoon holders as round-bottomed vases raised on short, slender pedestals. Of course nothing says that these original spoon holders could not have been put to use for holding paper spills, too, and it is unlikely that modern collectors will stop using the long-popular term spill holder to refer to this group of attractive pieces.

Old glass catalogs also show that, for the first time, glass manufacturers gave some of their patterns a specific name designation. In some cases these original factory names are still in common use among glass collectors. In other cases, where no original name is known or has not been discovered, collectors tacked on their own names for patterns. Over the years a number of original pattern glass names have been discovered or rediscovered, and some researchers feel these old names should now be instituted. I believe, however, it will be difficult to replace a popular, long-used collector name with the original one, especially since many of the new names are much more descriptive of the design than were the originals.

To give you some idea of the popularity of these early designs, the original seventeen colonial patterns are listed according to the main motifs used in their design. When the name is the original manufacturer's name for the pattern, it is noted in parentheses after the name with "o.n." for "original name."

The Colonials

1. Designs composed of large, indented circles or oval panels:

Ashburton (o.n.)
Argus (o.n.)
Bigler
Colonial
Excelsior (o.n.)
Oval Mitre (o.n.)

2. Designs composed of circles (thumbprints) with indented straight or curved lines:

Block with Thumbprint
Diamond Thumbprint
Four Petal
Loop (Petal and Loop; originally O'Hara or Leaf)
Pillar (o.n.)
Pressed Block
Sandwich Star
Waffle and Thumbprint (originally Palace)
Washington (o.n.)

Fig. 5-2 Spooner or spill holder? The *Diamond Point* spooner on the left shows the typical shape associated with spooners, while the *Sawtooth* piece on the right usually is referred to as a spill holder, even though it probably was originally sold as a spoon holder.

Fig. 5-3 A small *Loop* pattern open compote.

3. Designs composed of plain, long panels:

Flute

Huber (o.n.)

Some interesting points regarding these patterns are worth mentioning.

The *Ashburton* pattern was called by that name as early as the late 1840s, and records indicate pieces in that line were shipped to the California gold fields as early as 1849. One of the most popular glass patterns of the mid–nineteenth century, it was made in a wide range of pieces until the 1880s. After the mid-1860s, however, it was not produced in the heavy, ringing flint of earlier years.

The *Washington* pattern is another interesting one. Besides being one of the first patterns named for a famous person—George Washington—it is also a pattern name that can lead to confusion among beginning collectors because two other Washington patterns are available. The second Washington pattern was produced around 1876, at the time of the U.S. Centennial Exhibition in Philadelphia. Collectors usually refer to it as the *Washington Centennial* pattern. The third Washington

Fig. 5-4 The first of the *Washington* patterns. This celery vase dates ca. 1850–1860.

line was part of the late 1890s *States* series of patterns and actually referred to Washington State rather than the father of our country. The story of American pressed glass is full of such interesting and sometimes confusing little asides, which will be touched upon later.

Other Early Tableware Patterns

In addition to the first seventeen colonial patterns discussed, several dozen other fairly simple and elegant designs also date from the 1850s and 1860s. The following list is not meant to be complete or comprehensive, but it should give an idea of the variety of the most popular glass still available to collecters.

Several patterns feature a row of small circles (bull's eyes) as part of the design. These include *Bull's Eye* (originally called *Lawrence*), *Bull's Eye and Diamond Point* (originally *Union*), and *Bull's Eye and Fleur de Lis*.

A pattern reminiscent of old lacy glass is composed of a row of cornucopia standing upright on their tails and is called *Horn of Plenty* by collectors. It was originally sold as *Comet*. To make life interesting, there is another early pattern collectors call Comet that is totally different, and—hold on—there's a third nonflint pattern of the 1880s and 1890s known as *Halley's Comet*. A pattern marketed originally as *Ray* is another flint design reminiscent of older lacy glass and includes what looks like a pair of crossed cornucopias around the sides of pieces (see Fig. 4-19).

Other less-confusing patterns include *Tulip* (original name), *New England Pineapple*, *Gothic*, *Hamilton* (and the similar *Hamilton with Leaf*), *Pillar and Bull's Eye* (originally called *Thistle*), *Buckle*, *Magnet and Grape*, and *Wedding Ring* (also known as *Double Wedding Ring*).

The *Lincoln Drape* and *Lincoln Drape with Tassel* patterns feature a swagged band around the top and were, according to tradition, produced to

Fig. 5-5 On the right is a *Bull's-Eye* goblet, while on the left is a *Bull's-Eye and Diamond Point* piece.

Fig. 5-6 A row of three comet designs. On the left is a goblet in M'Kee's early *Comet* pattern, today called *Horn of Plenty*. In the middle is a goblet in the early *Comet* pattern, and on the right is a wine glass in the *Halley's Comet* pattern of the 1890s.

Fig. 5-7 A covered sugar bowl in the flint *Gothic* pattern, ca. 1860.

Fig. 5-8 This goblet is in the *Lincoln Drape with Tassel* pattern.

commemorate Abraham Lincoln's death. However, since flint glass was probably falling out of favor about that time, this commemorative tie-in may be a fiction. The *Cable* and *Cable with Ring* patterns, on the other hand, apparently were introduced to commemorate the laying of the Atlantic telegraph cable. Each pattern features a simple band of cable around the tops of pieces.

A widely produced pattern of this era was *Sawtooth* (originally *Diamond*), which is composed of an overall design of large, pointed diamonds. It should not be confused with *Diamond Point* (originally called *Sharp Diamond*), which is made up of a design of overall small diamonds (see Fig. 5-2).

Two patterns that were first introduced in the flint glass era but continued in production for decades were the *Thumbprint* pattern and the *Honeycomb* pattern. The Thumbprint pattern was origi-

nally called *Argus* by the Bakewell Company, although it is totally different from the earlier *Argus* pattern listed. The Honeycomb pattern derives its name from the overall motif featuring the hexagonal compartments of a comb of honey. It also was produced for decades in both flint and nonflint glass and, actually, never has gone out of production. The same design appears on contemporary drinking ware today, especially those used in restaurants. During the 1920s and 1930s nearly identical patterns also were produced by a number of glass firms. Honeycomb is a pattern that requires a good deal of study to know the truly old from more recent pieces. In flint glass, however, the weight and bell-tone ring are easy giveaways.

The *Waffle* pattern is composed of overall small, square blocks around the sides of pieces. A similar pattern, *Waffle and Thumbprint*, is one of

Fig. 5-9 The *Waffle and Thumbprint* pattern in a large decanter.

the colonial grouping. Finally, for music lovers, there is the *Harp* pattern, which features an ancient hand-held harp on the paneled sides of pieces.

One little-known pattern is today called *Madison* by collectors. However, in studying copies of some old glass catalogs I realized that this pattern originally was produced around 1860 by James B. Lyon and Company of Pittsburgh as its *Crystal* pattern. The Crystal pattern listed previously was produced by M'Kee and Brothers and is a simple, paneled design. On the other hand, Lyon's Crystal (Madison) is more complex. Actually, there appear to be several variations to this Crystal. In one variation (#1) pieces generally have hexagonal rims above rounded, hexagonal sides (see Figure 5-10). Each panel of the side is centered by a raised ring surrounding two short bars. On a slight variation (#2), the rings are framed by narrow ribbing while on #1 the background is plain. The third variation (#3) has the rings, but they are filled with three-bar crosses instead of parallel bars. This variation is also known today as *Lined panel* and also was made with the fine ribbing around the rings (#4). These four variations, according to catalog illustrations, only came in a small range of pieces. Variant #1 had a creamer, covered sugar bowl (two styles), spooner, seven-inch-wide covered bowl and seven-inch-wide covered compote. Variant #2 is shown only in a six-inch-wide and seven-inch-wide covered compote. Variant #3 (Lined Panel) is shown only as a celery vase, spooner, and a seven-inch-long and eight-inch-long oblong covered bowl on a low foot. Finally, there is a group of large, open compotes (#5) in a totally *different* rib and diamond point design that Lyon also called Crystal.

The Ribbed Group

Another group of patterns from the flint era features a band of design, usually a plant motif, against a background of fine vertical ribbing. These patterns were made from the late 1850s through the 1860s and are found in both flint and nonflint, so check each piece carefully as the heavier flint examples generally are more desirable. Some of these patterns were made in a wide range of pieces and will show up on the market fairly frequently. Others were made on a limited scale and are much scarcer today.

The plainest of the ribbed designs is called *Fine Rib* (an original name) and consists of only fine ribbing around the body. The most common and popular of the ribbed group is *Bellflower*, which features a single or entwined double vine of pointed leaves and bell-form flowers around the middle of the ribbed body. This abundant pattern was made by factories in New England and Pittsburgh and was offered originally as *Ribbed Leaf* by the makers. It can be found in several variations, including one with a background of fine ribs and another with

Fig. 5-10 A page from the 1861 Lyon and Company catalog showing several of its patterns. In the upper right corner is a *Crystal* (*Madison*) pattern spooner, sugar bowl, and creamer. Note that the term "spill holder" is not used in this ad. Courtesy of the Rakow Library of the Corning Museum of Glass.

thicker (coarse) ribbing. Different styles of stems also appear on the goblets, wine glasses, and other drinking vessels, some plain and some with knobs in the center of the stem. Collectors of Bellflower must know exactly which variation they are looking for. All the variations go together well, but some people prefer the single vine over the double vine variation. It is all a matter of personal taste, and this lovely pattern gives one a real selection from which to choose.

Less-common ribbed patterns include *Ribbed Grape* (with a grapevine, of course), *Ribbed Palm*, and *Inverted Fern*. These last two can be a bit confusing because they each feature scalloped palm-type leaves in the design. On *Ribbed Palm*

(originally called *Sprig*) a row of large leaves extends up from the bottom edge of the sides of pieces, while on *Inverted Fern* similar leaves alternately extend from the base rim or the top rim around the sides.

Ribbed Ivy and *Ribbed Acorn* are the last two of this ribbed group. Ribbed Ivy, with its band of ivy leaves on a vine, is fairly abundant and was made in a large range of pieces, while Ribbed Acorn was produced on a limited scale with only a small range of pieces including a covered butter dish, various compotes, a small three-and-a-half-inch-diameter dish (called a "honey" dish) and a larger sauce dish.

A Little More Light on the Subject

For many people a sideline to collecting pressed glass tableware is the acquisition of some early lighting devices also produced, in whole or in part, by means of mechanical pressing. As discussed in the lacy glass section, from the 1820s to the 1840s early lamps and candlesticks were made with pressed glass bases combined with free-blown fonts, the two parts joined by a glass wafer. Such wafers continued to be used to join separately pressed pieces to form a single object right into the 1870s. It took glass designers that long to begin to develop molds that could press larger pieces of glass, such as compotes and lamps, in one piece.

Beginning about the 1850s a much wider variety of lamps and candlesticks was being pressed. Lighting technology was moving ahead fairly rapidly. The discovery of large reserves of crude oil in Pennsylvania in 1859 soon led to a tremendous growth in the petroleum industry and, within a few years, kerosene, a new and safer fuel for lamps, was available widely. It remained the standard lighting fuel throughout the remainder of the nineteenth century and well into the twentieth.

Before the arrival of kerosene other liquid fuels were used. They were, however, fairly expensive and dangerous to use, which limited their appeal. In the late eighteenth century Swiss chemist Aimé Argand invented a special oil-burning lamp that was the first to surpass candlelight, but such lamps were rare and expensive in early America. Usually of cast bronze, they were more common by the 1840s when they often were used in matching pairs on the mantels and sideboards of the affluent. Refinements to the Argand lamp in the early nineteenth century included the Astral, Sinumbra, and Solar, lamps which were also available by the 1840s. They were, again, rather expensive metal lamps that used round or pear-shaped clear and frosted blown-glass shades.

Of more practical benefit to the average American consumer was the growth of the American whaling industry, which boomed from the 1820s through the 1850s. Although today considered an environmental disaster, the massive exploitation of the world's largest mammals did supply the high-quality whale oil that fueled early lamps. The oil of the sperm whale and the right whale (named because it was the "right" whale to hunt) were the choicest and provided a clean-burning and nonvolatile fuel. This oil was not cheap, but it was superior to wax candles and tapers. The other major household fuel for lamps before the development of kerosene was the very dangerous mixture of turpentine and alcohol called *camphine*. Many types of table lamps could be fitted with burners fueled by these substances, and by the Civil War many households probably had a lamp or two. The candle, however, remained an important secondary lighting source. Generally only larger cities had gas lines in place to provide household and street lighting in the better parts of town in the pre–Civil War period.

In the pressed-flint-glass era, roughly 1840–1865, a wide variety of table lamps and candlesticks became available.

Candlesticks, unlike many lamps of this period, usually were not made in patterns that matched tableware lines. The sticks, however, generally did feature simple and restrained designs similar to the flint tableware patterns.

Probably the most famous candlestick of this period is the "dolphin" model, often associated with the Boston and Sandwich Glass Company. This popular style was composed of a base with a figural dolphin, its head resting on a usually square base and its tail raised in the air to support the candle socket. Even though the Sandwich dolphins

Fig. 5-11 A small plate in the *Ribbed Grape* pattern.

Fig. 5-12 The classic Sandwich "Dolphin" candlestick in clambroth color is on the left. A twentieth-century milk glass reproduction is on the right.

are the most famous, other glass firms in New England and Pittsburgh made similar models. It can take a trained eye to differentiate between the dolphin sticks made at Sandwich and those made elsewhere. However, any of the originals in flint glass is desirable, especially in colored glass.

Probably the most commonly found socket is the "petal" socket, which derives its name from its resemblance to a flower blossom with the petal tips curled back. It also can often be found on a base composed of a circle of long loops. When combined they form the *Petal and Loop* candlestick. Other forms of bases that might turn up were pressed to resemble reeded columns or large leaves, and a simple, flaring, hexagonal base is also quite common. Any of these bases could be combined with a variety of candle sockets by means of the glass wafer technique.

Another candlestick pattern made at Sandwich and elsewhere in the nineteenth century is the "crucifix" model. It is actually in the form of the cross with Christ, which forms the pedestal below the candle socket. These sticks were widely produced in flint glass in various colors, especially milk glass, and they continued to be produced for a number of years after flint glass was no longer commonly used in glass pressing. Although very popular with the

Fig. 5-13 This *Petal and Loop* pattern candlestick was made from two separately pressed pieces joined by a wafer of glass.

Victorians, this design is less appealing to today's collector and generally sells for less than other styles of the same vintage.

In contrast to candlesticks, table lamps of the flint glass era, originally called "stand" lamps, quite often were produced in the simple, bold patterns also found on tableware. Patterns such as Argus, Bellflower, Sawtooth, Tulip, and Waffle and Thumbprint can all be found on footed table lamp fonts. The large fonts, often cylindrical, hexagonal, round or pear shaped, usually were raised on a handsome baluster-form pedestal with a square or hexagonal foot. Since the glass font and footed pedestal had to be pressed separately, once again the wafer of molten glass was used to join them together into a single lamp.

A vast majority of these lamps, as with the candlesticks, were made in clear glass, but companies such as Sandwich did produce lovely examples in colored glass, with the milky white *clambroth* color and the yellow-green *vaseline* color being

Fig. 5-14 A close-up of the glass "wafer" at the center of the *Petal and Loop* candlestick.

Fig. 5-15 This clear all-glass lamp has a *Tulip* pattern font joined by a wafer to a hexagonal base. Note the neck opening in the font, which would have taken a cork stopper with burner tubes through it.

more common than other hues. In rare examples one color of glass was used on the font or candle socket while another was used on the base. These two-color combinations, such as clambroth and blue or clambroth and green, made striking pieces

and such lighting devices are among the most expensive pieces of flint glass one will find today.

Another method of producing lamps without the use of a glass wafer was to combine a pressed-glass font with a hollow metal pedestal, often made of brass, and then joining the two parts to a square, white marble foot. An iron rod ran up through the foot and the center of the pedestal and screwed into a metal ring connector attached to a peg at the base of the font with a coating of plaster of paris, which made a solid adhesive. This method made it easy to assemble parts with various designs to produce a wide range of closely related lamps.

If this sounds a bit complicated, it is. The system worked, but it certainly was possible for a font to come loose unexpectedly if the plaster seal broke. Today collectors must use extra caution when handling such lamps. Remember not to submerge them in water for a long period when cleaning or that old plaster bond may melt. If this does happen, however, the parts can quite easily be rejoined with a new batch of wet plaster of paris. Also, when handling such lamps, pick them up with both hands, one on the font and one on the base. A sudden jerk could cause the plaster bond to give way.

Another variety of lamp of this period features a pressed font joined to a pressed base by a metal connector. This ring was attached to the pegged base of the font and the top of the base. Most often, again, plaster of paris was used as an adhesive to join the font and base to the ring, although some rings were designed with wide threading into which threaded posts on the font and base could be screwed. Many of these lamps have clear fonts attached to milk white bases, although other color combinations are known and one may find bases of black, blue, or other colors.

The metal connector was common on table lamps through the 1870s, but by the 1880s more pressed lamps were pressed in one piece, or the two glass sections were joined together directly with a peg on the font fitting into the top of the base. Even though metal connectors were used right through the 1890s, one will find many lamps of the later nineteenth century made of all glass. More and more colors were used in lamp production, and shades of blue and amber were especially popular. Sometimes one finds some unusual color combinations, too, with blue fonts attached to amber bases or vice versa. These late-Victorian colored glass lamps are especially popular with collectors today, with their popularity spurred by some excellent reference books, most notably the two-volume work *Oil Lamps: The Kerosene Era in North America* by Catherine Thuro.

Although pressed-glass lamps became the norm in the second half of the nineteenth century, a wide selection of lamps was produced from the 1850s onward with blown-glass fonts joined to pressed-glass, blown-glass or metal and marble bases. Space does not allow an in-depth study of

Fig. 5-16 A lamp with a pressed *Hearts and Stars* pattern font attached with a brass ring to a pressed milk glass base, ca. 1870–1880. It is shown with a typical kerosene burner.

these lamps here, so refer to the Thuro books for further information.

This discussion of lamps and candlesticks concludes with another important component: burners. Most collectors today are familiar with the typical kerosene burner, still available in many hardware stores, that requires a wide cloth wick and is controlled by a little handle extending from the side that raises and lowers the wick and thus controls the size cap extended one or, more often, two short tubes through which was fed the stringlike wick. Whale oil was fairly thick and not too volatile, so the short distance between the lighted flame and the fuel in the font was not a problem. On the other hand, camphine, originally referred to simply as "burning fluid," was highly volatile and lamps were known to explode while being lit. Because of this danger, another type of burner was developed that had two

Fig. 5-17 This early lamp has a free-blown font on a pressed base; ca. 1830–1840. It is shown with a whale oil burner.

of the flame. With the earlier types of fuel—whale oil and camphine—no such efficient system was available. Both these fuels required specific types of burners that had no handy mechanism to control the wick.

The whale oil burner was simply a thin screw cap that screwed into a metal collar fixed on the neck of the lamp's font, usually with plaster of paris. Some caps, though, simply attached to a cork inserted into the neck of the font. Through the metal

Fig. 5-18 This lovely ruby-flashed lamp font is cut with a Gothic arch design and is shown with an early camphine burner, ca. 1850.

long, angled wick tubes extending through the burner cap. These tubes kept the lit wicks apart so they produced less heat and also kept the flames further away from the filled font.

Most whale oil and camphine burners were not designed to use lamp shades. The lamps just had the open flames from the wick, basically a brighter form of candlelight. Such burners also were used on nonglass lamps of the era, especially pewter and brass pieces, and the burners were pretty much interchangeable with the threaded caps fitting either glass or metal lamps.

Surprisingly, quite a number of these original burners still can be found on old lamps, but reproductions have been made over the years, so buy them with care.

The other component of the lamp font is the metal collar into which the burner was screwed. These were most often of brass and were very simple in design, either undecorated or with just a couple of thin indented or raised parallel bands around them. Plaster of paris was again the bonding agent that joined them to the narrow neck of the font. These collars can be a guide to the general age of the lamp, but over the years the old collars could have worn out and been replaced by later versions. Reproductions of the collars are also available. Although it is preferable to have the original collar on a lamp, a replacement is not a great detriment to the overall value. The collars were originally produced with various-sized openings, and some sizes may be harder to find today. For years electric converters have been available that screw right into the old collars and thus convert an old lamp to an electric lamp without any need for drilling the font, as was sometimes done by early collectors. Drilling, by the way, does lower the value of all but the rarest of lamps drastically.

It takes a bit of care to determine if the collar on a lamp is original, or at least old. Reproduction collars and antique-style lamps have been produced since the 1920s and may have aged naturally over the decades. Basically, it pays to look at the incised lines around the collar. It will be even and sharp on old collars but often shallow and more rounded on reproductions. Collars with raised bands around them are much more difficult to date.

For antique collectors it is always desirable to have some antique lamps and candlesticks around to decorate one's home, and, thanks to the abundance of lamps mass produced since the 1850s, a wonderful variety is still available to choose from today. With careful conversion they can continue to serve the lighting needs of another century while charming us with their grace and beauty.

Production Centers

The years between 1840 and the end of the Civil War in 1865 saw a notable growth in American industry, which was reflected in the increasing number of glass factories established. Pressed glass tableware and lamps became increasingly important as America's population grew and expanded westward. To meet these demands established factories in New England and Pittsburgh continued to churn out a wide selection of wares and strong markets led to growing competition. Quite a number of factories opened, especially in the Pittsburgh region. Easier access to raw materials and markets meant that, within a few years, glass production in Pittsburgh outstripped that of its competitors along the East Coast and in New England.

The Boston and Sandwich and New England Glass Company continued going strong, but fewer and fewer new glassworks were set up in the East.

In Pittsburgh and vicinity, on the other hand, established firms such as Bakewell, Pears and Company, continued to prosper even with increasing local competition from nearly a dozen new glass factories opened by the 1860s. Several other factories also were established in nearby Wheeling, West Virginia, during this period, adding to the overall prominence of the midwestern glass industry.

One outcome of this increasing rivalry for the consumer dollar was the issuance of a number of wholesale catalogs by glass companies in the late 1850s and early 1860s. Before this time there are practically no illustrated records to show what pieces or patterns a specific glass firm might have produced. Now, happily, we can refer to a number of preserved catalogs, some of them recently reprinted, to see exactly which firm made what pattern.

This research material certainly adds an excit-

Fig. 5-19 Two variations of the flint *Bellflower* pattern. On the left is a goblet in the single vine, coarse rib, plain stem, rayed base variation, while on the right is one in the single vine, fine rib, barrel-shaped, knopped stem, plain base variation. Both ca. 1860.

ing element to the collecting of early pressed glass and can provide extra pleasure to the search for fine flint glass. However, these catalogs show that many popular patterns of flint glass were produced by more than one company. Certain designs were borrowed (stolen, really) or adapted by two or more competing glass firms. Bellflower, for example, was produced widely in New England and also shows up in the 1864 M'Kee and Brothers catalog under its pattern name *Ribbed Leaf*. Several other popular patterns of the 1850s and 1860s also are known to have been made by two or more rivals. Keep in mind that most of these designs were not patented as they would be today, and since glassworkers and moldmakers might move from company to company, it is easy to see how the popular patterns of the day also could move around. Although these catalogs are a boon to researchers and collectors today, keep in mind that they originally were not intended to be used by the buying public. They were wholesale catalogs, meant to be seen by merchants who sold the glassware to the public. Unlike today's mail-order catalogs, the average person on the street could not order directly from a factory but had to purchase an item be it glass, china, or furniture, from a local dry goods store or, in larger cities, a department store. If a glass pattern sold well, the wholesalers spurred its production through wholesale orders to the factory.

Today only a handful of original glass company catalogs are known from this period, including three from M'Kee and Brothers (1859, 1864, and 1868), one from Bakewell, Pears and Company (circa 1875), one from James B. Lyon and Company, Pittsburgh (1861), and one from the New England Glass Company (1868–1869). In addition, an illustrated advertisement for Curling, Robertson and Company in the Pittsburgh-Allegheny directory of 1856–1857 documents a number of patterns and pieces it apparently produced.

Desirability and Values

The factors that determine which pieces of flint pattern glass are most desirable and valuable are similar to those that relate to lacy glass: size, form, pattern, color, and condition.

Size generally is not quite as significant for this type of pressed glass simply because much more of it was produced in a wider range of sizes and pieces. Small pieces, such as sauce and honey dishes, are among the more common items in flint patterns since they originally were produced in large sets. Large pieces, such as covered compotes and decanters, are desirable and are quite common in some patterns. Most drinking vessels, such as goblets and tumblers, are fairly abundant in all flint patterns, especially in clear glass. Some of the more unusual forms such as wine, champagne, or cordial glasses

are a bit scarcer. Scarce too are certain sizes of tumblers (such as whiskey tumblers) and tumblers with applied handles, but, again, in clear glass they are readily available. For most flint patterns only one or two forms are rare. For instance, in the common Bellflower pattern, there is a rare sugar bowl with a flaring, octagonal bowl and a pyramidal cover that is totally different than the common rounded form. Syrup jugs with hinged tin lids are rare in most flint patterns, and a milk glass example in Bellflower is choice. Open-footed eggcups are quite common in flint glass, as are the smaller footed salt dips, but to find one with an original cover is a real triumph.

Certain patterns made in flint are quite rare today, since they were made in fewer pieces and for shorter periods of time. Even though such patterns may be rare in terms of scarcity, that does not necessarily mean they are more valuable than commoner lines. The old rule of supply and demand comes into play. If no collector is especially interested in a pattern the demand is low and so, correspondingly, is the market value. A few patterns were made in only a few pieces and are little known to collectors and dealers today. Such items sometimes can remain undiscovered or unappreciated and offer the careful shopper a chance at a real find.

The single most important factor in determining the desirability of a piece of flint glass is color. As in lacy glass, anything in a color is considered scarce, and certain pieces in certain colors are extremely rare and will sell for huge sums. Some patterns are nearly unheard of in any color, while other patterns will show up in a few colors quite often. One of the most common colors in flint glass is opaque milk white (called *opal* [o-pál] by nineteenth-century glassmakers). Shades of yellow and vaseline are also frequently seen. A color today called *fiery opalescent* has shades of milky white at the rims and raised areas of the pattern to almost clear near the center. It shows up fairly often in some patterns. Always in demand are shades of blue (cobalt, teal, or electric), purple or amethyst, and green. The blue and purple pieces are among the most expensive one will run across today, but green is actually scarcer. Since the greens are often very dark and not always showy, they do not appeal to as many collectors. Amber is also very rare in flint pattern glass, and red is practically unknown.

For an idea of how color can affect the market value of a piece of flint glass, consider a "bar lip" decanter in the Ashburton pattern. The bar lip decanter has a thick, rounded lip that was not meant to hold a glass stopper but was fitted originally with a pewter and cork spouted closure. In clear glass one might expect to pay $50 to $75 for a quart-size bar lip, but in canary yellow the range will more likely be $500 to $700. An example in dark blue or purple would cost $1,000 or better. Quite a spread!

This color factor is important for all pieces and patterns in flint glass. In general, a piece in a commoner color will sell for one hundred to two hundred times more than its clear counterpart. A choice color may well bring five hundred to a thousand times more.

Condition is the final factor to consider and is very important in valuing a piece. Unlike lacy glass, where a few small edge chips and flakes are fairly common, in pressed flint glass any chips or cracks have a drastic effect on market value. Common pieces in clear with noticeable edge chips or bad cracks are hardly saleable at all. Enough of it exists that collectors want perfect examples. A minor base flake on the foot of a good piece, such as a goblet or compote, will reduce the value somewhat, possibly 10 to 30 percent, depending on how noticeable it is. A sizeable chip or running crack makes it nearly worthless except as a fill-in piece, and it should bring only a few dollars. A very rare form or colored piece will retain some value, but serious damage can cut the sale price by half or more. Glass, of course, is all but impossible to repair invisibly, so it pays to seek out perfect or nearly perfect pieces or to pay very little for pieces with damage. Cracks, by the way, can be difficult to see in some patterns, since they may follow the pattern or mold lines. Keep in mind that a badly cracked piece of flint, such as a compote, may still ring like a bell when tapped.

Value Ranges

The following is a brief survey of price ranges for clear pieces of flint pattern glass in the most common and popular patterns.

$15—$30 range: Sauce and honey dishes.

$20—$50 range: Open eggcups, salt dips, small plates

$50—$100 range: Most drinking vessels such as goblets and tumblers; spooners and spill holders; some open compotes and bowls and some celery vases.

$100—$300 range: Covered sugar bowls and creamers; larger bowls and covered compotes; rare stemware like champagne, wine, and cordial glasses; covered butter dishes.

$300 and up: Many pitchers, very large compotes and rare covered dishes; syrup jugs or pitchers and almost anything in color. Colored vases and lamps can be in the $800 to $1200 range, and a rare deep purple open-edged large compote attributed to Sandwich sold for more than $25,000 in mid 1991.

Finally, keep in mind that a number of the popular flint glass patterns, especially Bellflower, Ashburton, Thumbprint, Honeycomb and Princess Feather, continued to be made in nonflint glass. Nonflint examples are only worth about one-third to one-half their flint-quality equivalents.

Old Versus New

As far back as the 1930s collectors and dealers were faced with the problem of reproductions in pressed pattern glass, including some patterns originally made in flint glass. Even in the 1920s some glass pieces were produced that closely resembled old items, a noteworthy example being the always-popular dolphin candlesticks.

Glass-writing pioneer Ruth Webb Lee was one of the first to publicize this problem widely, and her standard reference, *Antique Fakes and Reproductions,* was first published in 1938 with a revised and enlarged edition appearing in 1950. Through careful analysis and good photographs, Lee presented a comprehensive survey of reproduced flint and nonflint pattern glass known to be on the market at that time. Unfortunately, many more reproductions have hit the market since 1950, and for a more up-dated listing one should locate a copy of Dorothy Hammond's valuable references, *Confusing Collectibles: A Guide to Identification of Contemporary Objects,* and its sequel, *More Confusing Collectibles.* Both volumes were published in the early 1970s. A more recent reference that lists reproductions for many patterns is *Early American Pattern Glass: 1850–1910: Major Collectible Table Sets with Prices* by Bill Jenks and Jerry Luna (Radnor, PA: Wallace-Homestead Book Company, 1990).

Although these references are invaluable in listing and illustrating some pattern-glass reproductions, there are some guidelines a collector can follow to help avoid many of the reproductions of flint glass, even pieces fifty or sixty years old that may show good signs of age from years of usage.

The simplest and probably most effective way to determine whether a piece is old flint or a later copy is, again, the pinging test. This technique works especially well for pieces such as goblets, tumblers, and compotes, all of which should give a resounding ring when tapped gently. More difficult to sort out are objects such as candlesticks and oil lamps since the thickness of the glass, even on the bases, does not allow for much ring. When tapped, however, the base of an old candlestick or lamp should give a "pink-pink" sound and not just a dull thud. The weight of the old flint pieces made with lead oxide will also be greater than most modern copies, especially stemware.

Another test that can be very helpful, especially when examining a piece such as a lamp, compote, or candlestick put together with a thin wafer of molten glass, is to look carefully at this wafer. Most reproductions were pressed in one piece, so if one sees a mold line running right through the wafer it is not a flint-era piece.

The finishing of early flint glass was also important to glassmakers, who used a technique called *fire-polishing* to remove the prominent mold seams on the bowls of objects such as goblets, compotes, creamers, and sugar bowls and on the fonts of lamps. In this technique a pressed piece, while still hot, was held in the open glory hole of the furnace just long enough to smooth out mold seems and give it a glossier finish without distorting the pressed pattern. Because of this mold seam lines run up the foot and stem of a goblet or compote but end at the base of the bowl. Many reproductions were not finished that carefully, and more prominent mold seams can be one way to help identify a copy.

In flint patterns the most commonly reproduced pieces were goblets and tumblers, as well as other stemware. Modern collectors want matching sets, so there always has been a demand for stemware pieces. This strong market demand made it practical to reproduce antique molds and issue copies in accordance with the law of supply and demand. Unlike stemware, pitchers and creamers have been reproduced less often because of the difficulty in successfully replicating the lovely blown and applied wide strap handles found on nearly all of the originals. Because the molds of the 1850s and 1860s were not able to press the handles and bodies of pitchers and creamers in one piece, an extra step to apply these by hand was needed before the pieces were annealed. Remember, these applied handles always ended in a curlique or squiggle tail, and if an old piece has this tail missing, it was probably broken off at a later date.

Certain patterns of early lamps and candlesticks have also been reproduced widely, and checking the wafer joint and trying to determine how "flinty" it is may be the best tests a novice can employ. Once one becomes more familiar with the patterns that have been reproduced, one will know to proceed with caution when considering a purchase. Dolphin candlesticks, for instance, always should be carefully examined. Lamps in the *Three Printie Block* pattern and some heart-pattern lamps were reproduced in the 1920s and later. The tall acanthus leaf pattern lamps, on columnar glass or metal standards with square marble bases, were available as far back as the 1940s. With the passing of decades the wear they show can make them appear older than they really are. It is very important for collectors and dealers to examine pieces they are offered today very carefully. Color sometimes can be a help in this, since some reproductions were made in modern pastel shades, especially pale pink and green, which were never used in old flint glass. For lamps, a close examination of the burner collar may be helpful. As discussed earlier, reproduction collars usually are not as carefully finished as the originals and, even though they may have been artificially aged or darkened, they can be recognized with a little care and practice.

Early flint patterns have not been as widely reproduced as some of the later nonflint patterns. Below is a brief listing of the most often seen reproduced patterns and pieces.

Argus: The Imperial Glass Company reproduced the butter dish in a new mold and the Henry Ford Museum authorized Fostoria to make a four-piece table set in the pattern, but these pieces carry the marking "H. F. M." for "Henry Ford Museum."

Ashburton: Many new pieces in this pattern have been produced, especially in the 1960s and 1970s. Copies do not have the weight and ring of the old.

Fig. 5-20 The sugar bowl on the left is an original flint *Diamond Thumbprint* piece, while the one on the right is a reproduction by the Viking Glass Company. Note the darker hue of the old piece due to the refractive quality of the heavy flint glass.

Bellflower: The Metropolitan Museum of Art in New York had a number of pieces reproduced beginning in 1970, but these were marked with the museum's initials, "MMA."

Diamond Thumbprint: The Sandwich Glass Museum in Sandwich, Massachusetts, authorized the Viking Glass Company to make a number of forms, but they carry the initials "SM" for Sandwich Museum.

Honeycomb: Many copies have been made over the years and many modern patterns are adaptions of this line in nonflint glass.

Horn of Plenty: A goblet was reproduced years ago as was a tumbler and a look-alike creamer from a tumbler mold; also a tall-pedestaled oil lamp was made.

Inverted Fern: Watch for a reproduced goblet.

Magnet and Grape: A goblet was made in the early 1960s and later the Metropolitan Museum of Art authorized several pieces that will carry its "MMA" mark.

New England Pineapple: A cordial glass, goblet (knob and faceted stem), and wine glass have been copied.

Ribbed Palm: The Imperial Glass Company produced a new goblet.

Roman Key: Several new items have been imported.

Sawtooth: Many pieces were reproduced by the

Fig. 5-21 An early *Thumbprint* pattern goblet on the left with a green Fenton reproduction based on the *Baby Thumbprint* pattern on the right.

meant to be exact reproductions of old lines, but they often used old patterns for inspiration. In the early years of this century, circa 1900 to 1910, American glassmakers began to market lines of glass meant to appeal to the growing interest in early Americana. Although the 1920s saw the largest boom in the modern antiques business, as far back as the 1890s pioneer antiquers, especially in New England, were searching out furniture, ceramics, and glassware from their ancestors. By the first decade of the twentieth century this Americana trend was well enough established for reproductions or adaptations of what was then thought of as colonial pieces of furniture, glass, or china to be manufactured. For instance, in the first two decades of the twentieth century no fewer than six large American glassmakers were marketing very similar patterns under the name *Colonial*. All of these resembled, to a greater or lesser extent, the Flute, Huber, and Crystal patterns of the 1850s and 1860s.

Westmoreland Glass Company; some will carry its ''WG'' monogram. Other pieces were made by the L. G. Wright Glass Company.

Thumbprint: Fenton Art Glass Company made a similar pattern but the shapes are unlike the old ones.

Tulip with Sawtooth: A goblet and wine glass have been copied.

Waffle: A goblet was reproduced in the late 1930s but is unlike the old one.

Wedding Ring (Double Wedding Ring): A toothpick holder (not in the original selection) was made. Dalzell-Viking Glass Company has reissued in several colors of flint glass a goblet, a six-inch and eight-inch-diameter plate, a seven-inch-diameter covered compote, footed sherbet, covered sugar bowl, and two styles of toothpick holders.

As can be seen, serious collectors of pattern glass of the flint glass era must become familiar with the various items known to have been made in a pattern originally. Some reproductions have been made of pieces that never appeared in the nineteenth century.

Becoming familiar with the patterns and the pieces produced in those patterns also will help sort out another area of confusion for beginning collectors: twentieth-century glass patterns adapted from nineteenth-century ones. These patterns were not

Fig. 5-22 The *Honeycomb* pattern in modern glass. This deep ruby goblet was made by the Viking Glass Company in its *Georgian* pattern in the 1960s.

The Honeycomb pattern, probably never completely out of production since the 1860s, saw a renewed popularity in the early twentieth century, and this appeal has never waned (check out the water goblets in your favorite restaurant the next time you dine out). Six American glass manufacturers in the early decades of this century produced a nearly identical pattern that they all named *Georgian*, which was basically the Honeycomb pattern under a new guise.

Once again, that these adapted patterns were not and are not made in flint glass is the easiest way to tell the old from the new. Also, many pieces and forms, unlike the originals, were made in colors unheard of in the 1850s and 1860s. These twentieth-century patterns are fine in quality and very collectible in their own right, but do not pay flint prices for twentieth-century revivals.

In closing, some twentieth-century reproductions and revivals one should be on the lookout for are listed and briefly described.

Confusing Candlesticks and Lamps

Several well-known glass companies have reproduced dolphin candlesticks. Westmoreland as far back as the 1920s was making dolphin-based lamps with simple Flute pattern fonts. The nine-inch and ten-inch-tall dolphin candlestick (no. 1049), quite often seen in milk glass, had hexagonal bases, with each side of the base curved in.

The Heisey Glass Company also made what it called the *Sandwich Dolphin* (no. 110), and this piece is sought eagerly by Heisey collectors.

The Cambridge Glass Company also issued dolphin candlesticks in 1926, but its version has a domed base with a Diamond Point pattern, which is unlike anything originally made.

Westmoreland Glass made quite a series of reproduction lamps in the 1940s, and ones to be aware of include the type with a Three Printie Block font (no. 185), an English Hobnail pattern font on a square, white pressed-glass base, a Gothic Arch pattern font on a square base (found in various color combinations), and another in English Hobnail (similar to the old Diamond Point pattern) with a glass font and base.

Other reproduction lamps seen include an all-glass version with a Sawtooth pattern font on a hexagonal, shaped pedestal and foot, and another

dolphin-pedestaled lamp on a double-step square base, a form also made as a candlestick.

Following are some table glass patterns and the modern companies that produced them.

Confusing Modern Tableware Patterns

Anchor-Hocking Glass Company

Georgian (no. 215), circa 1930, resembles early Honeycomb.

Cambridge Glass Company

Mt. Vernon resembles Diamond Point

Georgian resembles Honeycomb

Colonial resembles Flute

Martha Washington resembles Pressed Block

Duncan and Miller Glass Company

Colonial resembles Flute

Georgian (no. 100), circa 1928, resembles Honeycomb

Early American Sandwich (No. 41) resembles early lacy glass

Victorian resembles Thumbprint

Fenton Art Glass Company

Georgian (no. 1611), circa 1930, resembles Honeycomb

Historic American Series, 1937, a ribbed background with oval reserves with vignettes of American historic sites

Plymouth, circa 1933, resembles Three-Printie Block

Fostoria Glass Company

Colonial (no. 2222), *Lucere* (no. 1515), *Lincoln* (no. 1861), *Puritan* (no. 143), and *Flemish* (no. 1913) all resemble Flute and Huber.

Hermitage (no. 2449) resembles Argus

Old English (no. 1460) resembles Honeycomb with little stars added

Wistar (no. 2620), a ribbed pattern with a large leaf band

Colonial Prism (no. 2183) resembles Prism

Heisey Glass Company

Heisey, beginning early in this century, produced a whole range of patterns in what it called the

Colonial line. Most of these were quite similar in appearance and resembled the old Flute and Huber patterns of the nineteenth century. Other distinctive patterns made include:

Old Sandwich (Thumbprint, *Early American* no. 1404) resembles Pillar

Provincial (Whirlpool, no. 1506) closely resembles Thumbprint

Ipswich (no. 1405) is based on the early Comet pattern but stemware pieces have a square foot instead of the round foot used in the old line.

Heisey also produced some pieces, such as the *Thumbprint and Panel* tall vase, of heavy and thick glass, though not flint, which at first resembles vases of the 1850s and 1860s, especially when found in color. Heisey marked much of its glassware, so look for the famous "H" in a diamond trademark.

Imperial Glass Company

Colonial resembles Flute and Huber

Cape Cod is vaguely reminiscent of Diamond Thumbprint. Imperial also produced several plates that resemble early lacy pieces in general design. These include the *Strawflower, Woodbury,* and especially, the *Blaise* patterns of the 1920s and 1930s.

Fig. 5-23 A twentieth-century adaptation of a flint-era pattern. On the left is a footed tumbler in Heisey's *Ipswich* pattern. On the right is an original flint *Comet* goblet that inspired the Heisey design.

Imperial also acquired molds from other glass firms and reissued some patterns. One it called *Old Williamsburg* was reissued from a Heisey pattern that resembles Flute.

Jeannette Glass Company

Harp (1950s) resembles a lacy design.

Jenkins Glass Company

Huck Finn resembles Flute

McKee Glass Company (circa 1904–1920s)

Colonial lamps (no. 20 line) resemble Flute and Huber

Colonial tableware (no. 21 line) resembles Flute

Colonial (no. 75 line) resembles Honeycomb

These Colonial patterns were all part of the Pres-cut series of the early twentieth century and pieces may carry that logo in the center of the bottom.

Old Colony (1904–1920) resembles Huber

New Martinsville Glass Company

Chateau (no. 714) resembles Huber

Georgian resembles Honeycomb

Placid (no. 712) resembles Flute

Plain Colonial (no. 725) resembles Flute
  No. 38 resembles Thumbprint

Westmoreland Glass Company

English Hobnail resembles Diamond Point

Princess Feather (1924–1960s) resembles early lacy designs

A dolphin-based console set, with dolphin candlesticks and a center bowl with a dolphin pedestal, came out in the 1920s. A child's set called *Little Jo Water Set,* with a pitcher and tumblers, came out in 1924 and closely resembles Flute. Remember: no toy or children's dish sets were widely produced in flint-era tableware patterns. Some lacy-period toy miniatures, like flatirons, simple candlesticks, and a simple Flute pattern pitcher and bowl set, did carry over into the flint glass era.

Red-Cliff Company Reproductions

I recently came across some interesting and good-quality reproductions of old flint patterns. Each piece is clearly marked "Red-Cliff" with the company logo on the bottom of the foot.

The Red-Cliff Company of Chicago operated from 1950 until 1980 and decorated and distributed copies of old chinaware, most notably pieces with the *Tea Leaf* pattern. These pieces are clearly marked and are quite collectible today. I was familiar with these copies of old china but had not been aware of any glassware with Red-Cliff markings.

I was fortunate to be able to visit personally with Frank Fenton of Fenton Art Glass of Williamsport, West Virginia, and learn the history of the Red-Cliff pieces.

According to Fenton, in the late 1960s or early 1970s Red-Cliff contacted Fenton about producing a series of five goblets based on early glass designs that Red-Cliff provided. Each goblet carries the

Red-Cliff marking, and some pieces had the rims flared to form small compotes. These were the only pieces in this limited line.

When Red-Cliff went out of business in 1980 Fenton took over the goblet molds in order to settle accounts with Red-Cliff. A few years later Fenton produced a line of unmarked bells using the goblet molds.

The series of goblets is illustrated here. One is a close copy of an early French lacy glass goblet, circa 1840, which was called *Sablé Arch*. Sablé (sábley) in French means "sanded" and refers to the sanded or stippled background design typical of lacy glass. The other piece is an adaptation of the *Magnet and Grape* pattern but should not fool anyone familiar with the old pattern.

The other three Red-Cliff patterns include a close reproduction of the pattern *Knobby Bull's Eye*. A pattern Red-Cliff called *Heirloom*, which appears to be a close copy of the *Heavy Gothic* pattern made by U.S. Glass in the early 1890s. Finally, Red-Cliff made a pattern it called *Sydenham*. This design features a band of wide petals around the base of the bowl and was based on the *Sydenham* pattern of early white ironstone

Fig. 5-24 A page from the 1972 Red-Cliff Company catalog shows its line of goblets and small compotes based on old pressed-glass patterns. Courtesy of Miriam Mucha.

Fig. 5-25 On the left is an original *Magnet and Grape* flint goblet, and on the right is a Red-Cliff adaptation in a pattern it called *Grape*.

china, a china pattern Red-Cliff also reproduced. Apparently each of these patterns was designed to complement the reproduction ironstone patterns that were a Red-Cliff specialty. The accompanying copy of a Red-Cliff catalog page from 1972 illustrates each of the five goblets and some of the compotes made from the same molds.

For collectors of old pressed glass these Red-Cliff pieces do not really pose a problem since they are clearly marked. They are of fine-quality glass and available in several colors, so they should be collectible in their own right.

Part IV
The Golden Age of Pressed Glass
1865–1915

CHAPTER 6

Dawn of the Nonflint Era

The decades between the end of the American Civil War in 1865 and the beginning of World War I in Europe in 1914 marked the beginning of the modern world. The Industrial Revolution continued all over Europe and America, and the age of colonialism (or imperialism) came into full flower. England, France, and Germany vied with each other to lay claim to what they considered to be the uncivilized parts of the world. There they could carry on the "white man's burden" of bringing proper culture to native people (and, of course, selling them the products of their home industries). By the turn of the twentieth century even the United States had laid claim to a colonial empire in Hawaii and territories wrested from Spain after the Spanish-American War of 1898 (Cuba, Puerto Rico, the Philippines). The Manifest Destiny of the 1850s now carried the U.S. flag overseas.

In the years immediately following the Civil War, the country went through the Reconstruction, bringing the Southern states and their citizens back into the Union fold. The North, of course, emerged from this conflict with its industrial strength greatly enhanced, and life north of the Mason-Dixon line was prosperous, the mood (tempered somewhat by the assassination of President Lincoln) optimistic.

Some industries had boomed during the war, but nonessential industries, such as glass manufacturing, had a harder time. Markets were disrupted and necessary materials harder to come by. Most consumers had other things on their mind than buying a nice set of china or sparkling glassware.

One of the necessary ingredients for the production of glassware up until this era was lead oxide, a key ingredient needed to produce flint glass. Since lead bullets and artillery shells were of critical importance to the war effort, there was less lead available for the glass furnaces of America. What saved the situation and opened up a whole new phase in American pressed-glass technology was the perfection of a new glass formula by William Leighton, Sr., a noted glassmaker who brought his skills to this country from Scotland in 1835. He had, for some time, been superintendant of the New England Glass Works, but in 1863 he joined Hobbs, Brockunier and Company of Wheeling, West Virginia. It was while with Hobbs, sometime in 1864, that he discovered a new formula for glass that eliminated the need for expensive lead oxide. His new "lime" (also called "soda-lime") glass was a mixture containing bicarbonate of soda instead of the soda ash used in flint glass. This new glass could be pressed quickly and in more detailed molds than the old flint glass, and it cost one-third less than flint. The drawback, at least by modern standards, was that the glass was lighter in weight and less light-refractive than flintware. From the manufacturer's point of view, however, it opened up many opportunities for expanding markets and developing new and novel lines.

The United States in the late Victorian age was growing by leaps and bounds, and the expanding middle class had pushed all the way across the continent. The transcontinental railroad connection was completed in 1869, and soon every corner of the country was connected by telegraph and railroad lines. By the turn of the century even the most isolated farmer in the Dakotas could order the latest in furniture, china, or glassware from a mail-order catalog and have it delivered by rail within a few weeks. The Gilded Age saw a tremendous growth in the number of very wealthy industrialists, and their manners and tastes were emulated everywhere by the bourgeoisie who wanted to give the impression of good taste.

More than ever, the products of the glass companies of the second half of the nineteenth century reflected the trends in tastes and manners of America's consumers. Initially the trends of the late 1860s and 1870s were fairly conservative in pressed-glass wares. Many flint patterns of the 1850s and 1860s continued to be produced widely in both flint and nonflint glass. Several new directions in glass design did evolve, however, including the introduction of numerous naturalistic designs (flowers, fruits, and berries), patterns featuring a finely stippled background, and several famous patterns featuring frosted effects achieved through the use of machine grinding and, slightly later, by exposing sections of a piece to hydrofluoric acid fumes.

But the 1880s marked the real heyday of American pressed-glass production, with more patterns and more pieces in the patterns being made than ever before. The discovery of gas fields in Ohio and Indiana lead to the opening of a large number of glasshouses in those states, where this clean, cheap fuel was abundant. Pittsburgh continued to be a major center of glass production, but more and more the glass factories of the Northeast experienced hard times as the cost of fuel, raw materials, and trouble with the growing labor movement led to the closing of such long-running companies as the Boston and Sandwich Glass Company and the New England Glass Works, which was relocated to Toledo, Ohio, and still operates today as the Libbey Glass Company.

A very notable change in pressed glass was the introduction of colored glass on a wide scale. Dozens of patterns now were commonly available

Fig. 6-1 A goblet in the famous *Westward Ho* pattern of the 1870s. This pattern features a naturalistic motif with its depiction of a deer and buffalo and also symbolizes America's move westward in the late nineteenth century. Courtesy of the Corning Museum of Glass.

in a wide range of color including blue, green, amber, and purple. Milk glass and novelty items of all types were rushed to a market hungry for whimsey and gewgaws, feeding the late-Victorian fancy for anything new and unusual. By the end of the 1880s, numerous patterns also were introduced that imitated the fine-cut glassware of the era we now call the Brilliant Period of American cut glass. Cut glass was always a luxury item, but the average homemaker could capture some of its sparkle in a nice pressed bowl or compote for a fraction of the cost.

The period from the 1890s to 1915 generally

continued the trends in pressed glass developed in the 1880s. However, during this era most glasshouses joined together to form *combines* (monopolies) to insure their survival and prosperity. In 1891 fifteen well-established glass firms formed the United States Glass Company, and later, in 1899, nineteen other glass firms combined to set up the National Glass Company. Although new patterns and lines were introduced during these years, these combines also reissued numerous patterns that member companies had introduced some years earlier. Novelty items and colored pattern glass continued to be major products of the time, and clear pieces were often decorated with dark amber or ruby stain to add to their eye appeal. These pieces, now called *amber-stained* or *ruby-stained*, remained popular into the 1920s and are especially collectible today.

Although Queen Victoria died in 1901, the Victorian age continued strongly to influence tastes in the decorative arts up until World War I. Many of the intricate patterns of the 1880s and 1890s, along with some new ones, were available well past the turn of the century. Also, new glassware, such as custard and carnival glass, made to imitate expensive art glass, became the rage. Countering the effusive decorative excesses of some of this late-Victorian pressed glass, some early-twentieth-century glassmakers began to follow a new trend toward simplicity and restraint. As noted earlier there was a growing interest in American history and early American antiques, and a number of glass firms introduced pattern lines with names like *Colonial* and *Georgian* that harkened back to the heavy, simple flint glass patterns of the 1850s. By the Roaring Twenties anything Victorian, including pressed glass, was considered passé. Glassware of the 1920s and 1930s reflected this evolution of the marketplace, as early American style patterns competed with modern Art Deco–inspired lines in the inexpensive and colorful pressed glass we now refer to as Depression glass. Not until the late 1930s, when collecting Victorian pattern glass became a major hobby, did the patterns of the 1870s, 1880s, and 1890s once again become popular. Soon reproductions and copies of these patterns appeared on the market to appeal to consumers seeking an old-fashioned look for their dining tables and, sadly, to confuse and mislead glass collectors right up to the present.

Collectors today should take heart, however, since a wealth of information is available to help avoid the relatively few stumbling blocks to be encountered in the search for lovely late-Victorian pattern glass. This book will help unravel some of the mysteries concerning this pressed glass and point the way to a better understanding and appreciation of the glass that has graced American tables for over one hundred years.

Up close with American pressed glass from 1830 to 1900.

Old and new ruby glass. On the far left is a ruby-flashed spoon holder cut with a diamond and bull's-eye design, ca. 1850. The small bowl in the center is a reproduction of the *Ruby Thumbprint* pattern. Note its pale color with its slightly iridescent finish. An original *Ruby Thumbprint* bowl is shown in the upper right of the photo. Directly below it is a *Dakota* pattern tumbler with ruby staining and the engraved name "Jack."

A colorful array of Victorian novelties from the 1880s and 1890s. These are all old pieces, but beware of reproductions—especially of slipper whimseys. See text for details.

Various colored pieces from the 1880s and 1890s. In the back row are a small *Gonterman* compote and a purple slag mug in the *Bird in Nest with Flowers* pattern. In front, left to right, are a blue opalescent *Hobnail* barber bottle, a *Red Block* butter dish, and a blue opalescent *Square-Footed Hobnail* pattern spooner.

Tea time circa 1890: An Austrian porcelain teapot and cup and saucer stand ready while some sweet treats are displayed on the little green *Ribbon Candy* doughnut stand. Cream will be poured from the *Snail* pattern creamer, and sugar is nearby in a *Scalloped Tape* sugar bowl.

Some classics in custard glass. Clockwise from the top: a spooner in Northwood's *Argonaut Shell* pattern; a creamer in *Chrysanthemum Sprig* by Northwood; a chamberstick in *Jewelled Vermont,* probably by the U. S. Glass Company; a Northwood *Grape and Cable* jar with original nutmeg trim; and, finally, another Northwood piece, a sauce dish in *Intaglio.*

Colorful carnival glass. In the upper right is a blue tumbler in Northwood's *Grape and Cable* pattern, and just below it is a green bowl in Imperial's *Pansy.* In the left front is a marigold milk pitcher in Imperial's *Windmill* pattern, and just behind it a blue plate in the *Three Fruits* pattern by Northwood.

Milk white and blue opaque Victorian glass. In the upper row are an original Atterbury "Owl" covered jar and a Challinor, Taylor and Company "Hen on Nest" dish. In the bottom row are a small "Lion" covered dish with its original gold trim, a decorated dresser jar, and a blue opaque covered creamer in Westmoreland's "Swan and Cattails" design. It retains some of its original painted trim.

A grouping of colorful 1890s pattern glass. On the left is a *Clematis* (aka *Flower and Pleat*) pitcher with a frosted band and light staining. Next to it is a *Daisy and Button with Thumbprint Panel* covered compote with amber-stained panels. On the upper right is a colorfully decorated *Bohemian* pattern sugar bowl and below it is a ruby-stained *Heart Band* creamer with a silver souvenir inscription.

Some post-1900 patterns in color. On the left is a toy creamer in green in Cambridge's *Colonial* pattern. The tumbler beside it is in the *Narcissus Spray* pattern with color staining. The green mug in the upper right is in the *Lacy Medallion* pattern, a close relative to *Colorado*. The tumbler on the lower right is Northwood's *Cherry and Lattice* pattern with stained cherries and gilt trim.

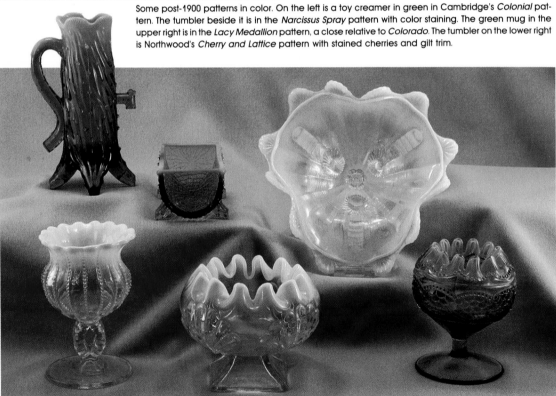

Opalescent pressed glass. In the upper row are Northwood's "Town Pump" and "Trough" novelties and a dish in Northwood's *Fluted Scrolls* pattern. In the front row, left to right, are an old *Opal Open* rose bowl, probably by Northwood; a *Beaded Fan* rose bowl from the Jefferson Glass Company; and another rose bowl from Northwood in the *Pearls and Scales* pattern.

CHAPTER 7

Forms and Styles in Late-Victorian Pattern Glass

Although much of the tableware produced since the late 1840s continued to be seen in the new patterns of the late nineteenth century, certain changes illustrate how the food-serving habits of Americans evolved after the flint glass era.

Common and useful forms such as compotes, bowls, pitchers, creamers, and sugar bowls all remained, and the four-piece table setting, first introduced in some old flint patterns, expanded so that nearly every nonflint pattern had these pieces and many more.

One interesting trend is the number of drinking vessels produced in flint and nonflint patterns. During the flint era all the popular patterns were made in a large range of glasses, goblets, and tumblers. For instance, pieces common to most of these patterns included an ale glass, a champagne glass (often two forms), a claret glass, a cordial glass (often two forms), a tall "flip" glass, a goblet (two or three forms), a mug, a tumbler (several sizes), and several sizes of wine glasses. Not all flint patterns had all these pieces, but a majority did.

By contrast nonflint patterns from the late 1870s through the turn of the century saw a much smaller range of drinking vessels. Most patterns had one form of goblet, a tumbler, and a wine glass, and many had either a champagne, cordial, or claret glass and sometimes all three. Cups (what we call "punch cups") became quite common, especially as punch bowls became more popular. In those patterns having the largest number of stemware items, the pieces generally look identical with the only difference being one of size. The goblet was the largest, followed by the champagne goblet, claret, wine and the cordial. The cordial glass (roughly equivalent to our "liqueur"-size glass) was the smallest piece. By the 1890s most patterns included just a goblet, tumbler, and wine glass. Other drinking vessels were seen much less frequently. One might wonder whether the strong temperance movement of that age influenced the numbers and kinds of stemware the average consumer used.

Another example of change is the number of bowls and compotes available in flint and nonflint patterns. Bellflower, one of the most popular and long-lived flint patterns, has been found in fewer than fifteen sizes and shapes of bowls and compotes, with and without covers. By contrast the popular *Broken Column* pattern of the 1890s has over thirty known different sizes and shapes of bowls and compotes.

Quite a number of new forms of tableware became common in later pattern glass but were rare or unknown in the flint period. Cake stands (round plates on a pedestal base) are very rare in flint glass patterns but very common in nonflint patterns, often available in two or more sizes. What we now call "banana" stands (cake stands with two sides turned up) were not made in flint patterns but were very popular by the 1890s. More serving plates also became common in nonflint patterns, and bread plates and pickle dishes, sometimes with appropriate pressed inscriptions, were popular as were larger round plates with open handles on the sides, which we call "cake plates." A large-covered jar, what today we call a "bisquit" or cracker jar, is also found in some late-Victorian patterns but not in flint glass lines. Rose bowls, for potpourri, were another late-Victorian innovation popular in American parlors of the 1880s and 1890s. Toothpick holders, very popular with collectors today, were unheard of in the 1850s and 1860s. They really did not come into their own until the middle to late 1880s, when dozens of novelty forms appeared. Salt shakers,

Fig. 7-1 The late-Victorian *Fleur-de-Lis and Drape* pattern shown on four sizes of stemware. From left to right are the goblet, champagne glass, wine glass, and cordial glass.

which we take for granted today, were not made in flint glass patterns. Small open dishes, salt dips, were used. Salt in the mid–nineteenth century was crude and unrefined by today's standards, and there was no known way to keep it from becoming lumpy during damp weather. It simply would not pour as it does today and so had to be served from little dishes with little silver spoons. The inventive American mind did begin to work on the pouring problem beginning in the late 1860s. Quite a number of nonpattern glass salt shakers was developed with built-in "agitators" attached to the inside lid to break up the lumpy salt so it would pour through the openings. In some cases matching pepper shakers with smaller lid openings were also produced, but not until the patterns of the 1890s do we find matching salt and pepper shakers, without the agitators, available in some patterns. Even then the old-fashioned open salt dip remained in common use. Another piece thought of as typically late Victorian is the sugar shaker (what the English call a "muffineer"). Resembling an oversized salt shaker, it served cinnamon sugar and was made in some patterns, as were covered jars for serving jams or marmalade. These two latter pieces are actually more common in the art glass lines of the late nine-

teenth century than they are in pressed glass, but they were widely popular then and are eagerly sought by collectors today.

The shapes of pieces in nonflint pattern glass also were changing in the late nineteenth century. Pitchers and creamers, for example, often had applied glass handles, but these were no longer the flattened "strap" handles with a curlique end. Instead plain, rounded bands of glass were attached to the rim near the top and bottom of a piece. These handles, heavier near the bottom than near the rim, tapered gradually. Such handles were common after the late 1870s and are a good indication of later production. Pitchers also began to evolve some new shapes. Flint glass pitchers often had graceful rounded shapes, either raised on a slender pedestal with a plain foot or sitting flat on the table. Many later patterns had blocky or heavy cylindrical bodies. The tall and graceful cylindrical pitcher we call a *tankard* was another popular innovation.

Novelty became very important to glassmakers as they vied to capture the fancy of the buying public. Patterns such as *Three Face* and *Frosted Lion* featured the pattern only on the bases of the pieces, and other lines had pieces held aloft by such unlikely forms as horsehoes, hands, or full-figured classical maidens, and now and then the dolphin reappeared from the flint glass era.

Late-Victorian pressed patterns often had pieces raised on a short pedestal or with short legs or feet at each corner of the base. Putting legs or little feet on patterns became quite popular as can be seen by patterns such as *Classic* and *Colorado*.

The bases and pedestals of many patterns also became more ornate with knobs and bands of pattern matching the design on the body of a piece. No longer were all bases simple and round. Many were scalloped, ruffled, lobed, or even square. All these elements give them the fussy look we associate with things Victorian.

CHAPTER 8

Pattern Glass of the Post-Civil War Period 1865–1870s

The Reconstruction roughly coincides with the restructuring of the American glass industry. Glass factories once again were able to increase production and feed the growing demand of war-weary Americans for consumer goods. The introduction of the nonlead (soda-lime) formula meant that glass goods could be produced more cheaply and, although the phasing out of flint glass was gradual, by about the mid-1870s most patterns were made in soda-lime glass or with greatly reduced amounts of lead oxide in the glass batch. Quite a few of the popular flint patterns of the prewar period remained in production, but if one compares a piece from circa 1860 with the same piece circa 1870, one will note quite a change in its weight and its resonance when tapped.

A number of innovative patterns developed in the 1870s were produced in more complex and detailed molds than those used for flint-era patterns. Soda-lime glass was easier to mold into such detailed designs, and the charm of the pattern helped mask the lighter weight and lesser brilliance of the glass itself.

Several style trends can be noted beginning in the late 1860s and following through patterns of the 1870s.

Naturalistic patterns, those featuring plants and animals in fine detail, became popular in the 1870s. Previously some stylized plants (Bellflower) or parts of plants (Pressed Leaf) were found in flint patterns, but in the 1870s a whole gardenful of fruits and flowers was featured. *Barberry, Bleeding Heart, Holly, Lily-of-the-Valley, Cherry, Currant, Cabbage Rose,* and *Grape and Festoon* are some patterns in which the beauties of the garden and woodland were captured. Birds like the cardinal,

insects (*Grasshopper*) and mythical creatures (*Dragon*) also found themselves on the tableware of the era.

Another major design trend might be called Americanism. These glass patterns reflected a renewed pride in all things American. The centennial year of 1876 strongly influenced this movement, and dozens of novelties and some tableware lines featured patriotic themes and scenes at the Centennial Exhibition in Philadelphia. Stars and stripes, the Liberty Bell, and patriotic mottos were all the rage during this burst of patriotic fervor. This period also saw a reawakening of interest in early American antiques, especially the furniture of the Revolutionary War era.

The beauty of the American landscape was captured on the *Cape Cod* pattern (a rustic coastal scene) and the opening of the American West inspired popular and distinctly American lines such as *Log Cabin* (with pieces actually modeled after a primitive log cabin) and *Westward Ho* (originally called *Pioneer* by the maker), which was highlighted by vignettes of the soon-to-be-decimated American bison as well as deer and log cabins in the wilderness. (A Westward Ho pattern goblet can be seen at the beginning of Chapter 6.) In what might be considered an ironic twist, the designer included a Native American as the figural finial on the covers of pieces in this pattern. However, the figure is shown in a crouching position instead of standing tall and proud. This pose could be just a matter of design practicality, but it may have been the designer's subconscious reflection of the Native American's status in the white society of that era.

Other patterns, of course, do not fall neatly within this trend. A number of simple geometric

Fig. 8-1 An unusual pattern that may have appeared first in the 1870s, *Grasshopper* came in two variations. On the left is the creamer without insects, and on the right is the spooner with insects going up the sides.

designs such as *Ribbon* were introduced featuring the frosted highlights popular on several patterns of the 1870s, and patterns like *Drapery* and *Beaded Mirror* featured a softly stippled background. Plain geometric motifs are found on patterns such as *Jacob's Ladder, Chain,* and *Palmette* (see Fig. 8-7).

One other factor to consider is that color was rarely used in these new patterns of the late 1860s and 1870s. During the 1870s the blues, greens, purples, and ambers found so often in the following decades almost never were featured on pressed-glass tableware.

Important Manufacturers and Patterns

Although it is impossible to include a comprehensive history of each manufacturer of late-Victorian pattern glass in a book of this scope, some of the most famous and successful will be touched on here. Several pioneering glass-pressing firms of the 1830s–1860s have already been discussed. Quite a number of them continued to grow and expand through the final decades of the nineteenth century, and a couple, like McKee and Gillinder, survived well into the twentieth century.

Following is an alphabetical list of the major

manufacturers of pressed-glass tableware during the period immediately following the Civil War. Many of them went on to even greater glory in the 1880s, but here are included patterns these companies are believed to have produced during the late 1860s and through the 1870s. Keep in mind that many of these firms also produced other types of glassware such as lamps and lighting accessories (lamp chimneys) and novelty ware in addition to their tableware lines. When known, patterns that have been reproduced are indicated.

Adams and Company, Pittsburgh

Considered one of the largest American glass-makers in the early 1860s, this firm had continued success in the 1870s, especially in lamp production.

Recent research by Jane Shadel Spillman, curator of American glass at the Corning Museum of Glass, has shed new light on the pattern glass production of Adams during the 1870s, including some surprising discoveries. In her article "Adams & Company: A Closer Look," published in *The Glass Club Bulletin* of the National Early American Glass Club (Winter 1990-1991), Spillman outlines her research into Adams's production during the 1870s and 1880s.

Using an Adams catalog that she dates to circa 1871–1872, Spillman is able to confirm only a handful of patterns made by this firm. Among these are several naturalistic patterns, including *Grape and Festoon* (which they called *Myrtle*), *Magnet and Grape with Stippled Leaf,* and a pattern they called *Medallion,* which appears identical to *Beaded Acorn,* featuring an oval reserve with an acorn cluster against a stippled background. *Chain* (or *Beaded Chain*) is a well-known geometric design that shows up in this catalog, as does *New York Honeycomb.* Included are several holdover patterns from the flint era, but they also offered a new line they called *Log Cabin,* which is different from the better-known pattern that features square, cabin-shaped forms and is attributed to the Bryce Brothers firm.

Most surprising of all was the discovery that the famous *Liberty Bell* pattern produced at the time of the U.S. Centennial in 1876 is an Adams product. For decades it was assumed that this line was produced by Gillinder and Sons of Philadelphia. Although Gillinder did produce a number of Centennial souvenirs as well as a *Centennial* tableware line, Spillman found reports on the Centennial regarding Adams's production that clearly describe

Fig. 8-2 The sugar bowl and creamer in Adams's *Liberty Bell* pattern. Note the "bell" finial on the sugar lid and the applied reeded handle on the creamer.

pieces in the Liberty Bell pattern. Adams then called this its *Independence Centennial Ware,* and collectors recognize its prominent raised design of the famous cracked bell on each piece. The set includes a group of oval platters that are especially desirable. The most common version of the Liberty Bell platter is probably the *Signer's* platter, which features the Liberty Bell in the center and the names of each signer of the Declaration of Independence around the outer border. Another variation features the names of the original thirteen states around the border. A final, scarcer variation is highlighted by the bold reproduction of John Hancock's signature in the border and has twig handles at the ends. This latter version is especially rare in milk glass.

Fortunately for collectors this pattern was not reproduced until the U.S. Bicentennial in 1976, and the maker was careful to change the date on the originals, 1776–1876, to 1776–1976. Marked this

way such pieces will become the antiques of the future and, although widely produced in the mid-1970s, in about a century they too should be very collectible.

Bakewell, Pears and Company, Pittsburgh

This firm was one of the glassmaking pioneers in Pittsburgh and was known early on for its top-quality blown and cut wares. It was also a major glass presser and produced many of the best-known flint-glass patterns, which they kept in production into the 1870s. It also introduced several completely new patterns in the 1870s.

Cherry showed a cluster of cherries in the naturalistic vein. The *Icicle* pattern, patented in 1874, featured a staggered band of narrow ribs running up the sides. It was produced in both clear and milk glass and resembles the earlier *Stedman* pattern by

Fig. 8-3 The *Liberty Bell* "Signer's Platter" features the names of the signers of the Declaration of Independence around its lower border.

Fig. 8-4 The three "Ribbon" patterns of the 1870s. Left to right are goblets in Bakewell's *Ribbon*, King's *Frosted Ribbon—Double Bar* and Duncan's *Frosted Ribbon.*

McKee. Not too well known to modern collectors is the *Etruscan* pattern also patented in 1874. It is a simple paneled design closely related to earlier flint patterns.

Probably one of its handsomest patterns of this decade is *Ribbon*, circa 1870. Featuring alternating narrow bars of frosted and clear glass, the pieces had flat, slightly flaring sides. The pattern, sometimes mistakenly called *Frosted Ribbon,* should not be confused with a later and less well-known pattern by that name. The frosting of the bars on Ribbon was achieved by machine grinding rather than the use of acid fumes. The goblet and an open compote with a figural "Rebecca at the Well" pedestal base are the reproductions to beware in this pattern. A rarity to look for is another open compote with a figural dolphin pedestal base.

Finally, the *Princess Feather* pattern (originally called *Rochelle*) continued to be popular. It was carried over from the flint era and widely produced in both clear and milk white.

Boston and Sandwich Glass Company, Sandwich, Massachusetts

The Sandwich company, famous for so many popular patterns in the flint-glass era, apparently did not introduce a large selection of new patterns in the late 1860s and 1870s but continued production of its time-tested favorites. A few lines often ascribed to this factory are discussed here.

A couple of very collectible patterns of the 1870s have tentatively been attributed to Sandwich.

However, as of this writing there exists no good documentary evidence that firmly ties them to this factory. Lee, in her pioneering work on Sandwich glass, did not note either pattern as coming from this firm.

The *Cape Cod* pattern has long been associated with Sandwich, although no fragments of it were found there. Probably early collectors thought the oval reserve on the side featuring a sailing boat was meant to represent a scene on Cape Cod, where Sandwich is located. The oval panel on the reverse of the pieces features a lighthouse and cove scene, and each panel is framed by floral sprigs and ivy vines against a stippled ground.

A pattern closely related to Cape Cod is today called *Canadian.* Instead of seaside scenes this pattern has arched, vertical panels featuring various rural landscapes, but each panel again is surrounded by floral sprigs and ivy matching those on Cape Cod. Shards of this pattern have been found at the site of the Burlington Glass Works in Hamilton, Ontario, in Canada, and that probably accounts for its name among modern collectors. However; no conclusive proof exists that it was made there, and it may have been introduced first in the United States although no American maker is known at present. Lee speculated that Cape Cod and Canadian originated at the same factory; what factory is not known.

Canadian has been reproduced or adapted to make a footed vase or candlelamp featuring similar arched panels that include varied rural and seaside scenes. This piece appeared in the 1970s in a milk-white or clambroth color. On the inside bottom of this piece is a round indentation that might hold a small candle or flower stems.

Sandwich is thought by some researchers to have been responsible for a version of the popular *Tree of Life* pattern also made at the Portland Glass Company in Portland, Maine. Another variation was produced in the Midwest.

The Tree of Life purportedly made at Sandwich features what resembles a slender, leafless tree running up the sides of a piece against an overall background of fine hatched lines resembling a frosted window pane. Of the pattern variations Tree of Life is the only one that truly features a treelike design.

Collectors should be careful not to confuse this pressed pattern with an art glass line called *cra-*

Fig. 8-5 This handsome piece is a covered sugar bowl in the *Bradford Blackberry* (or *Grape*) pattern attributed to Sandwich.

to find this pattern and, although produced with some lead, it is not as heavy as earlier flint patterns. It also was reproduced heavily years ago, particularly the goblet and wine glass.

Other botanical lines that Lee attributed to Sandwich include *Bradford Blackberry, Stippled Fuchsia, Flowered Oval, Grape Band Variant,* and *Beaded Acorn.* The *Frosted Leaf* pattern likely was made during this time by Sandwich but apparently also by the Portland Glass Company. Shards of the *Gooseberry* and *Leaf and Dart* patterns were found at the Sandwich factory site, but since loads of such fragments (called "cullet") were shipped from one factory to another to be used in mixing fresh batches of glass, these fragments alone do not prove conclusively that those patterns were made there. Of the listed patterns, some pieces of Frosted Leaf and Gooseberry have been reproduced.

Other patterns of the 1860s and 1870s attrib-

Fig. 8-6 *Powder and Shot* is a pattern that may have been made at Sandwich.

quelle or *overshot,* which was definitely produced at the Sandwich plant about this same period. Craquelle resembles Tree of Life but has a rougher surface texture and does not include a tree design. Pieces of craquelle were blown and, while still hot, rolled in a bed of fine, crushed glass that adhered to the surface. This technique is totally different from the one used to make another type of art glass called *crackle* glass. In crackle glass a blown piece, while still very hot, is dunked in cold water, which causes it to develop a fine internal webbing or "crackling," giving its present name.

A number of naturalistic patterns have also been attributed to the Sandwich factory. The most famous of these is *Morning Glory,* which was produced in only a limited range of pieces and apparently for only a short period of time. It is a hard uted to Sandwich are *Dickinson, Beaded Mirror,* and *Divided Heart.* Shards of the *Powder and Shot* pattern, which features what appears to be an old powder horn pouring beads of shot, also have been found at Sandwich. Other designs, like *Beaded Acorn* and *Beaded Mirror,* include an oval surrounding the design against a stippled background. Once again fragments of Powder and Shot also have been found at the Portland Glass Company site.

One noteworthy piece from the 1870s can be attributed safely to Sandwich. It is a little mold-blown salt shaker popularly known among today's collectors as the "Christmas salt" because around the rim of the metal top is stamped "Patented December 25, 1877." This patent was for the special agitator top, a pronged bar that fit down into the shaker. When one twisted the little pointed finial on the lid, it turned the agitator to stir up any lumps of salt inside. As mentioned getting salt to pour was a challenge during this era. Although nothing in the simple, barrel-shaped design of this little item reminds one of Christmas, it is available in a range of attractive colors, and the holiday date, plus the fact it can be attributed safely to the Sandwich factory, add to its collector appeal.

The only reason the lids carry the December 25th date is that all U.S. patents were registered on the Tuesday of each week, and that week in 1877, Tuesday happened to fall on Christmas Day. It is not a very romantic story but one of those little historical coincidences that add interest to collecting.

Another related salt shaker also attributed to Sandwich can be found with a similarly marked lid. It is a tall, twelve-paneled cylindrical form and is scarcer than the short, barrel-shaped one.

Special note: Jane Shadel Spillman, curator of American Glass at the Corning Museum of Glass, has shared information from an early notebook that belonged to the Gillinders, a noted glassmaking family. This notebook covers some of the products of New England area glass factories, including Sandwich. The Sandwich entry is dated 1865 and lists eleven patterns as being made there. These are listed below, but keep in mind that these are the original pattern names and only four of them are still in use today. The other patterns are as yet unidentified but might possibly represent some of the patterns Lee attributed to the Boston and Sandwich Glass Company.

The patterns are: Ashburton, Comet (same as M'Kee's?), Flute and Split, Finger and Diamond, Huber, Mirror, Mt. Vernon, Mt. Washington, Old Colony, St. Lawrence, and Zouave.

Bryce Brothers, Pittsburgh

Another well-established glass company responsible for many fine flint glass patterns, which they continued to produce into the 1870s, Bryce Brothers patented several new plant designs during those years. These lines are not too well known to collectors today but include the patterns *Grape Band, Curled Leaf* (both circa 1869), and *Strawberry* and *Thistle,* circa 1870 and 1872, respectively. This Thistle should not be confused with the early-twentieth-century pattern known as *Paneled Thistle.* The early Thistle features a band of thistle leaves and blossoms around the body rather than the wide panels with a single thistle stock found on the late Higbee company pattern.

Bryce patterns based on geometric motifs include a design collectors call *Diamond Sunburst,* patented in 1874, and its best-known pattern of the period, *Jacob's Ladder,* patented in 1876. The latter line originally was called *Maltese* by the makers and later was reissued as *Imperial.* It features vertical wide bands of a crisscross, trellislike design alternating with horizontal bars suggesting a ladder. This pattern continued in production into the first decade

Fig. 8-7 *Jacob's Ladder* by Bryce is on the left while *Cord and Tassel* by Central is on the right.

of this century, which should mean there is an abundant supply out there to be collected. The best part is that so far it has not been reproduced.

Campbell, Jones and Company, Pittsburgh

Founded in the 1860s, this firm produced some interesting patterns in the 1870s.

In 1871 Mary Campbell, wife of James W. Campbell, one of the owners, patented a plant design called *Currant Ware,* known to collectors today simply as *Currant.* One interesting feature of this line is the figural log finial on the covers.

Jenkins Jones, another owner, patented *Dewdrop with Star* in 1877. This line featured a design of heavy stippling or "pearls," as Jones called them. A star-shaped formation of pearls in the base of some pieces may relate to the "star" in the name. The wide selection of plates in this pattern features a star design in the middle. Plates were a rather unusual form in the pattern glass of this era, and some thirteen sizes are found in this pattern ranging from four and a half inches in diameter up to nine inches. Originally only made in clear glass, some pieces have been reproduced in both clear and color including plates, a footed master salt, a footed sauce (dish), and a goblet (never part of the original set). Another plate in this line was a bread plate featuring the Biblical quote "Give Us This Day Our Daily Bread" around the beaded border with a sheaf of wheat in the center. This plate reportedly also was made for the Central and South American markets with the quote in Spanish.

Another "dewdrop" pattern from this firm is *Paneled Dewdrop,* which features the pearls again but arranged in wide bands alternating with plain bands.

Campbell, Jones and Company also patented its own *Flute* pattern in 1878, but this is a clear, nonflint pattern and would not be confused with the heavier flint *Flute* pattern.

Central Glass Company, Wheeling, West Virginia

Starting as a modest company in 1863, this firm went on to introduce some of the most distinctive patterns in American pattern glass in the late nineteenth century.

About 1870 it issued its *Rose* pattern, which is called *Cabbage Rose* by collectors. It features a wide band of realistic rose blossoms and leaves. In the 1960s the goblet and spoonholder were reproduced in clear and colored glass but the new pieces are heavier than the old and lack their fine detail.

In 1872 Central patented its *Cord and Tassel* pattern (see Figure 8-7), which shows a pair of heavy rope cord bands flanking an undulating rope band hung with tassels around the middle of each piece. This pattern has not been reproduced.

Probably the highlight of its 1870s pattern-glass lines, at least as far as today's collectors are concerned, is its *Log Cabin* pattern issued around 1875. This figural ware has pieces molded to resemble log cabins, with the covers on pieces formed as a shingled roof with center chimney. Some of the large pieces are raised on a figural tree trunk pedestal base. A scarce and desirable pattern, the covered sugar bowl, creamer, and spooner have been reproduced fairly recently in clear, cobalt blue, and chocolate glass, so be on the alert. Reportedly the door latch handle is missing on the doors of reproduced pieces. Also, the horizontal boards in the end gables of the roof-shaped covers of old pieces are missing on the reproductions. These should be helpful clues.

Fig. 8-8 A *Dewdrop with Star* plate. This pattern came in a wide variety of plate sizes but, unfortunately, has been reproduced widely.

Doyle and Company, Pittsburgh

This glass firm established in 1866 really came into its own in the 1880s, but a couple of noteworthy patterns were issued by Doyle in the 1870s.

Drapery, which it patented as *Lace* in 1870, is a collectible line. It consists of a band of pointed curtain swags with scalloped edges trimmed with tassels. *Grape and Festoon,* which has an undulating band of leaves framing grape clusters, was introduced in the mid-1870s and appears in several variations: with clear leaves, with stippled leaves, with veined leaves, and with a stippled grape cluster. A closely related pattern called *Stippled Grape and Festoon* has a stippled background behind the grape clusters. Shards of this latter pattern also have been found at the site of the Boston and Sandwich Glass Company. It remained in production through the 1890s, and neither of these lines has been reproduced.

Fig. 8-9 *A Grape and Festoon pattern spoon holder. This pattern is found in several variations but all feature a stippled background typical of several 1870s patterns.*

George Duncan and Sons, Pittsburgh

The founder of this company, George Duncan, had been associated with glassmaking in Pittsburgh for many years before the firm of Ripley and Company took this name in 1874. It went on to produce a large number of well-known patterns in the 1880s as well as numerous novelty items. In the 1870s its fame is due to its one major pattern: *Three Face.*

One of the most famous of late-Victorian pressed-glass patterns patented in 1878 by John E. Miller, Three Face has long been a top pattern in collectibility. For many years it was thought the three identical women's faces forming the stems of pieces were the face of Miller's wife. More likely, he was inspired by an earlier French design that featured four women's faces around the bases of pieces. Most famous with an acid-frosted base, all-clear pieces also were produced as were pieces with engraved designs trimming the upper clear portions.

Sadly, not long after collectors began gathering this pattern, reproductions hit the market and have plagued collectors since the 1930s. Some of these will be touched on a little later, but for the general collector it is best to follow the old adage: Know the glass or know the dealer.

A lesser-known Duncan pattern of the late 1870s today is called *Frosted Ribbon* and should not be confused with the better-known Bakewell pattern discussed earlier (see Figure 8-4). The Duncan line, originally called simply "no. 150," was made in both all-clear and with the wide panels alternating clear and frosted. The sides are slightly flaring and the knob on the pedestal bases of some pieces feature small thumbprints. The clear pieces often were decorated with engraved bands of leaves around the body. Unlike the Bakewell line, this pattern has not been reproduced.

Gillinder and Sons, Philadelphia, Pennsylvania

Founded in 1864, this glass firm, one of the few major concerns of the period not near Pittsburgh, was well established by the 1870s. It was in fact responsible for several famous pressed-glass patterns and pieces of the 1870s.

It patented a *Star* pattern in 1870 that today is called *Stippled Star* because of its stippled back-

Fig. 8-10 Close-ups of the bases of the *Three Face* (left) and *Baby Face* goblets show the design differences.

ground. In 1874 it patented its *Mellor* pattern, a design with bold, overlapping circles also known as *Block and Circle*. Stippled Star has been reproduced.

With the coming of the American Centennial celebrations in 1876, Gillinder really hit its stride. It is famous today with collectors because of the numerous glass souvenirs it produced at a factory set up right on the grounds of the Centennial Exhibition in Philadelphia in 1876. Many of these pieces actually bear the name of the company itself, stamped in the bottom, a very rare occurrence on pressed glassware of the late nineteenth century. In addition to pieces such as a figural bust of Abraham Lincoln and a woman's shoe, which were best-sellers at the Centennial Exhibition, it also introduced a tableware line related to this event.

The Centennial tableware line Gillinder put out around 1876 is known today as the *Washington*

Centennial pattern, the second pressed-glass pattern named in honor of the first president. This elegant design consists of a band of large, overlapping circles, down the middle of which runs a band of three diamonds. Graceful applied handles with curlique tails are found on the pitchers and creamers. For collectors this pattern offers a chance to make a find, as it is not as well known or easily recognized as the Adams Liberty Bell pattern.

Continuing its pattern achievements in the 1870s, around 1877 Gillinder released another new pattern well known to collectors today. The *Lion* pattern, usually referred to as *Frosted Lion* or *Lion Head,* is another design where the actual pattern is restricted to the lower half or base of the pieces, or is used on cover finials. The upper sections remained clear or sometimes were engraved with leaf or flower bands. Most Frosted Lion pieces feature a molded rope band around the rim.

Fig. 8-11 Gillinder's *Washington Centennial* pattern of 1876. This is the second pressed pattern named after George Washington.

Fig. 8-12 A large *Frosted Lion* covered compote, 14½" tall and 8¾" in diameter. This size has not been reproduced in this pattern. Note the rampant lion finial.

Several variations are found in the pieces in this line, but they all blend together well in a collection. Though most of the stemware pieces in the set have a frosted stem molded with three lion faces, there are also plain, clear, low pedestal bases. Some pieces have a flaring, frosted, collared base featuring a recumbent lion. The other major variation involves the finials on the covers of pieces: one type features just a frosted lion's head, while its cousin has a full-figural rampant frosted lion. This latter type can be found in several sizes. As far as collectors are concerned, pieces with figural lions are worth somewhat more than those with just the head.

Another piece that Gillinder produced and sold at the Centennial Exhibition is a frosted paper-weight with a figural recumbent lion. However, this was not part of the tableware set, though many collectors will include it there.

The Frosted Lion pattern, widely popular in the late nineteenth century and with glass collectors of this century, fell victim to numerous reproductions beginning in the 1930s. It never was made originally in color so avoid any of those pieces. Since numerous pieces have been copied over the years, the best way of separating the old from the new is to check the detailing, which is poor on the new, and the frosted finish, which is rough and chalky on twentieth-century pieces. Especially helpful is to check the lion's mouth, since on newer pieces the corners droop down, giving him a sad or angry expression. On originals the mouth is a

Fig. 8-13 A large *Westward Ho* covered compote, 15" tall and 8¾" in diameter. Again, this size of compote has not been reproduced.

straight line. This wonderful pattern remains a collector's favorite, but beginning collectors must proceed with caution.

Topping off a decade of glorious innovation, about 1879 Gillinder released another of the top ten patterns of late-Victorian pressed glass—*Westward Ho.*

Originally called *Pioneer* by the maker, this line features, as mentioned earlier, a mixture of design elements meant to capture the spirit of the opening of the American West. Frosted scenes with a buffalo, deer, mountains, pine trees and a pioneer's cabin circle the bodies of each piece below a clear rim band. Footed pieces have a fairly plain, clear pedestal base with a simple, round foot. Extensively reproduced since the 1930s there is, unfor-

tunately, no easy way to tell the old from the new. Checking the details of the design and finish are the most helpful guides. On early reproductions the frosting, as on Frosted Lion, is rough to the touch. Later reproductions have a much smoother finish but the details of the design, such as the fur on the animals, is very poorly defined. It is a pattern that requires great care in collecting but that probably best captures the essence of America's nineteenth-century pioneer spirit.

Hobbs, Brockunier and Company, Wheeling, West Virginia

The founders of this glass factory had a long association with glass production in the Pittsburgh-Wheeling region before setting up a company under this title in 1863. In that year they also acquired the services of William Leighton, Sr., who, the reader will recall, was responsible for introducing the soda-lime formula that ended the flint-glass era of pressed glass. Leighton and his son, William, Jr., had a long and successful association with this company, which in 1879 was considered the largest glassmaker in the United States.

Hobbs is well remembered among glass lovers today for the many innovative and lovely pressed and art glassware it brought out, especially during the 1880s, but during its heyday it was also famous for lamp production and other patented glass production improvements.

During the 1870s it introduced several interesting patterns in pressed-glass tableware including *Blackberry* (circa 1870) and *Paneled Wheat* (circa 1871), both of which mirror the naturalistic trend of that period. *Blackberry* has been reproduced.

One of its most noteworthy lines of the era was another pattern produced to mark the U.S. Centennial in 1876. It produced its own *Centennial* line that year, but today it usually is referred to as *Viking* or *Bearded Head.* Surprisingly, Hobbs's Centennial includes no motif that might be considered the least bit patriotic. It is basically a very plain, clear line with rounded shapes. Its only remarkable feature is that the round, collared rims of the bases have four short feet embossed with the rather fierce visage of a helmeted warrior, which collectors have decided is probably a Norse Viking. Although every true

Son of Norway like myself should be intrigued by this connection, I must confess that I find the pattern rather homely. In addition to the faces on the feet, the domed covers have finials with a pair of the same faces, back to back. Since the historical significance of this Centennial pattern cannot be denied, it is quite collectible today. A goblet and tumbler, never part of the original set, have been made in recent decades.

For many years the midwestern version of the famous *Tree of Life* pattern, referred to as *Pittsburgh Tree of Life* or *Tree of Life with Hand*, has been attributed to the firm of George Duncan and Sons of Pittsburgh. However, recent research by writers Neila and Tom Bredehoft confirms that this variation was actually a product of Hobbs, Brockunier and Company.

In their article "Is Pittsburgh Tree of Life

Fig. 8-14 *Tree of Life with Hand* is known now to be a Hobbs product. This spooner features a frosted base.

Really Pittsburgh Glass?" published in the December-January 1989 issue of *Glass Collector's Digest*, the Bredehofts report that no research has been able to verify that the Duncan firm ever made this line. However, they cite an article in the September 4, 1879, issue of the trade publication *Crockery and Glass Journal* that describes a new Hobbs set (no. 898) of frosted ware featuring a hand grasping a snowball. This hand and snowball certainly could refer to the hand and ball found on the pedestal bases, handles, and finials of pieces in the so-called Pittsburgh Tree of Life pattern. As the authors point out, this line should now probably be referred to as Tree of Life with Hand, since it apparently was not made in Pittsburgh itself.

Tree of Life with Hand, like its sister patterns made in New England, also features a design of crisscross webbing filled with a textured background of hatched lines. Another major difference between this and other Tree of Life lines is that pieces in this version have melon ribbing on the bowls of all pieces. This ribbing gives the rounded forms of some pieces the appearance of a large cantaloupe, the surface texture resembling the skin of this fruit.

The melon ribbing and hand with ball bases, finials, and handles of Tree of Life with Hand make this a truly distinctive and appealing pattern. In addition, this pattern variation has not been reproduced.

King, Son and Company (King Glass Company), Pittsburgh

This company produced some noteworthy patterns in the 1880s and 1890s, but in the 1870s only a few lines were produced that are of special interest to collectors today.

Its first significant pattern of this decade was patented in 1871 and was called *Maple*. It consists of a band of overlapping maple leaves within parallel bands segmented by a diamond panel, within which is a four-petal florette. The finial on covered pieces resembles a pointed pine cone or perhaps a hop, which may explain why it has become known to collectors as *Hops Band*.

Around 1875 a catalog from this firm shows a number of patterns that are sought by collectors. Probably the best known today is the *Bleeding*

Fig. 8-15 Another realistic floral pattern of the 1870s is *Bleeding Heart*, shown here in the spoon holder from the set.

Heart pattern, which it named *Floral Ware*. It represents that popular spring flower. Another design that collectors seek is *Banded Buckle* (its *Union*), which is very similar to the *Buckle* pattern. However, Banded Buckle includes a narrow band of crosshatching above the band of large crosshatched ovals (buckles) that circumscribe the body.

A pattern that might confuse some beginning collectors is its "no. 13" line, which today is referred to as *Frosted Ribbon Double Bars* (see Figure 8-4). As the name implies, the pattern is similar to the Bakewell and Duncan patterns of the same era except that pairs of ribbons run up the frosted side instead of just one. This ware also was made unfrosted.

In addition to these pattern lines King also produced a wide variety of plain, simple tableware sometimes decorated with acid etching or engrav-ing. Several simple children's sets were also in its lineup as was an alphabet plate featuring a hen and chicks in the center and the raised letters of the alphabet around the rim.

In spring 1875 King patented a special innovation in glass pressing: a method to press curved and ribbed feet for pieces. This type of foot became known as a "shell" foot. The new shell feet were used most notably in 1876 on King's own *Centennial* pattern. Other than these unusual feet the pieces in this pattern are completely plain, with fat, rounded shapes and simple, ruffled rims on the open bowls. The covers also feature a shell finial that matches the feet. For those looking for an early pattern with historical associations, this little-recognized Centennial line should prove an interesting challenge to locate.

M'Kee and Brothers (McKee Glass Company), Pittsburgh

This company (it actually spelled its name M'Kee at that time) was an offshoot of Bryce, McKee and Company. The McKees went off on their own in 1854 and became well known for producing the fine flintware so well documented in its surviving catalogs.

In the 1870s the firm was still going strong and would remain one of America's leading glassmakers into the twentieth century. Although it carried over many of its flint patterns into the 1870s, it also introduced several new ones during the period. About 1870 McKee produced a rare and strange pattern called *Dragon*, which is most notable for the large, long-snouted flying dragon with a large, curling tail featured on pieces. The finials on this line feature a large conch-type shell that also showed up on some of its other patterns. Also in 1870 M'Kee introduced *Barberry*, which is highlighted by lifelike clusters of this plant. Collectors call a line they patented in 1874 *Block and Honeycomb*. It features a band of large hexagonal blocks above a honeycomb design around the base of pieces.

A sister pattern of Duncan's *Three Face*, M'Kee introduced its *Cupid* pattern at about the same time (see Fig. 8-10). Today called *Baby Face* by collectors, the stems of pieces in this limited pattern consist of three cherubic children's faces. The figural bases and finials on this line are acid finished, like those on the Three Face pattern. The goblet and wine glass in Baby Face have been reproduced, but the new pieces lack the fine detailing and workmanship of the old, and the acid finish is too smooth and shallow. An electric lamp with a ball shade was produced a few years ago, but as it was not part of the original line it should not fool collectors.

Many companies issued glass novelties in the 1880s and 1890s, and one such popular item was the bread tray. However, one of the earliest of these novel trays was patented in 1873 by the McKees. It was basically oval with a large sheaf of wheat in the middle and smaller sheaves at the ends forming a portion of the handles. Around the outer border band of this piece is raised the Biblical quote "Give Us This Day—Our Daily Bread."

New England Glass Company, Cambridge, Massachusetts

Famous for its fine-blown and pressed wares from previous decades, this glassworks continued producing its flint glass patterns into the 1870s. However, it did not produce many new pattern lines. It did, nonetheless, introduce some fine novelty pieces, such as a candlestick with a pedestal base in the form of a classically dressed woman of ancient Greece. Dating circa 1870, this handsome item is today called "Caryatid" or "Draped Lady." Also circa 1870 it produced a figural inkwell in the shape of a small rowboat raised on blocks. It was made in clear, milk white, and blue glass. Another famous Victorian novelty item, the "Double Hands with Grapes" dish, was made by this firm around 1875. It was modeled as a pair of cupped woman's hands with grape clusters at the wrists. This piece, later produced at other firms including Atterbury, was made in several colors but is best known in milk glass. However, it has been reproduced, so collectors should be wary when considering the purchase of this charming piece.

Portland Glass Company, Portland, Maine

Famous for the brevity of the life of the firm (1864–1874), this company in that short period did introduce a couple of noteworthy pattern-glass lines.

Fig. 8-16 Two variations of the *Loop and Dart* pattern. On the left is a *Loop and Dart with Diamond Ornament* goblet, possibly from Sandwich, and on the right is the *Loop and Dart with Round Ornament* goblet from Portland.

Fig. 8-17 A *Portland Tree of Life* creamer in a silver-plate frame.

Its first patent in 1868 was issued to J. S. Palmer for a pattern known as *Scalloped Flute*. It remains fairly scarce today. More famous are the two patterns patented by plant superintendent William O. Davis.

In 1869 Davis patented the pattern *Loop and Dart with Round Ornament,* which features a row of slender spear points alternating with oval loops suspended from a rim band and raised against a stippled ground. Another very similar pattern with a diamond ornament band was made elsewhere, possibly at the Boston and Sandwich plant. A related pattern, *Loop and Dart,* was issued in Pittsburgh about this time but does not have the teardrop ornaments of the first two. The Portland pattern originally was quite successful and is sought today especially because of its limited production period.

Probably even better known than Loop and Dart with Round Ornament is the pattern Davis brought out about the same time, which is now called *Portland Tree of Life* to differentiate it from similar patterns made elsewhere. This pattern closely resembles the midwestern version with its fine webbing of cracks throughout the walls of pieces. Again, the webbing is filled with a cross-hatched line design. What makes this pattern especially unusual is that some pieces can be found with the pressed marking "P. G. Co. Patent," and other items have the name "Davis" woven into the design. Another unique feature of this line is that some pieces were made to be set into special silver-plate footed stands with handles. These pieces have rounded bottoms so cannot stand alone. Portland Tree of Life was produced mostly in clear but also was made rarely in colors including amber, light and dark blue, canary yellow, green, cranberry, and amethyst. Some pieces have been reproduced in recent years.

Other glass factories operated during the period covered here, but most did not produce many significant pressed-glass patterns or, like Atterbury and Company of Pittsburgh, specialized in novelty wares and lighting.

Desirability and Values

The rules governing current market values for popular patterns of the late 1860s and 1870s are pretty much the same as those for early flint patterns. Form and color are two major factors, and scarce pieces and the few pieces in color bring higher prices.

For most patterns featuring naturalistic or geometric designs, values generally correspond to the following ranges:

$50 and under: A great many pieces are available in this range, especially smaller bowls and open compotes. In quite a few of these patterns stemware (goblets and wine glasses) can be found under $50 but will cost somewhat more in other lines. Small sauce dishes often can be found for under $25.

$50–$100 range: Almost all medium- and larger-sized pieces fall in this range, including covered pieces and scarcer pieces such as cake stands. Each pattern varies depending on the range of pieces made.

$100 and up: In most patterns only the choicest pieces, such as larger pitchers and rare forms, bring over $100.

In spite of rampant reproductions, the big name patterns of this era continue to bring premium prices for their old pieces. These choice patterns include Lion (Frosted Lion), Log Cabin, Three Face, and Westward Ho. In each most pieces will be priced in the $75–$200 range, with the rare pieces in the $300–$400 range. Only small sauce dishes may be found for under $25 in most cases.

Old Versus New

Earlier the major producers of pressed-glass tableware of this period were described, some of the most important and collectible patterns discussed, and reproductions noted.

To help collectors get a better grasp of what to look for and avoid in these patterns, the following list of reproduced patterns indicates what to watch for in the copies. Remember: reading books, visiting with knowledgeable dealers and collectors, and examining as much pressed glass, old and new, as possible, are the best ways to become confident in collecting Victorian pattern glass.

Baby Face: Watch for poor detailing and a thin, too satiny finish. Beware: goblet, wine glass, and a new electric lamp.

Blackberry: Watch for a blurry design and a pearly white color in the newer milk glass. The old was a denser white. Reproduced in clear and milk glass. Beware: butter dish, celery vase, creamer, single eggcup, goblet, sugar bowl, and water pitcher.

Cabbage Rose: See text. Beware: goblet and spoonholder. Reproduced in clear, amber, amethyst, blue, and green.

Canadian: See text. Beware: milk white footed vase.

Cardinal: Beware: goblet in clear, blue, and green.

Cherry: Watch for the sharper, more pronounced design on reproductions. Older pieces have a more rounded look on the cherries. Beware: butter dish, gobet, salt dip, sugar bowl, toothpick holder, and water pitcher. These were reproduced in many colors, including milk white and blue opaque as well as clear. Westmoreland reproduced milk glass pieces, plain and enamel decorated, but these carry the entwined ''WG'' company logo. It made: double-handled cookie jar, three-and-a-quarter-inch-high creamer, two-and-a-quarter-inch-high flat, double-handled sugar bowl, five-and-a-half-inch-high pedestal-base honey dish, ten-and-a-half-inch-high pedestal-base open compote with scalloped rim, and a twelve-inch-high double-handled covered compote.

Dewdrop with Star: Watch for the many sizes of plates in this pattern. The seven-inch-, seven-and-a-quarter-inch-, seven-and-a-half-inch-, and eleven-inch-diameter round plates have been reproduced as was a footed master open salt, footed round sauce dish, and a goblet not in the original set.

Frosted Leaf: Watch for pieces reproduced in lead glass for the Smithsonian Institution. They carry its ''S. I.'' monogram. Beware: butter dish, creamer, spooner, sugar bowl, and wine glass.

Gooseberry: Beware: goblet and wine glass, both reproduced in clear and milk glass.

Grasshopper: Beware: goblet in clear and color. There was no goblet originally.

Liberty Bell: Watch for the pieces made for the U.S. Bicentennial in 1976. They will carry the dates 1776–1976. Beware: seven-ounce goblet, ten-ounce goblet, and three different platters made in clear.

Fig. 8-18 This milky clambroth vase is a modern adaptation of the old *Canadian* pattern.

Lion: Watch for the rough, chalklike frosted finish on old reproductions and the sad-faced lion. Beware: four-inch-diameter sauce dish, ten-and-a-half-inch-diameter handled bread plate, butter dish, celery vase, oval high-pedestal covered compote, sugar bowl, eggcup, goblet, medium oval bowl, water pitcher, and spooner. Also, Imperial Glass Company made an amber compote with its entwined ''I. G.'' logo in the base and ''Patented August 6th, 1889'' inside the cover. A two-and-seven-eighths-diameter round dish with round foot was made that somewhat resembles the old master salt dip. Pieces have been reproduced in clear and frosted and some in color. Color was never used in the old pieces.

Log Cabin: See text. Beware: sugar bowl, five-inch-high creamer and spooner.

Morning Glory: Beware: goblet and wine glass, often reproduced in color. It was never made in color originally.

Portland Tree of Life: Watch for pieces made from new molds in the 1970s. Beware: five-and-a-half-

Fig. 8-19 A close-up of a *Frosted Lion* compote pedestal with lion heads. These heads are better defined and do not have the sharply downturned mouths of the reproductions.

and wine glass. Some copies were made in several colors; most old pieces were clear but a few have been found in blue.

Three Face: Watch for the many old reproductions in this famous pattern. The earliest reproductions had a chalky white frosting with a rough feel, but later ones were smoother feeling. Check the facial details: the nose is not sharp on newer pieces, the hair lacks good detailing, and the eyes can be almost almond shaped instead of more naturally rounded. Beware: footed sauce dish, six-inch-high covered compote, four-inch-diameter low-pedestal covered compote, sherbet dish, spooner, sugar shaker, toothpick holder, goblet, wine glass, butter dish, tall-pedestal cake stand, champagne glass, six-inch- and six-and-a-half-inch-diameter tall-pedestal covered compote, creamer, lamp, salt dip, salt shaker, and sugar bowl. Some pieces were authorized by the Metropolitan Museum of Art and were made from new molds. These are marked with the mu-

inch-diameter flat, crimped and flared bowl, nine-ounce goblet, four-inch-diameter three-legged round sauce dish, four-inch-high sugar bowl, and four-ounce wine glass. These were made in clear, amber, and blue.

Ribbon (Bakewell's): Watch for rough-feeling frosting on the panels and markings that appear to have been caused by filing or tooling. The ''Rebecca at the Well'' pedestal-based open compote has several details to watch for, including a flattened edge on the rim of the bowl (instead of rounded as on the old), and the nearly round holes formed by Rebecca's elbows (which are pointed and better defined on the old). Beware: goblet and open compote with ''Rebecca at the Well'' figural base.

Stippled Star: Watch for many pieces reproduced in new molds. They tend to be heavier and coarser in design than the old pieces. Beware: two-inch-high round, footed salt, goblet, creamer, master salt dip, sugar bowl, tall pedestal-covered compote, two-and-seven-eighths-inch-diameter individual salt dip

Fig. 8-20 A close-up of the finial on an authentic *Westward Ho* compote cover. Note the well-defined eyes and square jaw of this Native American as well as the fine detailing of his fur and especially his feathered headdress.

seum's "MMA" initials, but many reproductions are not marked at all.

Viking: See text. Beware: goblet and tumbler.

Westward Ho: See text. Watch also for the deer's mouth, which appears open on copies. The original animal had a straight-lined mouth. Check all detailing, especially the animal's fur. Also check the narrow band between the clear rim band and the frosted band with the design. On old pieces this band is often flattened and sharp edged, while on many copies it is rounded. On covered pieces check the detailing on the Native American. On the reproductions his chin is very weak and tapers off, while on old pieces he has a square jaw and good mouth and eye detail. The feathers on his head also have sharp detailing on old pieces. The reproductions often have heavy mold seams running down his back. Beware: celery vase, four-inch-diameter low-pedestal covered compote, five-inch-diameter low-pedestal covered compote, six-inch oval covered compote, six-inch-diameter low-pedestal round covered compote, tumbler, footed sauce dish, six-inch-diameter tall-pedestal covered compote, butter dish, goblet, water pitcher, wine glass, seven-and-a-half-inch-high creamer and ten-and-a-half-inch-high sugar bowl. Some pieces were reproduced in color, which never was used originally.

To sum up: although reproductions can be a problem with many of the most popular patterns of the late 1860s and 1870s, with care and study one should be able to avoid most of them. Remember: Many twentieth-century reproductions are heavier than their old counterparts, and design details are seldom as well done. Also, watch out for pieces that were not made in the original pattern line.

CHAPTER 9

The 1880s: Color Becomes King

If one decade can be accepted as the pinnacle of American pressed glass production, it is probably the 1880s. The 1870s saw strong growth and many innovations in design and technology, but it was also a transitional period leading away from the preceding flint glass era.

By the 1880s the United States was becoming a major industrial power with a fast-growing population spread coast to coast. A number of new states had joined the union by 1890, and railroads and telegraphy had united every corner of the country from Washington to Maine and Florida to California. Although there were years of struggle for western pioneers, the frontiers shrank dramatically in this decade and more and more Americans had time to think about the finer things in life and spare time and money to travel. People could even splurge a little by buying some little glass whimsey that caught their fancy as a memento of a special occasion or place.

American industry was booming, and the glass industry in particular was growing and evolving. More and more glass companies were taking advantage of the cheap natural gas supplies being discovered in Ohio and Indiana and moving further west, away from the Pittsburgh area. This was a boom period in plant growth spurred by a gas bonanza that, unfortunately, petered out in a few years, causing a real shake-up among glassmakers. The decade also saw growing strength in the labor movement. American glassworkers had organized, most notably as the American Flint Glass Workers Union ("flint" in this sense referring to finer tableware). Serious labor problems began to develop in the late 1870s as overworked factory hands struggled to keep pace with the production demands of a burgeoning industry and changes in technology that threatened some jobs. The famous Boston and Sandwich and New England Glass companies both closed during the 1880s in part due to labor turmoil, and things continued to be unsettled into the 1890s.

On the brighter side, in spite of labor troubles the decade was, without doubt, a watershed in glassmaking innovation. Art glass, as it is called today, became all the rage with the carriage trade, and exciting new lines like Amberina and Burmese came on the market in the mid-1880s. To compete with such wares and answer the needs of the less wealthy, many colorful and novel pressed ware were also introduced. This was the beginning of an age of color and novelty for American glass. A great many new patterns in pressed glass were introduced in soft shades of blue, green, amethyst, vaseline, and amber. Also, methods of highlighting clear glass with ruby and amber staining were patented late in the decade. Pressed and mold-blown glass with the innovative opalescent treatment reached the market late in the 1880s and was an immediate success. Milk white glass, previously made in a few patterns of tableware and novelties, now became common and was produced in an array of novel forms such as animal-shaped covered dishes, figural bottles, and lamps. New shades of opaque blue and green and mixed hues of purple and white (slag or marble glass) became the specialties of firms such as Challinor, Taylor and Company and Atterbury and Company. Within a few years there was something for every glass lover's taste and pocketbook, and the knickknack shelves of Victorian parlors bulged to overflowing with the charming, novel, and sometimes downright bizarre glass fantasies of the era.

Design trends of the 1880s closely paralleled those of the previous decade with a good number of naturalistic patterns (featuring plants, animals, and humans) being introduced. A variation is what I call realistic patterns, those designed to resemble some other object (like *Oaken Bucket*) or patterns that incorporated real objects in their design such as *Egg in Sand* or *Good Luck* (*Horseshoe*). Some patterns crossed over between these two styles, with the *Japanese* pattern incorporating fans as an important part of its design as well as birds and insects. There

Fig. 9-1 The bold design of this *Finecut and Panel* goblet is typical of the geometric patterns of the 1880s. Available in several colors, this piece is amber.

was even a dish in the shape of a fan included in the line. *Japanese* is also a good example of an exotic design inspired by the opening up of foreign lands through trade and exploration. Japan had hidden behind a veil of secrecy for centuries before being opened up rather forcibly to the West by Commodore Matthew Perry's armed arrival in 1853. By the 1870s and 1880s there flourished a great deal of interest in all things Japanese, and the arts and crafts of that country greatly influenced the Western art world, especially in France. The *Japanese* pattern represents an early attempt to commercialize a fad started in European art circles.

Another noteworthy design trend of the 1880s includes what I refer to as *classical* theme patterns. Renewed interest in the ancient world of classical Greece and Rome was spurred by such events as the discovery and excavations at the mystical city of Troy by German Heinrich Schlieman. This renewed fervor for the art and architecture of antiquity widely influenced the art world, and its motifs were adapted for such mundane objects as American pattern glass. Classically inspired patterns include *Minerva, Egyptian, Cupid and Venus,* and, most obviously, *Classic.*

The largest group of patterns introduced during the 1880s that often remained in production into the 1890s are the *geometric* and *abstract* designs. Nearly every geometric form imaginable was used in pressed-glass patterns, and many designs threw together a number of motifs. Toward the end of the decade a growing number of patterns was also being issued to imitate the ornate and brilliant cut designs found on the very best cut glass of the period.

Pressed glass, as will be seen, was presented in myriad forms and designs in the 1880s, and there was something for everyone. Glass collectors today are still reaping the benefits of the rich harvest of the glass-pressing ingenuity of over a century ago.

Important Patterns of the 1880s

Since dozens and dozens of pressed patterns were produced during the 1880s, it is not feasible in a book of this size to cover them all in depth. In this section a cross-section of especially representative patterns from this decade have been selected to give more background on them and their importance to collectors. In an accompanying chart is listed a more extensive selection of patterns introduced between roughly 1880 and 1890 and divided according to the general stylistic guidelines discussed in the previous section. A star indicates which patterns have known reproductions, and a cross indicates which were produced in color or had colored trim added to them. This chart gives an overview of what

IMPORTANT PATTERNS OF THE 1880s

Geometric and Abstract		Naturalistic	Realistic

Geometric and Abstract

+ Art (Job's Tears)
+ Atlas
+ Aurora
+ Beaded Band
  Beaded Oval and
    Scroll
+ Block and Fan
  Bow Tie
  Buckle with Star
+ Cathedral
  Chain with Star
  Chandelier
  Clear Diagonal
    Band
★ + Cottage
  Crow's Foot (Yale)
+ Currier & Ives
  Curtain
  Curtain Tie Back
★ + Daisy & Button
★ + Daisy & Button
    Single Panel
    (Ellrose or
    Amberette)
+ Daisy & Button
    w/Crossbar
★ + Daisy & Button
    w/Thumbprint
    Panel
+ Daisy & Button
    w/V Ornament
+ Dakota
+ Diagonal Band
  Diagonal Band
    w/Fan
★ + Diamond Quilted
+ Duncan Block
★ Eyewinker
  Fan with Diamond
+ Fine Cut
★ + Finecut and Panel
★ + Fleur-de-Lis and
    Drape
★ Frosted Circle
  Garfield Drape

Giant Bull's Eye
+ Gonterman
+ Grand
  Hand
    (Pennsylvania)
+ Hanover
+ Hartley
+ Henrietta
+ Hexagon Block
+ Hidalgo
★ + Hobb's Block
★ + Hobnail
★ + Hobnail-in-Square
  Late Buckle
+ Jacob's Coat
+ Jasper (Bent
    Buckle)
★ + Jersey Swirl
+ Kokomo
+ Mascotte
★ + Medallion
+ Melrose
+ Nailhead
+ One-o-One
+ Pavonia (Pineapple
    Stem)
★ + Pleat and Panel
+ Pressed Diamond
+ Raindrop
★ + Red Block
  Rosette
+ Scalloped Tape
    (Jewel Band)
+ Sheraton
+ Spirea Band
+ Thistle Shield
★ + Thousand Eye
★ + Three Panel
+ Torpedo
★ + Two Panel
+ Valencia Waffle
  Victoria (Fostoria's)
+ Zipper
+ Zippered Block

Naturalistic

★ Actress
★ Baltimore Pear
  Bamboo
+ Barley
+ Dahlia
★ + Deer and Pine Tree
  Fishscale
+ Flower Pot
  Flying Stork
  Frosted Chicken
  Frosted Eagle
★ Frosted Stork
+ Hummingbird
  Jumbo
  Lion and Baboon
★ + Maple Leaf
★ + Monkey
★ + Paneled Daisy
+ Paneled Forget-
    Me-Not
★ Polar Bear
+ Primrose
+ Queen Anne
    (Bearded Man)
★ + Rose in Snow
★ + Rose Sprig
+ Sprig
  Squirrel
★ + Swan
+ Wheat and Barley
★ + Wildflower
+ Willow Oak

Realistic

★ + Basketweave
+ Cane
+ Egg in Sand
★ Good Luck
    (Horseshoe)
  Horseshoe Stem
  Japanese (Bird in
    Ring, Butterfly
    and Fan)
★ + Shell and Tassel
+ Stippled Chain
+ Wooden Pail
    (Oaken Bucket)

Classical

  Classic
  Classic Medallion
    (Cameo)
  Cupid & Venus
★ Egyptian
★ Minerva
★ Psyche & Cupid

+ = Produced in color or with color trim

★ = Reproduced

79

sorts of patterns were big sellers a century ago, and one can see that an overwhelming majority of them were highlighted by color. Keep in mind, as mentioned earlier, that many of these designs continued in wide production right through the 1890s, and a good many were still for sale well past the turn of the century.

Geometric and Abstract Patterns

This category is by far the largest in the 1880s, so this survey begins with some noteworthy and popular examples. Most were produced by the same companies that led pressed-glass production in the 1870s, so specific makers are not discussed in detail here.

Art   Adams issued this bold and handsome pattern in 1889 under this name, but it is also called *Job's Tears* or *Jacob's Tears,* as well as *Teardrop and Diamond Block.* The variant names are actually more descriptive of the design, which consists of a double band of large diamonds around the rim above a band of very large teardrops extending down the sides of the pieces.

This pattern was produced widely by the U.S. Glass Company after Adams joined that combine in 1891, and it is found in a very large range of pieces. It is seen most commonly in clear, but pieces sometimes were decorated with ruby staining or frosted portions. Any other color treatments would be rare. Luckily for collectors, this pattern has not been reproduced.

Atlas   Another simple design released around 1889, *Atlas* has been called by other names including *Cannon Ball, Crystal Ball, Bullet,* and *Knobby Bottom.* As these secondary titles make clear, round balls play some part in the design and, in fact, a band of large spheres do encircle the base of each piece below the plain cylindrical top portion. Keeping in mind that in mythology Atlas is the giant who holds up the globe, one can see the tie-in with the original name.

Atlas became another popular pattern for the U.S. Glass Company in the 1890s and apparently was available as late as 1904. It was made in clear, clear with engraved designs around the top portion, and clear with ruby-stained trim. Again, the ruby pieces bring the premium prices. A nice selection of

Fig. 9-2 Similar in appearance, the goblet on the left belongs to the *Eyewinker* pattern, while the one on the right is from the *Atlas* line.

pieces is available to collect and nothing in the pattern has been reproduced.

Block and Fan   A number of popular geometric patterns of the 1880s can be identified by their blocky designs—designs composed of rows of large square or multifaceted blocks.

One of the most representative patterns of this type is *Block and Fan.* A dramatic band of large square blocks encircles the middle of pieces in this line, and these large blocks often are flanked by bands of tiny square blocks. The top of each piece is highlighted by a row of fanlike designs, which explains its popular name. Continued in production throughout the 1890s, this line can be found with the blocks trimmed with ruby staining to add to its eye appeal. It has not been reproduced.

Currier and Ives   Today this pattern takes its collectors' name from the famous nineteenth-century printmaking firm of Currier and Ives. It was originally sold as *Eulalia.* Why the unusual name? Probably because the unique round water tray features a pressed comic scene in its center, which must have reminded early collectors of some similar print published by Currier and Ives. A two-wheeled cart is stranded on a railroad track because the obstreperous mule pulling it refuses to budge even as a steam train bears down on the hapless passengers. Called

Fig. 9-3 A squatty rose bowl in the *Block and Fan* pattern, one of many blocky designs of the 1880s and 1890s.

Fig. 9-4 This 9½″ d. "Balky Mule" tray is part of the *Currier and Ives* pattern.

the "Balky Mule" tray it comes in two sizes, nine and a half inches and twelve and a quarter inches in diameter.

The pattern found on all pieces, but only along the edge of the "Balky Mule" tray, is a checkered design composed of a small plain dot or button alternating with a small square containing a starburst. The design is quite similar to other patterns of the period, such as *Cane,* and to probably the most famous of the 1880s pressed-glass patterns, *Daisy and Button,* discussed later in this section.

Curtain Tie Back This pattern has been dated erroneously as far back as the 1860s, even though it is a nonflint line. Recent research by Jane Shadell Spillman, curator of American Glass at the Corning Glass Museum, has established quite firmly that this pattern was produced by Adams and Company in the mid-1880s. In her research on the Adams firm Spillman found an advertisement in a glass wholesaler's catalog of the mid-1880s in which *Curtain Tie Back* was being offered for sale along with other known Adams products. Since such lots of glassware were packaged at the glass factory and not by the wholesaler, this pins down the production dates and maker for this line.

The pattern name seems to derive from the wide U-shaped arches filled with fine beading that divide the sides of pieces into four segments. To early glass collectors these arches may have resembled the old brackets used to hold Victorian draperies in place. The pattern was produced in clear only and has not been reproduced.

Daisy and Button The very epitome of the late-nineteenth-century pressed-pattern glass, *Daisy and Button* was produced widely in the late nineteenth century and appeared in over a dozen variations by numerous glass concerns. Its great popularity in Victorian America was, unfortunately, echoed by a vast range of reproductions and adaptations that have been flooding the market since the 1930s.

The origin of this design has a fascinating history. In 1882 a new pattern of fine cut glass was patented and immediately became a hit. During 1883 and 1884 pieces in this new cut-glass design were purchased by the Russian ambassador in Washington, D.C., and soon it was known as the *Russian* pattern. In a bid to emulate the costly brilliant cut pattern, glass-pressing companies soon were producing a close imitation that has become known as Daisy and Button since it resembles octagonal buttons alternating with starburst "daisies" in an overall design.

Daisy and Button also is one of the few pressed-glass patterns produced in a true art glass variation. Nearly all fine art glass ware of the late nineteenth century was free-blown or mold-blown, but it was found that Amberina, a heat-reactive glass that shaded from deep ruby to amber, could be pressed in a mold. The New England Glass Company patented the original Amberina line in 1883,

Fig. 9-5 Three variations of the *Daisy and Button* pattern. On the left is a regular *Daisy and Button* goblet, while in the center is an amber *Daisy and Button with Crossbar* goblet. On the right is a *Daisy and Button with Thumbprint Panel* goblet with rare blue staining on the panels and foot.

and not long after it licensed Hobbs, Brockunier and Company of Wheeling to produce a pressed version of this glass in what Hobbs called its "no. 101" pattern. This pressed line, most often seen in novelty boat-shaped dishes and a large squared dish with matching smaller dishes, originally was much cheaper to produce than the blown pieces, but today this pressed Amberina is as expensive and desirable as its blown cousin.

With the immediate success of the Daisy and Button design, various companies decided to introduce their own variations and copies of the Hobbs pattern. Today researchers have found over 150 pieces of old Daisy and Button (often abbreviated to "D&B") available. These include items made in an overall Daisy and Button design issued by competing companies. It would be very difficult to tell pieces produced by different companies apart, and most collectors would not bother since they all blend together well.

In addition to clear, Daisy and Button was

made in a wide range of popular Victorian colors including canary yellow, blue, amber, apple green, vaseline, and, of course, scarce Amberina.

Although Daisy and Button remains an appealing pattern, the nearly fifty reproductions that have been around for as long as fifty years really have dampened its desirability for collectors of old pressed glass. There is still plenty of the old glass out there, but it will take a good deal of practice and patience to sort out the old from the new. Ruth Webb Lee's *Antique Fakes and Reproductions* and Bill Jenks' and Jerry Luna's *Early American Pattern Glass: 1850–1910* do a good job of listing and describing the most troublesome reproductions, so only some notable reproductions are covered here. Probably most commonly seen are the figural top hats and women's slippers that first hit store shelves in the late 1930s. Similar in form to some old pieces, these were reproduced in several colors and sizes similar to those of the old. Other novelty dishes in the forms of antique kettles, sleighs, and whisk brooms were copied. So was a little figural vase in the form of a woman's hand holding a Daisy and Button pattern cornucopia. Various bowls, covered compotes, plates, goblets, and toothpick holders are also out there, and watch out for the fan-shaped plates, too. A castor bottle set in a silver-plate frame was made about 1970.

As noted, it will take care and experience to distinguish old Daisy and Button from newer copies, but one general guideline to consider is weight. Later pieces tend to be heavier and thicker than the old ones. The newer glass often is cloudier or muddier in quality, while the design itself may feel too sharp and slick. According to early glass researcher and author, Ruth Webb Lee, many of the newer pieces, at least before about 1950, have a crinkly appearance in the clear portions of the buttons, whereas the old pieces are smooth and clear. More recent copies may not show this same quality, but their heavier weight still would be a factor to watch for. The colors used in reproductions are often reportedly harsher and brighter than the older colors, and new pieces may not be as well finished as the Victorian wares. Check the feel of a piece. If it has a rough texture and crude mold seams, question its age.

With the remarkable number of old pieces made a century ago, plenty is left to collect. Those who love this pattern should study it and take up the challenge to beat the reproductions, as they will be rewarded with a lovely collection.

Daisy and Button with Crossbars If plain Daisy and Button seems just too confusing, *Daisy and Button with Crossbars* is one of several variations that captures the charm of Daisy and Button but is safer to collect.

It was issued originally by the Richards and Hartley Flint Glass Company of Pittsburgh as its "no. 99" pattern or *Mikado*, apparently a reference to the popular Gilbert and Sullivan musical of that era. Today collectors have given it a more descriptive name. Each piece consists of a "Daisy and Button" design broken up by large crossbars running up the sides of pieces. This pattern, made in a number of colors as well as clear, happily has not been reproduced.

Daisy and Button with Narcissus A later variation on the "Daisy and Button" theme, this pattern

dates from around 1910 through the 1920s. It features long-stemmed and long-leaved plants with a five-petal narcissuslike blossom shown against a "Daisy and Button" background. Not quite as popular as other Daisy and Button variations, this line was made in clear and clear with cranberry stain. Pieces also have been reproduced in other solid colors and clear, and these include flat oval bowls, vases, and wine glasses. Copies are heavier than old pieces and are duller with less clearly pressed designs.

Daisy and Button with Thumbprint Panels This handsome pattern is another choice for those who like the "Daisy and Button" design. Pieces consist of panels of "Daisy and Button" divided by corner bars with round indentations. Made in clear, it also often is found with amber, ruby, blue, or pink staining along the bars. Solid colors of amber, blue, green, and vaseline also were made. Heavier reproductions of the champagne glass, goblet, and wine glass are out there, but the other pieces are safe. Copies were made in clear with colored stain as well as solid amber and blue. Again, watch for a dull finish in the reproductions.

Daisy and Button with V Ornament Still another Daisy and Button cousin, this pattern has a background of "Daisy and Button" divided by large, plain V's running up the sides. Items were made in clear, amber, blue, and vaseline, and some may have copper wheel-engraved designs on their plain portions. A nice piece to watch for is the kerosene table lamp with a nonpattern-glass pedestal base and a square foot. The font has the pressed pattern. Another appeal of this line is that it is safe from reproductions.

Daisy and Button—Single Panel Called by this name or *Paneled Daisy and Button*, this is another nice adaptation of the plain "Daisy and Button" design. When issued by George Duncan and Sons around 1886 it was called *Ellrose* or *Amberette*, the latter name from the amber staining applied in many pieces to the clear panels dividing the panels of "Daisy and Button." Only the amber-stained pieces are referred to as Amberette by collectors. The Amberette name can lead to some confusion for beginning collectors because the Dalzell, Gilmore and Leighton Company of Findlay, Ohio, issued a pressed pattern by that name in 1898. This other Amberette often is called *Klondike* today, and it consists of a large cross filled with two bands of small square knobs that divide the plain background. The background can be found in plain clear or acid-finished (frosted) clear. The crosses were often amber-stained although all-clear examples also were made. The amber-stained pieces, especially those with a frosted background, are most sought today. Just to keep the collector guessing, the Northwood Glass Company in 1898 also issued its *Klondyke* pattern (note the spelling variation), which it produced in custard and opalescent glass. Today this Northwood design usually is called *Fluted Scrolls* or, when found in the custard variant design, *Jackson*.

Not too many pieces have been reproduced in this line, but in the 1970s a look-alike design came out in an eleven-inch-diameter berry bowl and matching individual berry bowls. They were made in clear and several colors. The Mosser Glass Company currently is making a very large punch bowl with undertray and cups in pale green and dark red, while the L. G. Wright Glass Company has a new star-shaped bowl in clear.

Dakota Simple and attractive, *Dakota* was issued by Ripley and Company in the late 1880s, possibly around the time North and South Dakota became states. Most of the cylindrical pieces are plain except for a band of small indented thumbprints around the base, which gives it another name, *Baby Thumbprint*.

Most pieces are tall and elegant, with the lovely tankard pitchers especially appealing. It was made in clear and clear with engraved designs. When ruby staining became popular a great deal of Dakota was made with this decoration too. In 1898 it was marketed as part of the U.S. Glass Company's States series. Considering its beauty and popularity, it is rather remarkable that it has not been reproduced.

Eyewinker To my mind this is a rather homely pattern, believed to have been introduced around 1889. The design consists of a band of large oval "eyes" with heavy beaded eyelids all around the tops of pieces and a row of large balls around the bases or edges. It was made in clear only and has been heavily reproduced since the 1960s.

Fig. 9-6 A scarce *Eyewinker* pattern syrup jug with metal top. Also see the goblet for this set featured with an *Atlas* goblet earlier in this chapter.

Garfield Drape This simple drapery pattern reportedly was issued to commemorate the death of President Garfield in 1881. The long, graceful swags are composed of three rows of tiny beads separated by tiny leafy bands on a stippled ground. It has not been reproduced.

Gonterman Elegant is probably the best way to describe the *Gonterman* pattern, introduced by George Duncan and Sons in 1887 as its "no. 95" line.

The graceful, rounded shapes of pieces feature narrow vertical ribs, with a plain rib alternating with a band of small knobs or buttons. There is a band of similar but larger knobs around the rims, and many of the pieces are raised on a pedestal base with another band of small knobs around its center. Especially unusual is the frosted finish on the bodies of the pieces and the amber staining decorating rim bands. The bases were left in plain clear. Three

Fig. 9-7 A *Garfield Drape* pattern goblet.

Fig. 9-8 The bold, clear *Hexagon Block* goblet on the left almost overpowers the pale blue *Finecut* goblet on the right.

finishes are combined on a single object, but the whole effect is decorative without being flashy.

Although Gonterman was made in a nice selection of items, it does not show up often on the market and commands high prices when it does. It has not been reproduced.

Hexagon Block Another attractive pattern with blocks that was issued in the late 1880s and remained popular during the 1890s is today called *Hexagon Block,* or sometimes *Henrietta,* although another similar and look-alike pattern also goes by that name.

Hexagon Block consists of a double band of large hexagonal blocks encircling the bases or bodies of pieces below a plain top band. It can be found with amber or ruby staining on the upper clear portions of pieces, and some pieces also have engraved designs such as fern and berry or bird and flower on the plain sections. Most pieces in this pattern have scalloped, round feet, and the pitchers and creamer have simple applied handles. This design has not been reproduced.

Another somewhat similar pattern that, along with *Henrietta,* can cause confusion is *Red Block.* Some pieces in this pattern also have a double band of hexagonal blocks, but these blocks are not elongated like those on Hexagon Block. Larger pieces in this line also have the blocks forming an overall design around the body. Examples often are found with ruby staining on the blocks and on the upper plain rims, giving this pattern its name. Although pieces also were made in all-clear and with amber stain, the ruby examples give it its name. The goblet and wine glass have been reproduced in Red Block and also were made in clear with light amber and blue blocks as well as with several iridescent shades never used on the old.

Hobnail A departure from more conventional geometric patterns, *Hobnail* consists of an overall design of small, rounded knobs or "hobs."

Most often produced in the mold-blown process, it is discussed here because some variations were machine pressed and it probably ranked second only to Daisy and Button in popularity in the

1880s and 1890s. Sadly, it also has been a longtime best-seller for reproducers.

Producers of this pattern originally referred to it as *Dewdrop*, and Hobbs, Brockunier and Company patented a line by that name in 1886 that they produced with an opalescent treatment, giving the tips of the raised hobs a pearly white color. Many other companies also came out with their own versions of Hobnail in the 1880s and 1890s. Since at least the 1930s reproductions and adaptations of old Hobnail have been on the market. Many of the reproductions are heavier and less well finished than the old pieces. A number of antique-looking bulbous barber bottles have been made in this pattern, and one good way to tell the old from the new is to look for a carefully polished pontil mark on the bottom. The reproductions either do not have the pontil mark or it is not polished smooth. Some twenty-plus forms such as pitchers, baskets, vases,

Fig. 9-10 A close-up of the nicely polished pontil on the base of the *Hobnail* barber bottle. This is one sign of its age.

Fig. 9-9 An authentic early *Hobnail* barber bottle in blue opalescent.

and bowls, many in several sizes, have been copied so there are dozens of newer pieces on the market. For decades the Fenton Art Glass Company, still operating today, has issued a wide selection of Hobnail pieces, many closely resembling their antique counterparts. These Fenton pieces have become collectibles in their own right, and the excellent books on Fenton, written by the late William Heacock, will be a tremendous help in sorting out the old from the new. Keep in mind that many of the newer Hobnail pieces are found in items never made in the nineteenth century or with design variations that set them apart from the old. There is a nice pressed Hobnail woman's high-heeled shoe with a cat's head at the top of the instep (called the "Puss-in-Slipper" or "Puss-in-Boot" design). Although the "Puss-in-Boot" shoe was made in old pressed glass (commonly in Daisy and Button), it was not made with the Hobnail design until the 1940s.

Another line of glass from the 1880s features the Hobnail motif. It was introduced by Hobbs in the mid-1880s under the name *Francesware*, and it is still known by that name. It is my guess that the Hobbs firm used this name as a commercial tie-in to the young first lady, Frances Folsom Cleveland, wife of President Grover Cleveland. The twenty-two-year-old Frances married her forty-nine-year-old guardian in the White House in 1886, and Cleveland remains the only U.S. president to be wed

Fig. 9-11 A *Francesware* pattern *Hobnail* creamer with amber rim and frosted body.

Fig. 9-12 This small amber compote in the *Diamond Quilted* pattern is 7″ tall and 7″ in diameter.

there. Because of the event's notoriety many American manufacturers sought to monopolize on the lovely young first lady's popularity. Francesware would have been a natural name for Hobbs to choose for its new glass line. Actually Francesware was made in two variations. One has *Hobnail* pattern bodies below a short, ruffled straight neck often trimmed with amber staining. The other has a body molded with wide swirled ribs below the rim. The bodies of both types appeared in all-clear or clear and frosted, with or without the amber-stained necks. The Hobnail variety, by the way, tends to be more collectible and a bit more expensive than its swirled sister design. Neither has been reproduced.

Hobnail offers some great opportunities to collectors of old glass, and many of the copies have an appeal of their own. If one wants the old, however, one must proceed with caution, caution, caution!

Pressed Diamond   If diamonds are a favorite geometric form, there are a number of old pressed patterns that feature them.

Pressed Diamond features an overall design of small diamonds that gives the pieces a waffled look. It was produced in a nice selection of clear, amber, blue, and canary yellow pieces and, happily, has not been reproduced.

A more subtle diamond design is featured in the *Diamond Quilted* pattern. An overall optic design of plain diamonds forms a low-relief lattice effect. Bowls and stemware pieces have graceful, slightly

flaring cylindrical sides with plain stems or low-footed bases. One unique piece in this design is a large clover-leaf-shaped tray with the Diamond Quilted motif on the low, scalloped sides. A series of plain diagonal bands alternate with wide diamond point bands in the bottom of this piece. Another pattern commonly found in color, it is available in clear, vaseline, light blue, amber, and pale amethyst.

The goblet, master salt dip, and tumbler have been reproduced but the new goblets have an elongated, rounded bowl and short stem unlike the old ones. The colors used on the copies also are harsher than in the old examples.

Diamonds also play a part in the *Diagonal Band with Fan* pattern. Probably introduced in the late 1870s, it continued in wide production in the 1880s. In this design wide bands of small diamonds swirl up the sides of pieces, and there is a rayed fan at the base of each band. Most often found in clear, it also was made in amber and apple green. It is safe from reproductions. Do not confuse it with the similar *Diagonal Band* pattern, which features a band of crosses and tiny fans curving up the sides and a band of chain loops around the top. This too is a safe pattern.

Thousand Eye   An attractive and popular pattern produced by Adams and Company, *Thousand Eye* features an overall design of tightly packed rows of low knobs running up the sides of pieces. Unlike the generally pointed and slightly spaced hobs of Hobnail, these knobs more closely resemble bands of bubbles. Apparently the Richards and Hartley Company also produced a very similar line, and pieces from the two lines are collected together. In the Adams pattern the flaring bases on some pieces feature three knobs spaced around the top of the base, while the Richards and Hartley version features plain-stemmed pieces with scalloped feet. Handles on both types are pressed as part of the piece rather than applied.

Thousand Eye was produced in a very large range of items in all the popular colors of the 1880s, including amber, blue, clear, vaseline, and green. Some pieces also have been found with an opalescent treatment. It has been a popular pattern with collectors for years, and a number of reproductions exist, so some care must be taken when making a purchase.

Torpedo Another pattern introduced near the end of the 1880s and carried over into the 1890s, *Torpedo* seems to get its name from the pattern band along the bottom edges of pieces, which resembles a row of torpedo bombs stood on end. These teardrop or torpedo shapes have an indented thumbprint in their heads, and the tapering tails are divided by

crossbars. It was made in clear and clear with engraving, as well as with ruby-stained trim. It has not been reproduced and neither has a sister pattern, *Reverse Torpedo,* made by a different maker a few years later. This close-cousin design also consists of teardrops in a band around the bottoms of pieces, but these drops hang down instead of being stood on their tails as in Torpedo. The teardrops also have a thumbprint in their heads but the tails are plain, without any dividing bars. On some pieces is a design of small diamonds between the tails of the teardrops (or torpedos). The other name for this pattern is *Bull's Eye and Diamond Point,* which may help in distinguishing it from the Torpedo line. This pattern was made in clear and in clear with engraving, but it was apparently not ruby-stained. It is another safe pattern, with no reproductions known.

Naturalistic Patterns

The naturalistic patterns of the 1880s are a much smaller group than those with a geometric theme, but there are nonetheless some very famous and popular patterns in this group.

I will divide this range of patterns into three subcategories: patterns featuring the human face or form, patterns featuring plants and flowers, and patterns featuring animals. Important patterns from each of these groups will be described and illustrated here.

Patterns with Humans

Actress Undoubtedly the most famous figural pattern of the 1880s and one of the most collectible of late-Victorian patterns, *Actress* recently has been proven to be a product of Adams and Company, circa 1880. A trade publication of the period refers to it as its *Opera* set.

The main feature of this varied pattern is that each piece carries the embossed likeness of a late-Victorian actress or actor. The names of the ladies are marked under the portrait on some pieces so that nontheatrical types could identify them easily. On most pieces the actresses are shown in bust profiles in the center of pieces, generally two portraits per piece. Some larger pieces carry a whole theatrical scene, such as the water pitcher, which has the "Romeo and Juliet Balcony Scene," and the large domed cheese dish, which has a seated male

Fig. 9-13 This *Reverse Torpedo* bowl is 8¼" across and 2" high.

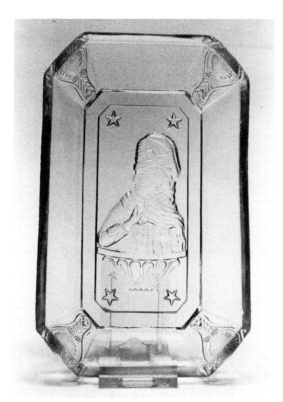

Fig. 9-15 The fascinating *Classic* pattern is illustrated by this log-footed pitcher. Note the wonderful detailing of the figure. Courtesy of the Corning Museum of Glass.

Fig. 9-14 One of the most famous of late-Victorian patterns is *Actress*. Shown is a 7″ l. rectangular relish dish with an actress's portrait in the bottom.

figure titled "The Lone Fisherman" on the cover and two figures in the flat base with the title "Two Dromios." Several pieces make reference to H. M. S. Pinafore, the famous vessel from the Gilbert and Sullivan comic opera of the same name. The portraits and scenes are the main features of the pieces, but some items also have rounded, shell-like drops down the corners or dividing the front panels. The pickle dish carries the quote "Love's Request Is Pickles."

Made only in clear and clear with frosted details, Actress surprisingly has had only a few pieces reproduced. The pickle jar and relish tray were reproduced from new molds in clear, amethyst, and blue. These copies will be heavier and lack the fine detailing of the old glass.

Classic One of the most unusual and most desirable patterns of the 1880s is *Classic,* a unique creation

featuring beautifully designed figures based on classical works of art.

Another noteworthy pattern from Gillinder and Son, who gave us several famous lines in the 1870s, Classic was also formerly dated to that decade. Recent research by collector and historian Melvin P. Lader has, however, firmly established that Classic must have been introduced about 1882.

The designer of this pattern has brought together a number of rather incongruous elements that give the pieces a unique charm. Each object is hexagonal in form, with each panel topped by a pointed Gothic arch. Three acid-finished panels containing raised classical figures alternate around the body with three panels featuring an overall "Daisy and Button" design. Introducing yet another design element, the designer added handles that resemble tree branches and, on some pieces, log-shaped feet. Later these log feet were done away with because they tended to break off easily and were found to be impractical. A mold featuring plain, round collared bases was used. Today the log-footed pieces bring a premium from collectors. To top off this unique confection, the covers of pieces such as compotes and sugar bowls feature a finial composed of a cluster of acorns and a short twig. Here in one pattern are the major design trends of the era—naturalistic, classical, and geometric—all together. *Classic* seems to fairly well epitomize what we might consider a Victorian design tenent that too much is not enough.

Although the mixture of designs may be a little overwhelming for some modern tastes, the mold work, especially on the figural panels, is outstanding. One particularly lovely piece in this pattern is a ten-and-a-half-inch-diameter plate with the arches around the rim. In the center of the most common version of this piece is shown a warrior on horseback spearing a lion. It is referred to as the ''Warrior'' plate. Adding to the appeal of this piece is the fact that the carver of the mold (and apparently all the Classic molds), Philip Jacobus, included his last name under a stone shown at the edge of the plate's design. It has long been assumed that Classic was designed by Jacobus, but this has not been proven conclusively and the pattern may have been a joint creation of the talented personnel at Gillinder.

For the presidential election of 1884 the Classic design was reworked to produce a series of four plates, each one featuring in its center the bust portrait of a presidential or vice-presidential candidate that year. Thus we find Democrat Grover Cleveland and his running mate, Thomas A. Hendricks, on two of the plates and their losing opponents, Republicans James G. Blaine and John A. Logan, on the matching pair. The busts, again engraved by Jacobus, are lifelike and beautifully detailed, making these plates some of the most unique and lovely pieces of pressed glass of the late nineteenth century.

Classic Medallion Carrying on the classical tradition, this simple pattern consists of a thin oval medallion containing a bust profile of a classical lady on each side of pieces. Everything else is very plain except for small tab handles on some pieces. It was made in clear only in a limited range of pieces and has not been reproduced. Collectors sometimes refer to it as *Cameo* because of the cameolike portrait.

Cupid and Venus Another pattern that may have first arrived in the late 1870s and that features figures from ancient mythology, *Cupid and Venus* has

Fig. 9-16 This little mug in the *Cupid and Venus* pattern is about 2½" high.

a large beaded oval on each side of the pieces. Inside the ovals are the standing figures of the goddess Venus and her son, Cupid. The ovals are joined by a narrow patterned band around the middle of the pieces, but otherwise the pieces are plain. It was produced mainly in clear glass with some pieces in amber or vaseline, and no reproductions exist.

A similar pattern dating from about the same period is *Psyche and Cupid,* which, again, features oval medallions containing a figural scene. This time the seated Psyche looks into a mirror held by Cupid. The ovals around the scene are rounder and plainer than the beaded ones found on Cupid and Venus, and the design overall is in very low relief, compared to the raised figures on Cupid and Venus.

Produced in a very limited number of pieces, Psyche and Cupid is found in clear only, and none of the original pieces have been reproduced, although a seven-inch-diameter milk glass plate with a similar design has been made. It was never part of the original set.

Egyptian One unique pattern now attributed to Adams and Company includes exotic and classical details together in one design. Today called *Egyptian,* the original maker called it its *Sphynx* set (no. 50) when it came out around 1882. Each piece features scenic panels on its flaring cylindrical sides, one showing the ruins of the Parthenon in Greece, and the other showing one of the pyramids of Egypt

Fig. 9-17 This panel of an *Egyptian* pattern goblet features a sphinx and a broken column.

with a camel and a tiny human figure. The large oblong platter in this set is highlighted in the center by a large profile portrait of the seated Cleopatra overlooking a landscape background. This platter is fairly common, but a much rarer variation features a center scene of the Salt Lake Temple, the spiritual home of the Mormons in Salt Lake City. This latter piece has been reproduced in clear.

Minerva This classic-inspired pattern was also made by Adams and Company. The Roman warrior goddess of wisdom is featured in this line standing in a round or oval reserve with scalloped bands of beading above and below. Her figure also is fea-

tured in the center of a thirteen-inch-long oval platter. A ten-inch-diameter plate in this line featuring a running armored warrior in the middle is called the "Mars" plate. In another version this plate is found with the motto "Give Us This Day—Our Daily Bread" in the center. Another motto piece is the oval pickle dish, which has in its center "Love's Request Is Pickles," the same quote found on the Actress pattern pickle dish. Minerva has not been reproduced.

Queen Anne This pattern, although it carries the name of an English queen, has only a very tenuous claim to being a figural pattern, but since it is also known to collectors as *Bearded Man* I felt I would list it here.

Queen Anne is the original name given by the maker, the La Belle Glass Company. The pieces have simple cylindrical bodies with bands of fine diamond point design in the bottoms or in the lids. The bottoms are rather unusual and consist of three blocky, curved branches forming a tripod base, each foot embossed with fine scrolls. The handles on the pieces are also angular, made up of two short, thick crosses joined by a crossbar, and they too are trimmed with scrolls. A short and thick cross forms the finial on the covered pieces. The "bearded man" face appears only under the lips of the pieces with spouts, such as the creamer and pitchers. Other than this bearded mask, there is nothing human in the pattern. Made mostly in clear, a few scarce pieces may be found in color. There are no reproductions in this line.

Patterns with Plants and Flowers

Baltimore Pear For many years considered a pattern of the 1870s, today *Baltimore Pear* is correctly dated to the 1880s. It is another popular pattern introduced by Adams and Company as its *Gipsy* line. The pieces are plain and rounded, their main design feature highly embossed pairs of juicy pears on a leafy sprig.

A longtime favorite of collectors, Baltimore Pear has been reproduced in a number of pieces to be listed later. The newer pieces are of poor quality and lack the fine detailing of the old, especially on the leaves. In the 1930s the Indiana Glass Company came out with its *Avocado* pattern, which features pairs of fruit resembling pears. The fruit is on an

Fig. 9-18 Two naturalistic patterns of the 1880s: a *Baltimore Pear* goblet is on the left and a *Rose in Snow* example on the right.

Fig. 9-19 *Dahlia* is a popular floral pattern from the 1880s. covered compote is 12½″ tall and 8¾″ in diameter.

overall overlapping leaf background unlike Baltimore Pear and the shapes of most items are unlike those of most Victorian glass. Also, Avocado is most often found in pale pink or green, colors never used on old *Baltimore Pear.*

Barley   The *Barley* pattern is another with very simple shapes to the pieces. Most items have plain, rounded bodies, and the only real decoration is a thin, undulating band of sprigged vine around the middle. Apparently this plant reminded someone of heads of barley, so it was given that name. It is not a very dramatic pattern and is rare in color.

One unique piece once thought to tie-in with this pattern is a figural glass wheelbarrow with leaf sprigs on the sides. It is now believed to be more closely related to the Adams and Company *Horseshoe* (*Good Luck*) pattern.

No pieces in Barley have been reproduced.

A pattern with a similar theme and name is *Wheat and Barley*. In this line the pieces are decorated with a hanging spray of grain stalks that could be wheat and barley. The sides of the pieces are flat and paneled, unlike the rounded shapes in Barley. This pattern can be found in amber, blue, and vaseline, as well as in clear, and it has not been reproduced.

Dahlia   Those who love flowers will enjoy this cheery floral pattern of the 1880s. Around each

piece is a wide stippled band featuring a clear, continuous band of dahlialike blossoms joined by leaf stems. Long attributed to the Canton Glass Company of Canton, Ohio, it may instead have come from Bryce, Higbee and Company of Pittsburgh. Shards also turned up at Canadian glass plants which may indicate it was also produced there.

A wide variety of pieces is available in Dahlia and it often is found in colors such as amber, apple green, blue, and vaseline, which also adds to its appeal. To top it off, it has not been reproduced.

Maple Leaf   One of America's favorite trees is represented by the *Maple Leaf* pattern, where stippled maple leaves make up the rounded sides of pieces which are raised on short log feet. The sauce dish in this line is in the form of a single leaf, and a band of overlapping leaves forms the borders of the plates. The ten-inch-diameter plate has an overall diamond design across the center, and a very collectible historical plate features the same maple leaf border with has in its center a bust portrait of General Ulysses S. Grant, who later became president. The plate also has the embossed inscriptions "Let Us Have Peace" and "Born April 27, 1822—Died July 23, 1885." Collectors refer to this as the "Grant Peace" plate, and it is prized even by those who do not collect other pieces in this pattern. Available in a wide range of colors, a number of the important pieces in this line were reproduced in the 1970s.

Paneled Forget-Me-Not Probably one of the best-known and collectible floral patterns of the 1880s, *Paneled Forget-Me-Not* was issued by Bryce Brothers as its *Regal* pattern. This design shows small sprigs of flowers in rectangular panels alternating around the body with wide panels featuring a checkered design.

Production continued into the 1890s and in a variety of colors including amber, blue, clear, amethyst, and green. Happily for collectors, it has not been reproduced.

Rose in Snow The lovely rose is captured on the sides of this pattern, where a large rose bud just opening on a leafy stem is shown against a finely stippled background (see Figure 9-18). It was available in several colors and is rather unique in that a number of the pieces in the set, such as the creamer, spooner, and sugar bowl, were made in both square and round forms. The pieces can be found with either a pressed handle or a simple applied handle. A mug with the inscription "In Fond Remembrance" was also made in this pattern and typifies the sentimentality of the Gilded Age.

A number of pieces of *Rose in Snow* have been reproduced since the 1930s, but on some copies two tiny leaves are missing from the leaf sprig on the lower right side of the flower stem. The stippling in the background of the copies also tends to be too light.

Wildflower This very popular late-Victorian floral pattern was long dated back to the 1870s. Current research, however, indicates that Adams and Company issued it as its "no. 140" pattern about 1885. Considering it was made in most of the popular glass colors of the 1880s, this dating certainly makes sense.

Wildflower pieces feature around the middle a horizontal, continuous band of stylized six-petaled

Figs. 9-20 and 9-21 Compare the finer stippling in the leaves and flowers in an authentic *Wildflower* goblet (top) to the same details in the reproduction piece on the bottom.

flowers and leaves with a crosshatched diamond band around the rim and a band of gadrooning around the base. Widely produced well into the 1890s, it has been extensively reproduced and must be collected with great care. It takes experience to tell the new from the old, but checking the fine stippling on the flower petals and leaves may help. This stippling is sharper and better defined on old items.

Patterns with Animals

Deer and Pine Tree One of several patterns featuring animals produced during the 1880s, *Deer and Pine Tree* is highlighted on the sides of pieces by a scenic vignette showing a standing stag in front of a doe with a pine tree in the background. It is also

Fig. 9-22 *Deer and Pine Tree* is a popular animal pattern from the 1880s. The stag and his mate can be seen in the front panel of this goblet.

called *Deer and Doe.* These figural panels alternate with fine diamond point bands or are trimmed with these pattern bands on most pieces. The pattern was made in several colors, and so far only the goblet has been reproduced in this line. Check the detailing to tell if the goblet is old or new, since the new one is missing such details as a vine climbing the tree and more defined details in the grass and shrubs across the bottom of the scene. The diamond point band on the reproduction looks more like small dots than diamonds. Finally, one of the deer's ears is missing on the new piece.

Another pattern, a bit earlier perhaps than Deer and Pine Tree, is *Deer and Dog.* This pattern features some pieces with an acid-etched design of a deer and dog in a wooded landscape. The pieces without this design are plain and completely unpatterned with slightly flaring cylindrical sides and pedestal bases. The unique feature of the covered pieces is that their finial is a standing figure of a handsome dog with a frosted finish. The pieces with the frosted deer hunt scene and those with the figural finials are very collectible, but the plain, unadorned items generally go unrecognized and unappreciated. No pieces in this line have been reproduced.

Another acid-etched design of the era is called *Flamingo Habitat* and features what resembles a stork standing amid lush foliage. It was made in a limited range of pieces with shapes similar to the Deer and Dog line, and no items have been reproduced.

Frosted Eagle *Frosted Eagle* is a plain pattern that gets its name from the acid-treated frosted figural eagle finial on the cover pieces. The bodies of items are plain and cylindrical with slightly domed bases. The perched eagle with its wings held back may represent the famous Civil War mascot, Old Abe, a real eagle carried into battle by the 8th Wisconsin Volunteer Regiment. He survived the war by a number of years and his stuffed remains were displayed at the Wisconsin State Capitol until it burned earlier in this century. Today this handsome bird is commemorated on this limited line of glassware. It has not been reproduced, but watch for a frosted jar with an eagle finial put out in 1976 to commemorate the U.S. Bicentennial. It features oval portraits of four Founding Fathers around the sides and is marked up inside the bottom. It was made as a special order for a private group by the Fenton Art Glass Company, which also made some other pieces in the same form and with eagle finials during the Bicentennial period.

Hummingbird Another naturalistic pattern that appeals to bird lovers, *Hummingbird* is also known by a number of other names. The design consists of a hummingbird hovering beside a floral sprig on one side, but on the opposite side another species of bird is flying by a large clump of fern leaves and flower blossoms. Since the design contains these varied elements collectors also have called the pattern *Bird and Fern, Fern and Bird, Flying Robin, Thunder Bird,* or *Hummingbird and Fern.* Because the delicate hummingbird is one of its most distinctive features, its name alone seems the simplest and most appropriate title for this line.

Made mainly in clear, it also can be found in solid amber, blue, or canary yellow. The quality of the impression, especially of the birds, can vary from piece to piece, so it pays to search for those items with the sharpest, best-defined impression.

Hummingbird was not made in a very large range of pieces, but with the various colors made there is a good selection to hunt for. The blue

Fig. 9-23 The namesake *Hummingbird* is shown hovering on this side of this pattern's creamer.

examples seem to be the most expensive, but any colored piece will bring 40 to 80 percent more than the same item in clear. This is another typically Victorian pattern that has not been reproduced.

Japanese This pattern, mentioned earlier, includes several naturalistic elements. The bodies of pieces are divided into ornate panels, one with a butterfly and fan device (hence another collector name *Butterfly and Fan*), and the other with a bird and ring (ergo a third name, *Bird in Ring*). To complete the exotic Oriental theme, the handles on pieces are molded in the shape of bamboo stalks. The panels are divided by diagonal bands with a zigzag design. A unique piece in this line is the plate made in the shape of a round Oriental fan with a short handle. A similar pattern called *Grace* by a different maker features different finials on the covers and has splayed feet rather than the pedestal bases on *Japanese.*

Made only in clear, Japanese has not been reproduced.

Jumbo A rare and unique Victorian pattern, *Jumbo* is named for the giant elephant displayed by showman P. T. Barnum in the 1880s. Here again the pieces are plain, and Jumbo is found as the figural frosted finial on covered pieces. Interestingly, on the pieces with handles, a human head, referred to as the "Barnum head," is molded under the base of each handle. A piece unique to this line is the pedestal-based spoon rack, which has, around the center of the pedestal, a wide disc with edge notches for inserting teaspoons. The top of the pedestal is highlighted by a figure of the standing Jumbo. All pieces in this pattern are scarce and expensive. Fortunately, no pieces in Jumbo have been reproduced.

Monkey Another circus favorite, the monkey, is featured on this rare pattern. A large seated monkey between small palm trees is shown on the sides of pieces in this pattern, and a figural monkey finial tops the lids of covered items. It originally was made in clear and opalescent, and sometimes in clear with enameled or amber-stained trim. Only thirteen pieces have been found in this pattern, and so far only the spoonholder has been reproduced in clear, amber, and other colors. Watch out for it, as all pieces in old *Monkey* are scarce and expensive.

Polar Bear This pattern takes us to the polar regions. Arctic exploration was big news in the late nineteenth century, and this pattern was designed to capture the arctic theme in pressed glass.

The slightly flaring cylindrical sides of pieces in this line are divided into three vignettes with animals. The first has a seal resting on an iceberg; the second, another seal with a smaller seal's head poking out of the water; and the third, the standing polar bear itself. The scenes are framed above by an arched design of icicles, and this top band and the animals in the scenes can be found with machine-ground frosting as well as in plain clear. The frosted examples are especially sought, but any *Polar Bear* piece is a prize. The small, flat-bottomed sauce dish is the only piece that shows up very often, and it is reasonably inexpensive. The goblet in this pattern

came in two variations, one with a straight rim and the other with a flared rim. A goblet with frosted details was reproduced in the 1970s by the Summit Art Glass Company, which, luckily, marked it with its trademark. This new piece also lacks the fine details of the old ones.

Squirrel A very limited number of pieces can be found in this pattern, which features an entwining tree branch design with a small seated squirrel in the middle. The finial on covered pieces features a figural seated squirrel in frosted glass. Only eight items are known in this pattern, which includes a tall pedestal-based kerosene lamp with the pattern on the font. The goblet in this line is extremely rare. Also, the Indiana Tumbler and Goblet Company (Greentown, Indiana) later produced a *Squirrel* pattern pitcher that may be confused with the one from this pattern line.

Swan The graceful swan highlights this pattern patented in 1882. The pieces feature an oval panel framing a swimming swan with an arched neck. On most pieces these ovals are surrounded by a finely beaded background, although in a variation the background is plain rather than stippled. The handles on some pieces are knob-ended bars running parallel to the body, and the covers of some pieces feature a figural swan finial. It originally was made in clear, amber, blue, and canary yellow, but the creamer and covered sugar bowl were reproduced in milk glass. The new pieces are heavier and less detailed than the old. Do not confuse this tableware line with the novelty milk glass dishes also featuring swans that were popular at the same time.

Realistic Patterns

A number of patterns popular in the 1880s were designed to simulate the shape or texture of some inanimate object, called here "realistic" designs. Some of the patterns actually were made in the shape of an object, while others just included an object in the overall design.

Basketweave This straightforward pattern has its name because the bodies of each piece look like the sides of a woven basket. A wide variety of pieces were made in a large selection of colors, including amber, blue, apple green, vaseline, and clear, and a

Fig. 9-24 This side of the *Polar Bear* goblet shows the bear walking across an icy landscape.

few pieces even came out in milk glass. On some of the covered pieces there is a stippled cat's head finial.

Unfortunately several pieces have been reproduced in various colors. The goblet, tumbler, water pitcher, and flat water tray (not the one with a molded country landscape in the center) are known to have been copied. Check the stems on the stemmed pieces, because the new items have a thinner stem than the old and the reproduced pieces generally are smaller and lighter in weight than the old ones. The colors, too, do not match the mellow old shades and appear pale and washed out beside their antique counterparts.

Bow Tie This pattern probably was not designed to resemble men's neckwear, but it does give the appearance of closely packed bow ties standing on end and marching around the sides of pieces. Actually, the design reminds me more of airplane propellers, but we do not want to start another name for this pattern. Produced in quite a variety of items, *Bow Tie* was made in clear glass only and has not been reproduced.

Cane *Cane* is another pattern that looks like woven material, but in this case the weaving resembles the pattern found on cane-seated Victorian chairs. The cane design covers the sides of pieces, and this is another pattern made in many colors. Unlike its cousin, Basketweave, Cane has not been reproduced.

Egg in Sand Here is another pattern named for what it resembles, that is, rows of eggs, slightly tilted, laying on a bed of fine sand. The two or three rows of eggs climbing up the sides of most pieces are raised against a finely stippled background. *Egg in Sand* was not produced in a large range of items, so it is not as widely collected as some other patterns. It was made chiefly in clear, with colored pieces being rare, and it has not been reproduced.

Good Luck The traditional symbol of good luck figures in the design of this pattern and gives it another collector name, *Horseshoe*.

Issued about 1881 by Adams and Company, the horseshoe forms the figural handles and finial on some pieces in this pattern and is shown in the

Fig. 9-26 This side of the *Good Luck* pattern goblet shows the prayer rug that gives it another name.

Fig. 9-25 The blue *Egg in Sand* (left) and *Cane* pattern goblets take their motifs from real objects.

center of a few pieces. However, many pieces in this line do not have any horseshoe shown on them. Instead, the bodies of most pieces feature a wide band decorated with floral sprigs. These sprigs alternate with a parallelogram tipped on end and molded with details to resemble a small Oriental rug, thus giving the pattern a third name, *Prayer Rug*.

A rather unusual piece of figural pattern glass, a wheelbarrow-shaped dish, has been tied recently to the *Good Luck* pattern.

The sides of the wheelbarrow are decorated with a thin vine with slender leaf sprigs, and for many years this design was believed to be part of the *Barley* pattern line of the 1880s. In fact, this leafy vine more closely resembles a design that is part of the Good Luck pattern. In addition, various quotes from trade publications of the early 1880s mention the Adams "unique butter dish in the shape of a wheelbarrow" (*American Pottery and Glassware Reporter,* November 17, 1881). James Dalzell designed and patented this piece on January 3, 1882, during his employment by Adams and Company.

The Good Luck pieces that feature the figural horseshoes are the most sought and expensive, but all pieces are quite collectible. Only the ten-by-fourteen-inch platter with horseshoe handles has been reproduced, so the pattern is fairly safe. It was made in clear glass only.

Another interesting pattern using the horseshoe theme is *Horseshoe Stem*. The figural inverted horseshoe forms the pedestal base on the limited line of pieces while the bodies are plain, slightly flaring cylinders. A small horseshoe finial tops cov-

ered pieces and half horseshoes form the handles on some. It was made in clear; sometimes the bodies were acid-treated for a frosted effect and then engraved with leaf sprigs. It has not been reproduced.

Oaken Bucket Also known as *Wooden Pail,* this figural pattern has pieces molded to resemble the slatted sides of an old oaken bucket. The bucket bodies are trimmed with two plain bands representing iron bands and some pieces have a plain, flaring collared base. Some items feature a molded bail handle for a further touch of realism.

This pattern was not made in a wide range of pieces, but some of the items can be found in several colors including amber, amethyst, blue, canary, and clear. It has not been reproduced.

Shell and Tassel This pattern combines a natural object—a shell—with a curtain tassel. Four ribbed cockleshells form lobes around the body of each piece, and a long tassel drops between each lobe. On many pieces the design on the shells closely resembles the slender threadlike motif on a stippled background found in the Tree of Life patterns discussed earlier, but on the pitcher and tumbler the

Fig. 9-28 A little *Oaken Bucket* pattern toothpick holder complete with its original wire bail handle.

Fig. 9-27 The figural "Wheelbarrow" novelty dish now is associated with the *Good Luck* pattern.

98

shells are easily recognized. *Shell and Tassel* was made in two forms: the more common is a square shape and the rarer a round form.

The round-bodied pieces have collared bases, smooth rims, and figural dog finials on the covers, while the square shapes have shell finials and scalloped rims. Values of the two forms are about the same, and they mix and match well. It was made in color only rarely.

A good-quality reproduction of the goblet was made as early as 1940, and another look-alike goblet appeared in the 1970s. Examine the center of the clear device between the lobed shells in the older reproductions. On original pieces this spot is clear and smooth, but on the early copies it looks wavy. It is not a dramatic difference, but it may help in recognizing a newer piece.

Desirability and Values

As a group, the pressed patterns of the 1880s very closely follow the value ranges of 1870s patterns. In the most popular patterns, which are widely available, the same range of pieces generally are found, and the prices for clear examples are quite steady.

Prices really escalate only for the rarest patterns. Commoner items of scarce patterns like Polar Bear or Classic, with a limited range of pieces, will sell for about twice what that item might bring in a pattern like *Pavonia* or *Fishscale*. A piece of Polar Bear with frosted details may bring another 20 to 30 percent more than an all-clear example. Classic pieces with log feet bring about 30 to 50 percent more than the same piece with a flange base. For Jumbo, probably the most expensive line produced in the 1880s, the small selection of pieces will sell for about three to ten times what equivalent pieces in a commoner pattern would bring.

Color is another factor that affects price. Some patterns were produced extensively in a range of colors, and the colored examples will sell for more than the clear pieces. Depending on the particular pattern and how scarce the colored pieces are, the differences between clear and colored examples may be as low as 30 percent or as high as 200 percent. A clear bowl might sell for around $10 while the same piece in vaseline or amber might bring $15, but the piece in choicer blue or green could go for $20 to $25.

Sometimes patterns that were made mainly in clear were also produced on a limited scale with ruby- or amber-stained trim. In the case of a pattern like Pavonia, the addition of this staining if in a piece in good condition, will increase its market value markedly. A Pavonia six-inch-diameter open compote in plain clear, for instance, might sell for around $35, but if found with ruby-stained trim it might bring about $75. A 200 to 300 percent premium is not uncommon in this and some other patterns with staining that are scarce. On the other hand, in a pattern like Block and Fan, which is much more common with the ruby staining, the price differential between an all-clear and ruby-stained piece might be only about 20 to 40 percent.

Engraved designs on the plain portions of patterns also became popular in the 1880s, and this engraved decoration usually adds somewhat to the value of a piece. In a clear item it might add from 10 to 20 percent to the value, but with combined ruby-staining and engraving, the value goes up to the level of the stained version or a bit more.

In the patterns of the 1880s many more sizes of pieces such as bowls, compotes, and cake stands were produced than in previous decades. Generally, larger pieces bring slightly higher prices. Scarcer forms, such as pitchers, cruets, baskets, and large covered compotes, will always be the most expensive pieces in a pattern, with the commoner pieces in the four-piece table set, bowls, and most stemware usually falling in the $50 to $100 range. Little sauce dishes, again, are nearly always the most common pieces in a pattern and sometimes can be found for only a few dollars.

There is a wide range of prices for the vast selection of pieces in common patterns of the 1880s. Because of this, collectors have many opportunities to make good buys in these patterns that, having reached the century mark, are truly antique.

Old Versus New

In the discussion of the popular patterns of the 1880s it was mentioned which ones have been reproduced and what to watch out for. Below is a concise checklist of these pieces. Remember: generally speaking, heavier weight and poor definition of design are the best details to consider when trying to distinguish the old from the new.

Geometric and Abstract Patterns

Cottage: See text. Beware: goblet and wine glasses.

Daisy and Button: See text. A very tricky pattern.

Daisy and Button with Narcissus: Watch for duller, heavier pieces. Beware: various sizes of flat, oval bowls, and the wine glass in clear and colors.

Daisy and Button with Thumbprint Panels: Watch out for heavy, dull reproductions. Beware: champagne glass, goblet, and wine glass.

Diamond Quilted: Watch for slightly out-of-shape pieces. Beware: goblet, master salt, and tumbler.

Egyptian: See text. Beware: "Salt Lake Temple" platter.

Eyewinker: Watch for many reproductions from new molds in clear and colors. Beware: covered butter dish, four-inch-diameter-high pedestal covered compote, six-inch-diameter, high-pedestal covered compote, five-inch-diameter, low-pedestal covered compote, five-inch-diameter tall open compote, seven-and-a-half-inch diameter tall open compote, creamer, six-inch-high goblet, six-and-a-quarter-inch-high goblet (10 ounces), flat covered honey dish, five-and-a-half-inch-diameter round covered honey dish, covered marmalade jar, milk pitcher (quart), water pitcher, four-and-a-half-inch-diameter plate (ashtray), flat and round salt dips, four-inch-diameter flat round sauce dish, three-and-a-half-inch-high sherbet, oval-footed soap dish, toothpick holder, six-inch- and eight-inch-high three-legged vases, and four-ounce wine glass. Note: the new goblet (with eyes), wine glass, and toothpick holder were not part of the original set, and many other pieces are in modern shapes.

Frosted Circle: Beware: goblet with oval frosted circles.

Hobnail: See text. Another pattern requiring much study.

Red Block: Watch out for copies with iridescent finishes. Beware: goblet and wine glass.

Fig. 9-29 This footed tumbler is in the 1940s opalescent *Moonstone* pattern. Do not confuse this line with early Victorian *Hobnail* pieces or other late *Hobnail*-inspired patterns.

Thousand Eye: Watch for subtle differences in the design of reproductions, especially the goblet, where the older pieces have a slightly longer and more graceful stem. New pieces have harsher colors and are heavier than their older counterparts. Beware: cruet, goblet, mug, oil lamp, six-inch-, seven-inch-, eight-and-a-half-inch-, ten-inch-, fourteen-inch- and eighteen-inch-square plates, toothpick holder, wine glass, string holder, and tumbler. Amberina and amethyst are new colors.

Naturalistic Patterns

Patterns with Humans

Actress: Watch out for heavier, less-detailed pieces. Beware: pickle jar and relish tray.

Psyche and Cupid: Watch out for the seven-inch-diameter milk glass plate, not original to the set.

Patterns with Plants and Flowers

Baltimore Pear: Watch for poor quality in the design of new pieces, especially the leaves. It originally was made in clear only. Beware: butter dish, cake stand, celery vase, creamer, goblet, milk pitcher, nine-inch- and ten-inch-diameter plates, water pitcher, sauce dish, and sugar bowl.

Maple Leaf: Watch out for colored and clear pieces from new molds. Beware: covered butter dish, creamer, tall-pedestal compote, tall-pedestal cake stand, goblet, spooner, sugar bowl, toothpick holder (not originally made), six-inch- and twelve-inch-diameter trays, tumbler, and water pitcher (half gallon).

Paneled Daisy: Watch for look-alike pieces and heavy, dull items. Beware: goblet, tumbler, footed toothpick holder, votive candleholder, tall-pedestal covered compote.

Rose in Snow: Watch for pieces with small leaves missing and light background stippling. Beware: mug with ''In Fond Remembrance,'' nine-inch-diameter plate, goblet, pickle dish, square covered sugar bowl.

Wildflower: Watch for the many pieces, especially in color, reproduced in this popular pattern. Care must be taken until one becomes familiar with the detailing. The reproductions lack the very refined stippling that fills the flowers, berries, and leaves on the old pieces. The vertical stems on the berries and leaves of new pieces are also often broken and do not continue uniformly around the sides. Colors in the copies are much harsher than the softer Victorian hues. Beware: goblet, wine and champagne glass, tall covered jar, four-inch-diameter low-pedestal covered compote, creamer, ten-inch square plate, flat rectangular salt dip, four-inch-diameter footed sauce dish, sugar bowl, tumbler, and turtle-shaped master salt dip.

Patterns with Animals

Deer and Pine Tree: Watch out for a lack of detailing. Beware: goblet.

Frosted Eagle: Watch out for bicentennial-era pieces with eagle finials. There are no reproductions of old pieces.

Monkey: Watch out for a look-alike four-and-three-

Fig. 9-30 Not really a reproduction, this Bicentennial-era covered jar features a frosted eagle finial. This piece was a special commission made by Fenton for a private group in 1976.

quarter-inch-high spooner. Old pieces in this pattern are rare.

Polar Bear: Watch out for a lack of details and the mark of the Summit Art Glass Company. Beware: goblet.

Swan: Watch out for heavier, less-detailed pieces in milk glass. Beware: creamer and covered sugar bowl.

Realistic Patterns

Good Luck (Horseshoe, Prayer Rug): Beware the ten-by-fourteen-inch platter with horseshoe handles.

Shell and Tassel: Beware: look-alike goblet.

CHAPTER 10
The Gay '90s in Pattern Glass

Gay '90s, the nickname for the decade between 1890 and 1900, has been popular for years and in many ways, does reflect the life and times of many Americans during the decade. Gay is certainly an appropriate adjective to describe the myriad patterns and colors popular in pattern glass during the closing years of the nineteenth century.

Although a larger number of patterns was introduced during the 1890s, most were geometric and abstract designs, with a growing number made to emulate the flashy, expensive brilliance of cut glass, the *de rigueur* gift for weddings and important occasions. Fewer new lines reflected a naturalistic and realistic bent, but a few notable ones, such as *U.S. Coin,* did appear. One noteworthy selection of patterns was produced by the U.S. Glass Company starting about 1898 and proved to be a marketing brainstorm. The *States* patterns began to make their appearance just before the turn of the century and buyers could select a design named for their home state, at least if they resided in one of the thirty-five included in the offering.

Much of the 1890s was happy and prosperous, with inventions like the motion picture and automobile being developed and the country looking ahead to an exciting new century, but there were also hard times. The depression of 1893 was extremely severe and was felt by all levels of society in towns and cities, large and small, around the country. The decade was basically one of retrenchment for the American glass industry.

There had been a boom in the late 1880s when many new glass companies opened up, fed by the promise of low-cost gas from the seemingly endless supplies in Ohio and Indiana. Unfortunately, by the end of the 1880s many of these gas fields were depleted severely, forcing the closure or relocation of a number of factories. The concerns of the growing labor movement were felt at all levels of the glass industry, and as unions became increasingly strong, glass factory owners decided to fight back. This led to the formation in 1891 of the United States Glass Company (U.S. Glass), a cartel of seventeen glass factories under a single umbrella. This merger allowed the various factory owners to form a solid front against the powerful unions as well as to give them a competitive edge against any nonmember glass companies. Production levels, innovations, prices, and distribution all could be carefully controlled by a central authority. Although the various member companies retained their names locally, they officially were designated by a letter only, such as Factory A, Factory B, and so forth. Many collectors today specialize in a pattern or group of patterns they know were made by a particular glass company, but keep in mind that during this period all the pressed wares of member glass firms were marketed under the heading of United States Glass Company.

U.S. Glass operated very successfully during the 1890s and continued to be a force in glass circles well into the twentieth century, but in 1899 it faced competition from another conglomerate of glass factories called the National Glass Company. Composed of companies that broke away from U.S. Glass as well as some independent firms, this group controlled fewer glass factories and did not operate as successfully as its larger rival. National was dissolved in 1904, and its various members again went their separate ways.

Because the production of most pressed glass was centrally controlled during this era, even larger volumes of glass at cheaper prices were able to flood the American market. Although a good variety of new patterns was issued, dozens of best-sellers from previous decades continued in wide production. Sometimes they were given a face lift by the addition of color, such as ruby and amber

Fig. 10-1 An early ruby-flashed spooner with a cut thumbprint and diamond design, probably made in England or the Continent ca. 1850, is on the left. On the right is a pressed-glass tumbler in the *Dakota* pattern with ruby staining, ca. 1890–1900.

Ruby Confusions　Do not confuse the terms *ruby-flashed* and *ruby-stained* when describing old glass.

Flashing involves dipping a hot piece of just-formed clear glass into a contrasting batch of colored glass, usually ruby. When the piece has cooled and annealed, a pattern is cut through the thin colored layer to the clear beneath, as is shown on the spooner on the left, circa 1850.

Staining involves painting an already-pressed piece of clear pattern glass with a ruby-colored stain and reheating it just long enough to dry the color coating. Shown on the right in the photo is a *Dakota* pattern tumbler with the upper portion ruby-stained. An amber stain also was used sometimes to decorate pressed pieces, and many examples with these added colors also were engraved with flower or leaf bands or souvenir inscriptions.

Flashing, a more durable but more expensive technique, was most often used on blown-glass pieces.

staining, and the application of flashy gold or colored enamel trim to highlight the design. If colorful glass rode a wave of popularity in the 1880s, it became a tidal wave in the 1890s. More and more pressed glass was marketed to attract those who might not have been able to afford the expensive colored art glass or clear cut glass of the period. Today unusual pressed lines such as custard glass, introduced in the late 1890s, have reached the value levels of many so-called art glass lines of comparable age. Glassmakers like Harry Northwood led the

way during this era and proved that stylistic pizzazz and innovation were not limited to artsy blown wares. Pressed glass could compete very nicely with its showy sister glass.

Now that patterns introduced in the 1890s have reached or shortly will reach their century mark and become true, legal antiques, there will be more impetus to collect the bright and sometimes bizarre patterns and forms in pressed glass that epitomize the glittering closing years of the Victorian era.

Important Patterns of the 1890s

As in the previous chapter on important patterns of the 1880s, this chapter will list some of the more notable designs of the 1890s, divided according to general subcategories. Here also is a separate chart that lists these and other period patterns. A star (★) or cross denotes which pieces were made in color or with color trim and which have been reproduced. In addition, a listing of the States series of patterns put out around the turn of the century is included. Even though some of these were issued after 1900, they are included here for easier reference.

Geometric and Abstract Patterns

Adonis　Although the original producer of this pattern gave it a name based on a figure from Greek mythology, there is nothing figural about it. The design consists of flaring, triangular ribbed fans against a horizontally ribbed background. Collectors often use two other names for this line—*Pleat and Tuck* or *Washboard*—that are a bit more descriptive of its appearance. Made in several colors, it has not been reproduced.

IMPORTANT PATTERNS OF THE 1890s

Geometric and Abstract

+ Adonis
★ + Amazon
+ Apollo
+ Austrian
★ Aztec
★ + Ball and Swirl
★ + Barred Oval(s)
+ Bead and Scroll
+ Beaded Swag
+ Beaded Swirl
+ Beveled Diamond and Star
+ Box-in-Box
+ Britannic
★ + Broken Column
★ + Button Arches
+ Champion
+ Cordova
★ + Croesus
★ + Crystal Wedding
  Cut Log
★ + Dewey
+ Empress
★ + Esther
+ Fancy Loop
★ + Feather (Indiana Swirl)
  Festoon
★ + Finecut and Block
+ Fleur-de-Lis
+ Halley's Comet
+ Heart Band
+ Heart with Thumbprint
★ + Heavy Gothic
+ Hero (Ruby Rosette)
+ Herringbone Buttess
+ Hickman (LeClede)
★ + Jeweled Moon and Stars
★ + King's Crown (Excelsior, Ruby
  Thumbprint)
★ + King's 500

★ + Klondike (Dalzell's
  'Amberette')
  Leafy Scroll
+ Loop and Block
  Loop with Dewdrops
+ Lorraine (Fostoria's)
★ + Mardi Gras (Duncan No. 42
  or Empire)
+ Millard
★ + Moon and Star (Palace)
+ Nail
+ Pillow and Sunburst (Elite)
+ Pillow Encircled (Midway)
+ Pineapple and Fan (Heisey's)
★ + Plume
★ + Priscilla (Dalzell's 'Alexis')
+ Priscilla (Fostoria's)
+ Quartered Block
★ + Queen
+ Ribbon Candy (Bryce)
★ + Roman Rosette
+ Royal (Co-op's)
+ Royal Crystal
+ Scalloped Swirl (York
  Herringbone)
+ Scroll with Cane Band
+ Shoshone
+ Shrine
+ Shuttle
+ Skilton (Early Oregon)
+ Snail (Compact)
  Strigil
+ Tacoma
+ Tepee
★ + Triple Triangle
+ Truncated Cube
+ Victoria (Pioneer's)
+ Victoria (Riverside's)
+ Xray

Naturalistic

Artichoke
★ + Atlanta (Clear Lion Head,
  Square Lion)
+ Beaded Tulip
+ Bohemian (Floradora)
+ Clematis (Flower and Pleat)
+ Double Daisy (Riverside's
  Chrysanthemum)
★ + Ivy in Snow
+ Leaf and Flower
  Magnolia
★ Strawberry and Currant
+ Stippled Forget-Me-Not
+ Sunken Primrose (Greenburg's
  Florida)
★ Valentine (Trilby)

Realistic

★ + Columbian Coin
+ Cord Drapery
+ Locket on Chain
+ Picket
+ Shell and Jewel
★ + U.S. Coin (Silver Age)

+ = Produced in color or with color trim
★ = Reproduced

Austrian One of the patterns of the well-known Indiana Tumbler and Goblet Company of Greentown, Indiana, this line hit the market in 1897 and was produced by other companies well past the turn of the century.

Austrian consists of large circular bands filled with an overall diamond button pattern. It was made in several colors with pieces in cobalt blue, opaque colors, and Greentown's famous "Nil green," which is rare, as are pieces made in choco late glass. Not all pieces were made in color. The have been no reproductions.

Broken Column A distinctive ribbed pattern intro duced around 1891 is today called *Broken Colum* The design consists of thick vertical columns rul

Fig. 10-2 The *Adonis* pattern is illustrated by a plate and covered sugar bowl on the right, while a *Shell and Jewel* pitcher is on the left.

Fig. 10-3 An *Austrian* pattern creamer. This piece also can be found with a cover.

ning all the way up the sides of pieces, each column deeply notched along its length, hence the "breaks" noted in the name. It must have been very popular when brought out, as it continued in production through the 1890s. A number of examples had the individual notches highlighted by ruby staining, giving them a polka-dotted appearance. Broken Column was produced mainly in clear or with ruby-stained trim, but a rare example or two, particularly a punch cup, may be found in dark cobalt blue.

Unfortunately its longtime popularity led to reproductions in recent decades, to be touched on later. Keep in mind that most of the copies are heavier in weight than the older pieces.

Button Arches A pattern still quite common today, *Button Arches* was introduced originally around 1898 and continued in production for many years. The design consists of slightly overlapping pointed arches around the bottom edges and covers of pieces, each arch containing tightly packed "but-

Fig. 10-4 *A Broken Column goblet.*

Fig. 10-5 Two examples of souvenir-decorated *Button Arches.* The wine glass on the left is in clambroth, while the toothpick holder on the right has a ruby-stained top and is engraved with a name and date. Note that it was sold in 1939. The pattern was introduced forty years earlier.

tons.'' Made in clear, clear with ruby staining and gold-stained bands, clambroth, and opaque white, one often finds this pattern highlighted with souvenir inscriptions. Small pieces, such as the toothpick holder, apparently were favorite giveaways or souvenirs from fairs, carnivals, and tourist spots. Because of its long production and wide distribution, it is a fairly inexpensive pattern to collect.

Some pieces with a thin ruby or cranberry stain have been reproduced, including a covered butter dish, cordial glass, individual and regular-sized creamer, goblet, spooner, covered sugar bowl, and toothpick holder. The old pieces have a deep ruby staining unlike the lighter cranberry, and clear or other colored pieces should be safe to collect.

Croesus One of the most collectible and expensive patterns of the late 1890s, *Croesus* was produced widely in a dark, rich green and purple. It was also made in clear, but these examples do not show up as often or bring prices near those of the colored items.

Croesus is made up of scrolled cartouches around the sides of pieces separated by panels of small diamonds. Footed bowls are raised on rounded, flat tab feet. On the choicest examples, the scrolls are trimmed with heavy gold paint, which makes a dramatic contrast with the colored ground.

Because of its long-standing popularity with collectors, this pattern has been reproduced. One set made from new molds includes a butter dish with cover, creamer, spooner, covered sugar bowl, toothpick holder, and tumbler. Another mold was used to reproduce another tumbler. All reproductions were made in clear and color.

Croesus can be a difficult pattern in which to separate the old from the new, but on the toothpick holder check the scroll at the top. On new pieces the scroll does not curl all the way up and under as it does on the old pieces. On gold-decorated pieces, reproductions have a more garish gold that was painted on cold rather than refired to bake the gold on as on old pieces.

Since this can be an expensive line to collect, collectors should know their glass or their dealer before buying.

Crystal Wedding This pattern is unusual in that the pieces were designed with square bodies instead of the commoner round ones. The bottom edges of bowls, the edges of lids, and the square pedestal

55144 *Croesus Green and Gold Assortment.* This is one of the most pleasing patterns of glassware ever made, the body of the ware is a rich green with the scroll work, top, edges and feet decorated with genuine gold, assortment is composed of the following pieces: butter dish, sugar bowl, cream pitcher, spoon holder, half gallon pitcher, half dozen tumblers, half dozen sauce dishes, one 8 inch dish, a vinegar bottle, tooth pick holder, two salt and two pepper shakers, pickle tray and condiment set containing one oil bottle, one each salt and pepper shaker and tray.

55144

Price $7.50

Fig. 10-6 A very early illustration of the *Croesus* pattern. Introduced not long before, this grouping was shown in the Sears, Roebuck and Company catalog of late 1898. In green with gold trim, this whole set was available then for $7.50. Courtesy of James Measell.

bases feature a band of large inverted teardrops that are tightly packed and give an undulating effect, like bands of hard ribbon candy. The finials on lids resemble large inverted acorns.

Made for a long span of years, *Crystal Wedding* was made mainly in clear and clear with ruby staining, and other colors are rare.

The goblet and covered compotes are the major

reproductions that plague this pattern. They have been made since the 1950s and later and will take some study in order to differentiate the old from the new. Reproductions were made in clear, clear with a light cranberry stain, blue lustre, and milk white. Detailing of the almond-shaped teardrops or thumbprints may be one way to tell old from new, as the newer pieces show these sharp and clear whereas on old pieces they appear to run together. On the foot of the pedestal-based compote look at the clear band just above the base band with the almond thumbprints. On old pieces this clear band has a scalloped edge, while on new pieces the edge is flat. Other detailing differences take some study to recognize, but in general the reproductions in clear have a light greenish tint unlike the fine clarity of the old.

Cut Log Another ribbed pattern that might at first be confused by some collectors with Broken Column, *Cut Log* was produced originally under the name *Ethol*. This design has less-pronounced vertical columns tightly arranged side by side and running only part way up the sides of most pieces. The columns are lower in relief than on Broken Column and, although broken up by notches, these indentations have small serrations in them unlike the plain notches on Broken Column.

Not as widely known or popular with collectors, this pattern has escaped being reproduced. It was made mostly in clear over a long span of years. A very similar pattern was put out by Westmoreland in the 1890s that it called its "no. 15" line.

Dewey Another famous pattern from Greentown, Indiana (the Indiana Tumbler and Goblet Company), *Dewey* was named in honor of the hero of the Spanish-American War of 1898, Admiral George Dewey, who destroyed the Spanish fleet in Manila harbor, thus securing the Philippines as a U.S. territory.

Pieces of Dewey have a background of fine horizontal ribbing divided by vertical bars with small leaves and large, round bull's eyes between the bars. The bases of pieces are scalloped collars with rounded tab feet with buttons. It is a popular pattern to collect, especially in the many Greentown colors, with rare examples in Nile green and chocolate glass.

The main piece to beware is the large covered

Fig. 10-7 A *Dewey* pattern sugar bowl in amber.

Fig. 10-8 Two decorated goblets from the 1890s. The *Finecut and Block* example on the left has blue-stained blocks, while the *Esther* piece on the right has a stained rim further decorated with little enameled stars.

butter dish reproduced by the Imperial Glass Company. It will sometimes carry Imperial's "I. G." monogram, but other examples are unmarked. It was reproduced in deep amber, clear, olive green, milk white, purple carnival glass, and purple slag, the latter two never used in the old glass. Greentown glass authority James Measell has noted that one way to tell the old base from the new is to check the vertical band on pieces with the small band of leaves in it. On reproductions the veins of the top leaf point down, whereas on old pieces the veins in all the leaves point up. It is a small detail but one worth remembering. The colors on the reproductions are also cloudier than on the old pieces.

Esther The *Esther* pattern is another nice one that features a band of design around the bases of pieces. In this case a curved row of small circles with starburst centers is mixed with short ribs and a curved, fanlike device in the pattern band, and the upper portions of pieces are clear and plain. Esther,

originally introduced as *Esther Ware,* was made in clear and emerald green as well as clear with amber- or ruby-stained trim or colorfully enameled flowers on the upper portion.

This attractive pattern has not been reproduced.

Feather The *Feather* pattern, originally sold as *Doric,* is also known today as *Indiana Feather, Indiana Swirl,* and several other names. This interesting design is available in a wide range of pieces.

The name derives from the long, round-tipped panels. Plain panels alternate with panels filled with a fine crisscross diamond design, giving the effect of long, slightly curved feathers. Made mostly in clear, it can also be found in emerald green and clear with amber staining. A rare water pitcher was also made in chocolate glass.

Feather continued in production past the turn of the century. A later variation has differences in quality, some pieces being bright and glossy while others are duller with a poor finish. There are also some variations in the bases, but all pieces blend together well. So far only the wine glass has been reproduced in clear with a pink stain.

Finecut and Block Blocky designs in pattern glass remained popular in the 1890s, and a new one introduced around 1890 was *Finecut and Block* (see Figure 10-8).

The sides of pieces have an overall design of small diamond-shaped blocks. A band of plain blocks is near the top edge and another one lower down, each band surrounded by small blocks with fine rayed ribs alternating with a fine-cut diamond. The stemware also has a band of fine-cut running around the middle of the stem, and the bases of all pieces feature the plain small blocks and rayed blocks on their round feet.

Produced in clear, amber, blue, and canary yellow, the pattern also included some pieces in which the plain blocks were decorated with amber, blue, or pink staining, giving them an unusual and decorative appeal. These stained pieces bring premium prices from collectors, as do the solid-colored items.

Unfortunately, a number of reproductions have been issued by the Fenton Art Glass Company, including the wine glass in clear and in color. The reproductions are heavier and less clear than original pieces. A study of examples in William Heacock's book, *Fenton Glass: The Third Twenty-Five Years,* should prove helpful in avoiding the new pieces.

Halley's Comet Another pattern with a comet theme, *Halley's Comet* should not be really confusing once one has seen it and compared it to the earlier comets (discussed in the Flint section). It was originally called *Etruria* by the glassmaker. The design features a pattern band around the bases of most pieces. The pattern resembles a wide band of circles with long tails resembling large sixes laid almost sideways (see Fig. 10-14). Halley's Comet was produced mainly in clear with some examples decorated with ruby staining. It is a safe pattern to collect.

Heart with Thumbprint This romantic pattern will appeal to those who enjoy the heart motif, a design not often used in pattern glass. Originally introduced as the *Hartford* line, it also is known by other collector names, including *Heart and Thumbprint*.

Each piece features a band of large, smooth hearts with a round bull's eye in the center of each. Between the hearts is a wide inverted V design filled with a diamond-point pattern. *Heart with Thumbprint* is found in clear and emerald green, and ruby-stained examples are found more rarely. A brighter pale green, cobalt blue, and custard color were also used on rare examples, and some pieces might feature gold trim.

This is a handsome and appealing pattern that, fortunately, has not been copied.

Hero *Hero* is apparently the original name for a pattern long confused with another very similar pattern of the same vintage, *Pillow Encircled* (originally marketed as *Midway*).

Both Hero and Pillow Encircled feature a band of circles around the bases and covers of pieces, and within each small circle is a large diamond with curved sides. The only real difference between the two lines is that in Hero the plain portion above the circles comes right down to their tops, forming a scalloped line. Pillow Encircled, on the other hand, has a straight dividing line above the row of circles, forming an obvious barrier between them and the smooth sides above. Otherwise the patterns appear identical.

When decorated with ruby staining the Hero pattern goes by the collector name *Ruby Rosette*. However, Pillow Encircled also was quite often decorated with ruby staining but is not called by that name.

Both patterns were made in a wide range of

Fig. 10-9 Two patterns with a somewhat similar design. On the left is a *Pillow and Sunburst* sugar bowl, while on the right is a *Hero* pattern sugar bowl with frosted sides highlighted by tiny enameled blossoms.

items and are often found with ruby staining and engraved souvenir inscriptions.

Just to keep things interesting, a third similar pattern called *Pillow and Sunburst* (originally Westmoreland's *Elite*) came out about the same time. This design also has the band of circles with diamonds, but here the large circles cover the whole sides of most pieces, and each circle is separated by a matched pair of rayed fans, or sunbursts. Also, the diamonds within the circles feature a fine diamond-point design, whereas the diamonds in Hero and Pillow Encircled are plain. Pillow and Sunburst shows up quite often in a toothpick holder and spooner but seems scarcer in other pieces. It is usually in clear but can be found rarely with ruby staining or gold trim.

King's Crown Another simple and handsome pattern featuring a band of large thumbprints around the bases of pieces, flanked by narrow serrated bands, this popular pattern was issued originally by Adams and Company as its *X.L.C.R.*, a cryptic spelling of its other early name, *Excelsior*. Collectors named it *King's Crown,* apparently because the thumbprints and serrated bands reminded someone of a regal crown. The same pattern was produced widely with ruby staining on the upper, plain portion, and this variation is called *Ruby Thumbprint* by collectors. Old pieces also were sometimes decorated with amethyst, gold, green, or yellow staining in the thumbprints, but only the ruby-stained pieces are called Ruby Thumbprint. The clear upper portions of pieces also could be decorated with engravings of flowers or birds.

Heavily produced from about 1890 through 1914, this pattern was made in over one hundred pieces originally but, unfortunately, has been plagued for years by reproductions. Some of the copies do not look at all like old pieces, but clear goblets, wine glasses, tumblers, and champagne glasses could prove confusing. New items tend to be thicker and heavier than old pieces, and many have a slightly greenish tint. Ruby Thumbprint also has been reproduced, but the ruby is actually more of a thin cranberry color and usually has a golden iridescent shine never found on the old deep ruby pieces.

A thin amber stain not used on the old pieces shows up on some reproductions, and others come in solid ruby red and green, colors never used to make the old pattern.

Since there are so many good, old pieces still on the market, one can collect a fine selection with a little study and care.

Klondike This pattern was discussed earlier when covering the Daisy and Button—Single Panel (or Amberette) pattern of the 1880s. Originally marketed as Dalzell's *Amberette*, this *Klondike* features a large cross filled with fine diamond-point bands intersecting the smooth sides of each piece. Some pieces are found in all-clear and clear with frosted smooth panels, but the choicest examples feature the cross with amber staining. On some pieces the amber cross will be found on pieces with plain clear panels, but even more desirable are examples with the gold cross against acid-frosted panels. The clear examples with an amber cross may sell for three or

Fig. **10-10** *Ruby Thumbprint*, old and new. The large berry bowl on the left is authentic, while the sauce dish on the right is a twentieth-century reproduction. Note the lighter shade of staining and the oval thumbprints on the copy.

Fig. 10-11 Decorative patterns of the 1890s. On the right is a *Klondike* tumbler with amber cross and frosted panels. The goblet is in the *Jewelled Moon and Stars* pattern with frosted moons and stained trim. Do not confuse this pattern with the similarly named *Moon and Star* line.

four times the price of the plain clear examples, and those with the amber cross and frosted background four to six times the plain, clear equivalent. The frosted and amber cross pieces almost qualify as art glass, at least in price, even though they probably did not cost much more to produce originally. The rarest piece in this pattern is the wine glass, and a frosted and amber cross example might sell for over $500, a very healthy price indeed.

Moon and Star A very popular late-Victorian pattern, the original name given to this line by the maker, Adams and Company, was *Palace*. Collectors, however, came up with a more romantic and descriptive title. The pattern consists of a wide band of oval moons with finely serrated edges directly above a band of smaller circles centered by a starburst. The design carries over to the covered and domed bases of pieces, and the oval moons are greatly elongated on some items in the set.

A rather intriguing story is sometimes told about this pattern, although I cannot vouch for its authenticity. It seems this pattern was a favorite of singer Kate Smith, a well-known radio star of the 1930s and 1940s. According to legend, Smith chose this pattern as a tribute to the popularity of her recording of ''When the Moon Comes Over the Mountain.'' When word of her collection got out, many other glass lovers supposedly were inspired to seek out this pattern, and it became a favorite with collectors of that era. Unfortunately, this popularity with collectors also inspired glass companies to reproduce the line, and it has been overrun with prolific reproductions for the past fifty years.

This pattern was never made in solid colors originally, although sometimes the moons were acid-treated to give them a frosted look. When ruby staining became popular, pieces were also trimmed in ruby. Many reproductions have been made in solid colors, so avoid anything in blue, pink, vaseline, ruby, or green if you are looking for antiques.

Priscilla (Dalzell's) This attractive pattern was introduced in 1895 by Dalzell, Gilmore and Leighton Company of Findlay, Ohio, under their name *Alexis*. The design consists of long, rounded ribs running up the sides of pieces, each rib with a small starburst or daisy design above and below a central thumbprint. It was made in clear and clear with ruby staining, and a large selection of items was produced.

Unfortunately, the pattern was reproduced widely in the 1950s and 1960s, so caution must be taken when buying pieces, especially in clear. Many reproductions were made in colors never used in the old glass.

Keep in mind, also, that several other Priscilla patterns were made in the late nineteenth century and early twentieth century by other glass companies that bear no resemblance to this early line.

Ribbon Candy For something a bit more sinuous in pressed glass, try the *Ribbon Candy* pattern, originally produced as *Bryce*.

The design, a meandering band of tightly packed loops that wind around the pieces, is totally different from the other straight ribbon patterns covered here. The design actually does remind one of the old-fashioned hard ribbon candy so popular at Christmas time. Again, it was mainly made in clear, but rarely may be found in deep green. No reproductions hamper the enjoyment of collecting this pattern.

Roman Rosette Another classic-inspired pattern, *Roman Rosette* features a band of small, swirled rosettes around the center of pieces against a wide,

Fig. 10-12 A *Ribbon Candy* pattern creamer.

stippled band. Produced in quite a selection of pieces right through the turn of the century, this pattern should not be confused with the lacy-era pattern given the same name. That flint pattern looks completely different. The late *Roman Rosette* was made mainly in clear but rarely may be found with staining in ruby or other colors.

Again, the goblet was the victim of reproductions in the early 1960s, but these are lighter in weight than the old ones and have poor-quality background stippling.

Snail One of my favorite patterns of later pressed glass, *Snail* (also sometimes referred to as *Compact*) was introduced in 1890 by George Duncan and Sons. It is a simple and elegant line with a band of graceful tight scrolls (resembling snail shells) wrapping around the bases of pieces and forming the covers on covered items. It was made in clear and clear with engraved designs on the smooth, plain upper portions of pieces, and ruby staining was also added to some of the "snails" on rare examples.

Fig. 10-13 Compare the early flint *Roman Rosette* sauce dish on the left with the late *Roman Rosette* small mug on the right.

Fig. 10-14 Do not confuse *Halley's Comet* pattern (the wine glass on the left) with the *Snail* pattern (the creamer on the right). Note that their scrolls go in opposite directions.

Made in a very nice selection of pieces, the line includes rose bowls that have a double band of the snails forming the rounded sides. This is one of the earliest patterns to include modern-looking salt shakers in its original selection of items. It is rather remarkable that such a lovely pattern has not been bothered by reproductions.

Xray Closing the list of geometric and abstract 1890s patterns is the little-known *Xray* line.

The pieces are very plain, the sides decorated only with some widely spaced narrow indented ribs running up the sides. It is found most often in clear and emerald green. Green examples may have ribs highlighted in bright gold, or the plain panels may have enameled decoration. Any color other than green is rare. Xray (or *X-ray*) does have the merit of never having been reproduced.

Naturalistic Patterns

Atlanta (Fostoria's) Few new patterns introduced in the 1890s featured animals, but *Atlanta* is one of them. It is also known by several other names including *Clear Lion Head*, *Square Lion* and *Late Lion*, which refer to the feline present on pieces.

Unlike the earlier *Lion* (*Frosted Lion*) pattern of the 1870s, this set features plain pieces with a square shape, the only decoration a scalloped band with a row of small bull's eyes around the base of

pieces and the stylized face of a lion at each corner. The covers on pieces such as the sugar bowl do have a realistic lion's head as the finial, but, again, such lids are square to match the square bases, unlike the round covers on the earlier Lion pattern.

Atlanta was produced mainly in clear and clear with frosted details, but a few rare examples with ruby or amber staining have been reported, and some pieces may be found with an overall frosted finish. In this pattern only the goblet has fallen victim to reproductions.

Beaded Grape (California) One of the States series, this pattern was introduced in 1899. The pieces all have a square form with rounded corners, and around the sides or down the panels run bold, leafy grapevines. The corners and rims of pieces feature a band of small beading referred to in the name. The water pitcher came in either a square or round form.

This very popular pattern was made in a wide range of pieces and was produced in clear and dark emerald green, often trimmed in gold, the latter being especially collectible.

Probably because of its great popularity, a number of pieces of *Beaded Grape* were reproduced in the original clear or green as well as in several additional hues. The new pieces do not have the definition and sharpness of design of the old and are generally of a poorer quality.

Beaded Tulip As with animals, not many plants were highlighted on patterns introduced in the 1890s. The tulip was one of the few, and on *Beaded Tulip*, originally issued as "Andes," the tulip is rather strange indeed. A very stylized tulip blossom and leaves do run up the sides of pieces in this pattern, and they actually strongly resemble the folk art tulips so often found in Pennsylvania Dutch folk art. If you enjoy the primitive charm of that art, you may also enjoy this pattern, which was made in only a limited range of pieces. It was made mostly in clear with anything in color being rare. None of the pieces have been reproduced.

Bohemian Another floral pattern, *Bohemian*, also called *Floradora*, was issued by U.S. Glass in 1899.

This showy design typifies the glitter and excesses of the Gay '90s. Around the bodies of cylindrical pieces is a wide band of horizontal blossoms on slender, leafy vines. Around the top and bottom edges are narrow bands of scrolls. The pattern was produced in clear, deep rosy red-stained, and emerald green, and in almost all cases the leaves, blossoms, and scrolls are highlighted by bright gold paint or gold-painted scrolls and colored staining on the blossoms.

A sister pattern put out at about the same time is one of the States series, *Delaware*. The major difference between these two patterns with flowering vines is that all the pieces in Bohemian, except the tumbler, are raised on short, blocky, and slightly flaring feet, while pieces in Delaware have flat bases. The blossoms are also somewhat different and the leaves on Bohemian are shorter than those on Delaware.

No reproductions have been reported for either of these patterns.

Clematis (Crystal's) This bold and simple pattern, also known as *Flower and Pleat,* was introduced around 1892. It features a vining band of large six-petaled blossoms wrapping around the rounded bodies of pieces. There is a narrow scalloped band around the top rim, while a band of short ribs extends up around the bottom rim. The heavy raised blossoms can be found in ruby or amber staining, as well as in an orchid-colored (light purple) stain. Reportedly this decorated line was meant to be a simulation of the famous *Pomona* art glass that features lightly stained decoration.

Ivy in Snow The original manufacturer's name for this pattern was *Forest,* but *Ivy in Snow* is much more descriptive since pieces feature a bold, leafy ivy vine curving down the sides on a finely stippled ground.

This handsome plant-inspired line is popular with collectors. It was produced mainly in clear, but rare examples are found with ruby or amber staining on the leaves, and a piece or two might show up in milk glass.

Beginning in the late 1930s, Ivy in Snow was reproduced heavily in both clear and milk glass, so beware. On clear reproductions watch for very thin background stippling that does not look nearly as pebbled as on the old examples. Most reproductions were made in milk glass, and this newer ware apparently lacks the density of white of the originals.

Fig. 10-15 A showy pattern of the 1890s, this *Bohemian* su bowl features cranberry-stained blossoms and leaves heavy gold trim.

Strawberry and Currant This pattern combi two popular fruits on the same piece. A lusci cluster of strawberries and leaves graces one s and a large cluster of currants appears on the op site. Other than these bunches, the pieces are s ple and plain. The designs are raised in bold re and are very realistic looking.

Another pattern produced in only a very l ited line of pieces, a few items have been rep duced including the goblet, wine glass, and a open compote with a crimped edge, a piece no the original selection. The original pieces cam clear only, but reproductions have been made i number of colors as well. Look for poor detailing the new pieces.

Valentine This romantic pattern, originally ca *Trilby* when it was introduced in the 1890s, is on

Fig. 10-16 A tall pitcher in the *Clematis* (or *Flower and Pleat*) pattern. The center band is frosted and the blossoms and leaves are lightly stained in color.

Fig. 10-17 The romantic *Valentine* (aka *Trilby*) pattern features a woman's bust portrait in the heart on the pitcher and goblet. This is a scarce and relatively expensive pattern.

the few new patterns of that decade to feature a human face or form. All the pieces feature a series of large hearts around the sides against a background of banded beading. On the water pitcher and goblet these hearts are enlivened by the bust portrait of a lovely young woman. Other pieces lack the portrait.

This pattern came out in only about a dozen pieces. The original line was made in clear glass only, although someone certainly missed a great decorative opportunity by not trimming it with ruby staining.

The Degenhart's Crystal Art Glass factory of Cambridge, Ohio, reproduced the toothpick holder from a new mold and made it in many colors instead of the plain clear of the old. Fortunately, most of its pieces will be marked with its trademark, a "D" in a heart.

Realistic Patterns

Cord Drapery This pattern is one of the limited number introduced by the short-lived Indiana Tum-

bler and Goblet Company of Greentown, Indiana. It was its "no. 350" line, which it also named *Indiana*, and it hit the market around 1898. The design consists of fine swirled cords running up the sides of most pieces, with the tips of the cords joined by a zigzag cord topped with an inverted fan-like "tassel." Since a *Cord and Tassel* pattern, already exists, collectors chose the name *Cord Drapery* for this line.

Cord Drapery was available in several colors including amber, blue, clear, and emerald green, with a few pieces in chocolate glass and milk white. The pattern was produced for a number of years but not in modern times.

Locket on Chain The well-known Heisey Glass Company introduced this pattern as its line "no.

Fig. 10-18 A *Locket on Chain* goblet.

160'' about 1896. The main focus of the design is a band of large oval medallions or lockets suspended from beaded swags around the edges of pieces. Between each locket is a beaded band running down the side and dividing the surface into panels. Each panel features a finely stippled background setting off the locket.

Collectors of early Heisey glass should be interested in this line, which has not been reproduced. It was made in clear and clear with ruby staining or gold trim, and any other colors would be rare.

Picket *Picket* or *Picket Fence*, as it is also known, was designed to resemble an old-fashioned fence. The pieces are square and footed, with the boards of the fence forming the sides. It was originally issued around 1890 by King Glass Company of Pittsburgh, which called the pattern *London*. Picket was made in clear and several colors and has not been reproduced.

Shell and Jewel First introduced by the Westmo[re]land Specialty Company of Grapeville, Pennsyl[va]nia, around 1893, several other glass firn[s] including some in Canada, apparently also p[ro]duced this design later.

Around the rounded base of each piece are f[our] large stylized ribbed shells, while around the rim[is] a band of large round buttons or jewels joined b[y a] swag and fan band (see Fig. 10-2). The midsect[ion] of pieces has a finely stippled surface that contra[sts] nicely with the shells at the base and the jew[els] around the top.

Mainly produced in clear, a few pieces m[ay] show up in color. So far it has not been reproduc[ed].

U.S. Coin Probably the most famous and hig[hly] collectible pattern of the 1890s, *U.S. Coin* was [in]troduced originally by U.S. Glass in 1892 as [the] *Silver Age* line.

This pattern is unusual because actual U[.S.] coins were used to produce the molds for piece[s in] this set, and each item features the image of th[ese] coins around the sides and bases. Because the U[.S.] Treasury Department at that time proclaimed [the] coin pattern constituted a form of counterfeit[ing,] the maker was forced to discontinue production [af]ter only three months. Since it was produced [for] such a short time, it is surprising that such a la[rge] supply of U.S. Coin still exists, but prices today [are] quite high, especially for rare pieces.

U.S. Coin was produced in all-clear or, m[ore] frequently, with the coins frosted. On very rare [ex]amples the coins or background were trimmed w[ith] ruby or amber staining, or sometimes gold pa[int.] These colored items are the crème de la crème [of] this pattern and command very steep prices.

Because this pattern has always been sca[rce] and desirable, reproductions have hit the marke[t in] recent decades. The square footed toothpick hol[der] is the most often seen reproduction, but any pi[ece] should be examined carefully before a purch[ase.] The glass of the new pieces may appear glos[sier] than old pieces, and some of the fine detailing of [the] old design will be lacking. An early reproductio[n of] the toothpick holder features seven stars under [the] eagle instead of the words ''One Dollar'' found [on] the original. A later reproduction of this piece [fea]tures letters on the coin that are blurred and [ill] defined, and the facial features of the woman are[...]

Fig. 10-19 A relish dish in the *U.S. Coin* pattern.

rounded corners is eight by ten inches, while the original is seven by ten inches. Both trays have dollar coins in the corners, but on the old ones the fronts and backs of the coins are shown at the same end, while on the reproductions the fronts are shown at one end and the backs at the other. Other pieces to watch out for will be listed later.

When the U.S. government halted production of U.S. Coin, the glassmakers hurried to salvage the market for this line by introducing a variant they called *Spanish Coin*. Today this pattern is called *Columbian Coin*. The coins in the mold were changed to include a variety of designs, including an eagle and shield, a crown and shield, two bust portraits of Christopher Columbus, and two with portraits of Amerigo Vespucci. This line did not catch on like U.S. Coin had and so was not produced for a very long period either. It was made in clear and with rare pieces trimmed in color. Two slightly different versions of the design can be found, but they are not nearly as sought after as U.S. Coin. The tumbler, toothpick holder, and goblet have been reproduced.

The Fostoria Glass Company came out with a line of coin glass in the early 1960s in clear and colors, but the shapes are totally different from the old line and the coins are not based on real pieces.

sharp and prominent. The eagle also is poorly defined and does not really resemble the stately national emblem. A rounded spoon holder on four scroll feet and with a flared, scalloped rim was also an early reproduction in both clear and vaseline glass. This form of spooner was not made in the original line. On the reproduction covered compote that is six inches in diameter with a tall pedestal base, and on a covered bowl that is six inches in diameter and five inches high, one finds a ribbon over the eagle's head on the coins. There was no ribbon on the originals. The reproduction tumbler with a paneled base band has a frosted coin dated 1892. The original featured a clear coin dated 1878. The reproduction rectangular bread tray with

Fig. 10-20 Two variations of the *Columbian Coin* pattern. The goblet on the left was trimmed with gold on the coins.

Fig. 10-21 A sherbet in Fostoria's *Coin* pattern from the 1960s.

The States Series

As mentioned in the introduction to this section, in the late 1890s U.S. Glass came up with the idea of marketing a series of glass patterns named for the various states. Quite a few of these patterns were new to this series, but some were reissues of earlier lines reintroduced as part of this line. The States series continued past the turn of the century. The approximate year of introduction as well as other pertinent information on the pattern are noted.

Most of the state patterns featured a geometric or imitation cut-glass design, but a few had a plant or flower motif that adds to their appeal.

Collectors should also be aware that a number of patterns of pressed glass carry a state name but are not part of the U.S. Glass States series. These are listed at the end of this section.

Alabama Part of the States series in about 1899, this pattern may have come out a few years earlier.

THE STATES SERIES FROM THE U.S. GLASS COMPANY

Before 1900	After 1900	Not Part of the States Series
★ + Alabama	Georgia (1902, Peacock Feather)	+ Alaska
★ + California (Beaded Grape)		Idaho (ca. 1891)
+ Carolina (reissue)	+ Iowa (1900)	+ Indiana (Greentown's, aka Cord Drapery)
★ + Colorado (Lacy Medallion)	+ Kansas (1901, Jewel and Dewdrop)	+ Florida (Greenburg's, aka Sunken Primrose)
+ Connecticut	★ + Michigan (1902, Loop and Pillar)	+ Georgia (Tarentum's, aka Little Gem or Georgia Gem, ca. 1900)
+ Dakota (reissue)	+ Nevada (1902)	
+ Delaware	+ New Jersey (1900)	New York Honeycomb
★ + Florida (Emerald Green Herringbone)	+ New Hampshire (1903, Bent Buckle)	+ Oregon (Early Oregon, aka Skilton, ca. 1891)
★ + Illinois	★ Oregon (1901, Beaded Loop)	Pennsylvania (O'Hara's, aka Hand, ca. 1880)
+ Indiana	★ + Texas	★ + Virginia (misnomer for the U.S. Glass Galloway pattern, aka Mirror)
+ Kentucky	Utah (1901)	
Louisiana	+ Virginia (1901, Banded Portland)	Wyoming (Ripley's, ca. 1891)
+ Maine (Paneled Flower)	+ Washington (1901, Beaded Base)	
+ Maryland	Wisconsin (1903, Beaded Dewdrop)	
★ + Massachusetts (reissue)	Wyoming (1903)	
+ Minnesota		
+ Missouri		
+ New York (U.S. Rib)		
Ohio		
★ + Pennsylvania (Balder)		
+ Tennessee		
★ + Vermont		

+ = Produced in color or with color trim
★ = Reproduced

Also known as *Beaded Bulls-eye and Drape,* it was made mostly in clear with some items found in emerald green or with ruby staining. It has not been reproduced.

California   See the description of Beaded Grape in the section on naturalistic patterns.

Carolina   Originally introduced around 1890, this simple pattern represents both North and South Carolina. It was made mostly in clear, with rare pieces highlighted by purple or ruby staining. It has not been reproduced.

Colorado   A very popular States pattern, the full, rounded bodies of pieces in *Colorado* are plain but rest on three flattened and pointed tab feet, each foot embossed with a lacy scroll design. A close cousin to Colorado is *Lacy Medallion,* which has

arched lacy panels around the bases of pieces but no feet. It is often collected with Colorado, and both patterns were made in clear, dark green, and sometimes dark blue. Other colors and items with ruby-stained decoration are scarcer. Both patterns often show up with souvenir markings, especially small cups and toothpick holders. The toothpick holder has been reproduced in Colorado, but the colors are harsher and the detailing poor compared to old pieces. Also watch for overly bright gold painted trim.

Connecticut   Not a very well known States pattern, pieces in *Connecticut* feature simple rounded or cylindrical sides. The only real pattern is a narrow band of diamonds around the rims, necks, or bases of pieces. It was made in a good range of pieces, mostly in clear, but some items may show up with engraved decoration or ruby staining. It has not been reproduced.

Fig. 10-22 Three States pattern goblets. Left to right: *Beaded Grape (California)* in green, *Carolina* with enamel trim, *Dakota* with a ruby-stained and engraved top.

119

Fig. 10-23 A *Florida* pattern goblet and a *Colorado* pitcher.

Dakota *Dakota* is a reissue of the popular 1880s pattern as part of the States series (see Figure 10-22).

Delaware Another showy pattern of the 1890s, *Delaware,* like its sister pattern, Bohemian, features stylized flower sprigs around the sides against a stippled background. it was produced in clear, amethyst, emerald green, opaque white, and custard glass and often featured bright stained detailing on the florals and borders. Sometimes known as *Four Petal Flower,* it has not been reproduced.

Florida Also known as *Paneled Herringbone* or *Emerald Green Herringbone* when found in dark green, this pattern was made most often in clear. As the alternate names suggest, pieces feature wide strips of a herringbone design running up the sides. The goblet (see Figure 10-23) has been reproduced in several colors as well as clear and green, but the new green is not as dark as the old and the new

piece is thinner and lighter in weight than the original.

Georgia Other names for this attractive pattern are *Peacock Eye* and *Peacock Feather* (or *Peacock Feathers*), which quite clearly describe the design—long featherlike bands running up the sides (see Figure 10-30). It was made mostly in clear, with all colored items scarce. It has not been reproduced.

Illinois Featuring a bold imitation cut-glass design, *Illinois* has a large starlike design around the sides. Most pieces have a square shape, and the handles can either be pressed or applied. It is most often seen in clear or emerald green, with ruby staining sometimes applied to clear examples. The covered butter dish has been reproduced in clear and in colors, but it lacks the sharpness of detail and brilliance of the old pieces. One special piece to look for is the tall, square straw holder and lid, a piece used to hold straws at turn-of-the-century soda fountains.

Indiana Another geometric design, *Indiana* is composed of blocks under rounded arches. It was made in clear or clear with ruby staining. It has not been reproduced.

Iowa This pattern is also known as *Paneled Zipper,* which more clearly describes the design. The plain rounded shapes feature narrow zipperlike stripes running up the sides. It was made mostly in clear or clear with gold trim and any colored pieces would be rare. It has not been reproduced.

Kansas *Jewel and Dewdrop* is another name for this pattern, which features wide clear stripes alternating with stippled stripes that have clear, round jewels flanking a clear, large oval jewel (see Figure 10-25). Most pieces are found in clear, with a few examples showing up with color-stained trim. This line has not been reproduced.

Kentucky This geometric design features long, clear fans running up the sides of pieces, each fan separated with pointed ovals filled with a fine dia-

Fig. 10-24 A cruet in the *Indiana* pattern.

Fig. 10-25 These three States pattern goblets are (left to right): *Iowa* (with gold trim), *Kansas* (with stained jewels), and *Michigan* (with a stained rim and enameled blossoms on the sides).

mond-point design. It can be found in clear and emerald green, and a few pieces show up in dark blue or clear with colored staining. It is similar to the *Millard* pattern, except that the oval panels in Millard are plain, without the diamond-point design. No reproductions plague this pattern.

Louisiana Another geometric design, *Louisiana* features a band of long, clear pointed ovals running around the sides with small diamond-point panels around the top and bottom between the ovals. It was made in clear or clear with a frosted finish and has not been copied.

Maine One of the few States patterns to feature a floral motif, *Maine* is also known as *Panelled Flower,* and it does indeed feature wide panels filled with a floral sprig resembling a morning glory. It was made in clear and clear with enameled trim on the flowers, as well as in emerald green. It has not been reproduced.

Maryland This geometric pattern has also been called *Inverted Loop and Fan* (or *Inverted Loops and Fans*). The design features a band of large loops around the tops of pieces and a band of large fans around the base, with large diamond-point-filled diamonds around the middle. It can be found in clear or clear with ruby staining and has not been copied.

Massachusetts An earlier pattern reissued as part of the States series, *Massachusetts* is an imitation cut-glass design featuring large diamond-point-filled arches around the sides. It was made originally in clear with a few pieces found in emerald green or other colors. It has been reproduced, so watch for the covered butter dish among other items. The new imported copies are as sharp and clear as the old pieces but heavier. One unique piece in the original line called a "rum jug" is a small, domed kettle-form piece with a short spout and closed top.

Michigan This simple design also is referred to as *Loop and Pillar.* Around the base of each piece is a row of large bulging oval loops below plain panels or pillars running up the sides (see Figure 10-25). It was made in clear and clear with various color enameling or staining. The toothpick holder is the only piece reproduced, and it was made from a new mold

by the Crystal Art Glass Company (Degenhart) of Cambridge, Ohio. Its piece was made in many colors and often has its "D" mark in a heart.

Minnesota This design again imitates cut glass with its overall diamond-point and hobstar pattern divided by arched bands. It is found most often in clear; any pieces in color or with color trim are much scarcer. It has not been reproduced.

Missouri Also known as *Palm and Scroll,* this pattern features long palmlike leaves running up the sides around the pieces. It is found most commonly in clear or emerald green, but other rarer colors are known. It has not been copied.

Nevada A very plain design introduced about 1902, this pattern is not widely collected today. Most pieces have a plain, bulbous shape with a slightly fluted rim. It was made mainly in clear but might be found with frosted or enameled decoration. It has not been reproduced.

New Hampshire Another name for this imitation cut-glass pattern is *Bent Buckle,* and the long diamond-point arches around the sides of pieces in this line do resemble a large belt buckle (see Figure 10-27). It was introduced around 1903 and is found most often in clear with some pieces trimmed with color staining. There are no reproductions.

New Jersey This pattern also has been called *Loops and Drops* The geometric design consists of a band of long, clear drops alternating with loops filled with a diamond-point design. It was made in clear and clear with ruby staining, and it has not been copied.

New York Recent research by writers Neila and Thomas Bredehoft verifies that there was indeed a States pattern for New York. Long known as *U.S. Rib,* the design consists of heavy vertical ribbing around the sides of the square pieces. It is found in clear and emerald green, and is sometimes trimmed in gold.

The original catalog for this pattern refers to it as the *State of New York* line, rather than just *New York.* Since it has not been reproduced and is now documented as being a States pattern, it should increase in collectibility.

Fig. 10-26 These three patterns represent, from left to right, *Massachusetts, Minnesota,* and *Missouri.*

Fig. 10-27 More States goblets. On the left is a ruby-stained *New Jersey* example, in the center is *New Hampshire,* and on the right an *Ohio* piece with leaf and berry engravings around the top.

Fig. 10-28 On the left is the *New York* goblet with a frosted band and enameled flowers. In the center is an *Oregon* goblet and on the right is the *Pennsylvania* goblet with a gold-trimmed rim.

State of New York, or No. 15061 Pattern.

Cream

Spoon   *Butter and Cover*

Fig. 10-29 A copy of a page from a U.S. Glass pattern catalog for its no. 15061—*State of New York* pattern. Courtesy of Neila and Tom Bredehoft.

Ohio A very plain pattern, the simple cylindrical shapes are only highlighted by a plain ring band around the neck, shoulder or base of the pieces (see Figure 10-27). Most items probably go unrecognized by collectors. It can be found with ruby-stained trim and it has not been reproduced.

Oregon The *Oregon* pattern is also called *Beaded Loop* (or *Beaded Loops*) because the design consists of a band of vertical clear loops around the sides of pieces, each separated by a band of small diamonds (see Figure 10-28). It was made in clear only. The goblet and sugar bowl have been reproduced. Do not confuse this pattern with the *Early Oregon* pattern, which came out much earlier and was not part of the States series.

Pennsylvania This imitation cut-glass pattern goes by two other names: *Balder* and *Kamoni*. The design consists of large diamond-point-filled diamonds alternating with sections of bold crosshatched banding (see Figure 10-28). It was produced in clear, clear with ruby staining, and emerald green. The handles on pieces can be either pressed or applied. A look-alike spoon holder has been made in this pattern, but it is heavier than the old and lacks its sharp detailing.

Do not confuse this pattern with the 1880s O'Hara pattern that it called *Pennsylvania* and that today usually goes by the name *Hand* because the covers on pieces feature a finial in the form of a human hand holding a bar.

124

Tennessee Also called *Jewel and Crescent* as well as other names, this interesting pattern consists of a band of large, paired crescents facing each other, with a small button in the center. On most pieces the pairs of crescents are separated by a short band of herringbone design. Found in clear, it can also have color-trimmed "jewels." It has not been copied.

Texas This geometric pattern has also been called *Loops with Stippled Panels* because the design features long, heavy loops running up the sides of pieces with each loop filled with a stippled design. Made in clear or clear with colored staining, the handles can either be pressed or applied. The individual-sized creamer and open sugar bowl have been reproduced in new molds in a variety of colors.

Utah Another early simple States pattern, *Utah* features a design of small, scattered six-point stars

around the bodies of pieces with simple paneling around the necks and bases (see Figure 10-32). Also called *Twinkle Star* as well as several other names, this design was made in clear only or clear with a frosted finish. It has not been reproduced.

Vermont This pattern has been called by several other names including *Honeycomb with Flower Rim, Inverted Thumbprint with Daisy Band,* and *Vermont Honeycomb.* Each of these names helps describe the overall design, which consists of an optic honeycomb body trimmed around the top rim with a band of daisylike blossoms (see Figure 10-30). Bold curled and ribbed leaves run down the sides and form the feet or the handle and foot on many pieces. It was made in clear and emerald green originally as well as more unique versions in custard glass, chocolate glass, milk glass, slag glass, and opaque blue. It is often found trimmed with enameled colors or ruby or amber staining.

The toothpick holder has been reproduced in a

Fig. 10-30 Three more States patterns. On the left is a *Tennessee* goblet, in the center a *Georgia* pitcher, and on the right a decorated *Vermont* goblet.

Fig. 10-31 A *Texas* pattern individual-size open sugar bowl.

wide variety of colors by the Crystal Art Gla
Company, but the new pieces are about one-quar
inch shorter than the old ones.

Virginia This simple pattern may be more wide
known as *Banded Portland* or *Maiden's Blush*, b
it was part of the U.S. Glass States series. The lo
narrow side panels curve out and flare at the top a
base. Around the center of each piece runs a ba
of fine diamond-point design. Pieces were made
clear and often given a rose-stained blush (hence
Maiden's Blush name). Some pieces also might
found stained with other colors. It was produced
quite a long period of time and in a very large asso
ment, so it is fairly easy to collect, especially si
it has not been reproduced.

Washington Another very simple pattern, *Wa
ington* was introduced after 1901. The pieces ha
simple cylindrical bodies with a ring around

Fig. 10-32 Four States pattern goblets: *Utah, Virginia, Washington* (with a frosted band and enameled trim), and *Wisconsin*.

126

base of each piece (see Figure 10-32). This ring features a tiny band of beading around its middle, and the ring and beaded band form the only design on pieces. It was made in clear but is often found with colored staining or enameled decoration. Very rare pieces may show up in custard glass. It has not been reproduced.

Wisconsin Also known as *Beaded Dewdrop,* this pattern features long, plain ovals around the sides of pieces, each oval separated by a narrow band of "dewdrops" (see Figure 10-32). It was introduced around 1903 and was made in clear. There are no reproductions.

Wyoming This rather strange pattern, also known as *Enigma* or *Bull's Eye,* consists of long oval panels up and down the sides of pieces, each panel separated by a narrow herringbone band. Inside the oval panel, at the top, is a rounded arch filled with a diamond-point design above a pair of small circles that resemble beady eyes. One can almost see some sort of strange helmeted Darth Vader–like creature in this part of the design. In the lower portion of the panel is a large, plain oval button or jewel. *Wyoming* was introduced about 1903 and made in clear only. It has not been copied.

Several patterns named for states are not part of the States series. Some of these include *Alaska* (an opalescent design); *Florida* (Greenburg's, aka *Sunken Primrose*); *Georgia* (Tarentum's, aka *Little Gem* or *Georgia Gem,* circa 1900), *Idaho* (circa 1891); *Indiana* (*Cord Drapery*); *New York Honeycomb; Oregon* (early Oregon, circa 1891); *Pennsylvania* (O'Hara's, aka *Hand,* circa 1880); *Virginia* (a misnomer for the U.S. Glass *Galloway* pattern also called *Mirror*), and *Wyoming* (Ripley's, circa 1891).

U.S. Glass also brought out, around 1905, a line it called *The States,* one pattern in honor of all the American states. This pattern consists of a band of large circles around the sides of pieces, including a circle with a starburst design alternating with one filled with diamond point. It was made in clear and clear with gold, and a few pieces are found in emerald green. It has not been reproduced.

Desirability and Values

Most patterns of the 1890s fall within the same value ranges as those for 1880s patterns. The same criteria for evaluating them hold true with scarce pieces or rare colored examples bringing top prices.

In most of the patterns in clear all but the rarest pieces can be found for under $100, with many under $50. If a pattern was made in color or decorated with amber or ruby staining, expect to pay at least 30 to 50 percent more than for the piece in plain clear, and double for some items.

As mentioned, U.S. Coin is the most expensive pattern from the 1890s, and it will be hard to find a plain clear piece for $100 or less. Most pieces in clear U.S. Coin will bring over $200. Pieces with the coins frosted will bring considerably more than those with clear coins. A majority of the frosted coin items will fall in the $250 to $500 range. Items with the rare ruby-stained, amber-stained, or gold trim bring even higher prices. This is a wonderful pattern but one that requires a great deal of study and a hefty pocketbook to collect seriously.

For the most part, however, the colorful array of patterns from the last decade of the nineteenth century can be collected and enjoyed by glass lovers with a modest budget.

Old Versus New

Since many of the reproductions were touched on in the pattern descriptions, below is just a brief alphabetical list of what pieces of which to be wary. Although some patterns have been reproduced widely, the number is really remarkably small considering the dozens and dozens of patterns available from that era.

Atlanta (Fostoria's): Beware: goblet.

Ball and Swirl: Watch for some pieces reproduced in milk glass. Beware: goblet and wine glass in milk glass, a covered candy jar in milk white, and an eighteen-inch-diameter plate in clear. The latter two were not in the original set.

Beaded Grape (California): Watch for many reproductions in milk glass produced by the Westmoreland Glass Company. Other pieces produced in clear and colors. Beware: square covered compote on tall pedestal, goblet, eight-and-a-quarter-inch-wide square plate, four-inch-wide square flat sauce dish, tumbler, and wine glass.

Broken Column: Watch for pieces with a heavier weight than the old ones. Beware: goblet and pieces reproduced for the Smithsonian Institution (marked "S. I.") and the Metropolitan Museum of Art (marked "M. M. A."), which include flat, open, round eight-inch and eight-and-a-half-inch bowls, ten-ounce creamer, nine-inch-high water pitcher, eight-inch-diameter plate, four-and-a-half-inch-diameter round sauce dish, four-and-a-half-inch-high spooner, five-and-a-quarter-inch-high sugar bowl, and six-inch-high wine glass. These marked items were offered right through the 1980s.

Button Arches: Watch for pieces with a light cranberry staining. Beware: covered butter dish, cordial, creamer (individual and regular size), goblet, spoon holder, covered sugar bowl and toothpick holder.

Colorado: Beware: toothpick holder, especially in color.

Columbian Coin: Beware: goblet, tumbler, and toothpick holder.

Croesus: Beware: covered butter dish, creamer, spooner, covered sugar bowl, toothpick holder, and tumbler.

Crystal Wedding: See text. Beware: eight-inch-high tall-pedestal covered compote, ten-inch-high tall-pedestal covered compote, six-inch-diameter low-pedestal candy dish and goblet.

Dewey: See text. Beware: large covered butter dish.

Feather: Beware: wine glass with pink staining.

Finecut and Block: Watch for extensive line reproduced by Fenton Art Glass. The pieces are heavier than the old and the pattern is not as sharp and clear.

Florida: Beware: goblet.

Illinois: Beware: covered butter dish.

Ivy in Snow: Watch for pieces reproduced in m[ilk] glass and some in clear. Beware: covered but[ter] dish, cake stand with tall pedestal, celery va[se,] creamer, covered compote, goblet, round pla[te,] sauce dish, spooner, covered sugar bowl, and wa[ter] pitcher.

King's Crown (Ruby Thumbprint): Watch [for] thicker and heavier pieces in clear, or with a cra[n]berry stain with a golden iridescence. Beware: go[b]let, wine glass, tumbler, and champagne glass, al[l] clear or colors; also a footed sauce, five-inch-dia[m]eter high-pedestal covered compote, cordial, [indi]vidual sugar bowl, individual creamer, footed sh[er]bet, flat sauce, eight-inch-diameter plate, cup a[nd] saucer, tall-pedestal cake plate, tall lemonade tu[m]bler, small tumbler, tall oil lamps with Kin[g's] Crown base, and Daisy and Button font, an[d] King's Crown base with a milk glass beaded fo[nt].

Klondike (Dalzell's): Beware: look-alike sugar bo[wl] in solid amber.

Massachusetts: Watch for new pieces imported a[nd] sold as Star Diamonds pattern in clear and col[or.] Beware: covered butter dish among other items.

Michigan: Beware: toothpick holder.

Moon and Star: Watch for anything in solid col[or] and pieces not made in the original set, such a[s a] toothpick holder. It has been profusely reprodu[ced] since the 1930s. Beware: butter dish, six-inch-dia[m]eter low-footed covered compote, four-inch-dia[me]ter tall-pedestal covered compote, six-inch-dia[me]ter tall-pedestal covered compote, creamer w[ith] pressed handle (the original had an applied hand[le,]) eggcup, goblet, salt dip, tall salt shaker, spoon[er,] sugar bowl, footed sauce dish, champagne gla[ss,] night lamp, footed tumblers, water pitcher, sev[en-]inch-, eight-inch-, and ten-inch-diameter plat[es,] punch bowl and cups, and toothpick holder.

Oregon: Beware: goblet and covered sugar bow[l.]

Pennsylvania: Beware: look-alike spoon holder[.]

Plume: Beware: goblet.

Priscilla (Dalzell's): See text. Beware: indivi[dual] creamer, goblet, and individual open sugar bo[wl] and wine in clear. Also in colors of amethyst, bl[ue] clear, green, ruby red, and opalescent colo[rs.] Fenton made a twelve-inch-high handled bask[et,] six-inch handled bonbon dish, ten-and-a-half-in[ch] diameter flared bowl, cocktail glass, various sizes of tall covered compotes, goblet, six-inch, eight-inch and twelve-and-a-half-inch-diameter plates, and eleven-inch-diameter rolled-edge plate, rose bowl, flat round sauce dish, sherbet dish, wine glass, covered sugar bowl, and toothpick holder. Later L. G. Wright Glass Company sold a four-and-a-half-inch-diameter covered compote in several colors and clear. Collect this pattern with care.

Queen: Beware: master berry bowl, cake stand with tall pedestal, and spooner.

Roman Rosette: See text. Beware: goblet.

Strawberry and Currant: Beware: goblet, wine glass, and tall open compote with crimped edge not in the original set.

Texas: Beware: individual-sized creamer and open sugar bowl.

Triple Triangle: Beware: goblet and wine glass.

U.S. Coin: See text. Beware: flat covered bowl (candy jar—not part of the original set); ten-inch-long bread tray with fifteen frosted fifty-cent coins; two-and-a-quarter-inch high candlestick (not in original set); nine-and-a-half-inch tall-pedestal covered compote with frosted coins; creamer with frosted coins; two-and-three-quarter-inch-diameter paperweight; four-and-three-quarter-inch-high footed spooner (not part of original set); seven-inch-high covered sugar bowl with frosted coins; two-and-seven-eighths-inch-high toothpick holder in all-clear, or with frosted or silver coins; and a two-and-seven-eighths-inch-high water tumbler with frosted one-dollar coins.

Valentine: Beware: toothpick holder in many colors.

Vermont: Beware: toothpick holder in various colors.

CHAPTER 11

1900–1915: Twilight of American Pressed-Pattern Glass

The waning years of the 1890s was a time of excitement and expectation for most Americans who looked ahead to the dawning of a new century. Progress was to be seen in all aspects of American life, and prosperity and economic stability were widespread. Americans were feeling good about themselves and their country. There was even a little war in 1898 to help stir up patriotic fervor. With the complete defeat of Spain in the brief Spanish-American War, the United States gained a real overseas empire and joined other leading colonial powers such as England, France, and Germany.

Americans were proud of their country's progress during the past century, and the future looked rosy too. That new contraption, the horseless carriage, was beginning to show up in some parts of the country, and other scientific marvels like the telephone and electric power for the home were becoming more widespread across the country.

However, as discussed earlier, there was no immediate shift away from the manners, morals, and tastes of the Victorian era. American taste in glassware closely followed that of the previous decades, and not until around World War I was there a major shift in what the buying public wanted. Many of the pressed-glass patterns of the 1890s continued to be produced and sold widely, and some innovations, such as custard glass and chocolate glass, attracted buyers, too.

Tableware designs did begin to change slowly right at the turn of the century as more patterns imitating fine-cut glass were marketed. Several glass firms even began to mark such wares with stamped trade names like Nucut or Pres-cut. On the other end of the design spectrum, very simple paneled patterns were introduced that recalled the elegant colonial designs of the 1850s and 1860s.

These two contrasting themes in pattern design continued in popularity into the 1920s.

The early twentieth century also saw an eclipse of the importance of the large American glass conglomerates that formed in the 1890s. U.S. Glass continued to operate into the 1960s, but with fewer plants and less impact on the glass market. The National Glass Company was dissolved in 1904, and some of its former members, including the Cambridge Glass Company and the McKee Glass Company, continued to operate successfully on their own. In addition, quite a number of independent glass companies were formed in the early 1900s, and firms such as Fenton Art Glass, Imperial Glass, and Federal Glass went on to become major producers for many decades.

Glassware of all types—commercial, industrial, and household—continued to supply growing markets during the early years of this century, and by the 1920s over two dozen glass factories, large and small, were producing vast amounts of glass. Tableware, in particular, was available in a plethora of colorful and affordable designs and styles to suit every taste and budget.

In the first fifteen years of the twentieth century, many established glass firms like U.S. Glass continued production of their older patterns. Most companies also began introducing a selection of imitation cut and simple paneled patterns, and soon the market was flooded with competing lines that were very similar. Everyone wanted to make a hot seller, and so copycat designs, nothing new in American pressed glass, became a major part of the offerings in those years. Because many of these turn-of-the-century patterns look so much alike, it can be difficult today to sort out what company made which pattern. To help beginning collectors with the

Fig. 11-1 A page from the Butler Brothers wholesale catalog of spring 1902. A variety of popular patterns were featured with pieces from the U.S. Glass Company's States series in the upper left and lower right. In the upper right is a selection of chocolate glass being made at the Greentown, Indiana, factory of the National Glass Company.

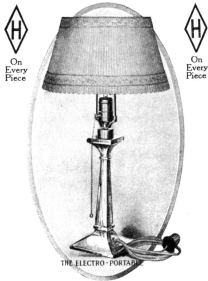

THE ELECTRO-PORTABLE

quandary, the following section gives a brief introduction to some of the most important early-twentieth-century glass factories and describes the types of wares they were producing, including the specific patterns.

As far as the sorts of pieces of glass tableware being made early in this century, most of the forms were carry-overs from the late nineteenth century. However, patterns generally were made in a smaller

Fig. 11-2 This Heisey Company advertisement from a 1914 magazine illustrates how colonial designs were again in demand. Here the company was promoting what it called "Ye Old Colonial Candle Stick . . . with the charming atmosphere of Great Grandmother Days." Note: great-grandmother's day would have been circa the 1850s, when colonial-style flint glass patterns were first in vogue.

This last addition to

Heisey's ⒣ Glassware

marks a new and wonderful epoch in the evolution of **Ye Old Colonial Candle Stick.** It combines the lighting efficiency of the 20th Century with the charming atmosphere of **Great Grandmother Days.** Makes an admirable addition to desk, table or dresser. Two sizes—19 inches and 21 inches over all. If your dealer cannot supply this **Electro-Portable,** we will deliver, prepaid, East of the Mississippi River, the smaller size for $3.75, the larger size for $4.75, without shade or bulb; West of the Mississippi River—add 50c. Insist on having this ⒣ trademark on the glassware you buy—then you have high quality without high price. Our free book contains helpful hints for the Hostess. Write for a copy.

A. H. HEISEY & CO.
Dept. 31   Newark, Ohio

selection of pieces and in more specialized sets. These included punch sets, water (or lemonade) sets, and berry (or ice cream) sets, which became especially popular, along with all sorts of decorative bowls and vases. A great deal of clear pressed glass was made, but colored glass in dark shades of blue, green, and purple, as well as color decorating with ruby and amber staining or gold paint and enamels, also remained popular.

New decorative pressed glassware took the American market by storm in the first decade of the 1900s. The showy ware today called carnival glass was meant to imitate the expensive art glass wares of makers like Louis Comfort Tiffany, and its bright iridescent finishes, obtained by spraying h[..] pressed glass with special metallic salts, became [..] immediate rage. Many glass firms of that peri[..] jumped on the carnival bandwagon, and for sever[..] years its popularity nearly overwhelmed all oth[..] types of pressed glass. Then, quite suddenly, i[..] market appeal waned and it was relegated to t[..] backs of cupboards for decades until, in the 1960s, [..] was rediscovered by a new generation of glass lo[..] ers.

Carnival glass is covered in a later chapte[..] now here is a look at the major glasshouses of t[..] early years of this century and their noncarniv[..] glass wares.

Important Glass Companies of the Early Twentieth Century

Cambridge Glass Company, Cambridge, Ohio (1901–1958)

The Cambridge Glass Company got its start when the National Glass Company built a large, modern factory in Cambridge, Ohio, in 1901. This plant was set up independent of the parent company but produced glass using molds from various other members of the National Glass combine. These pieces included milk glass and opaque turquoise blue items such as plates and salt shakers.

After 1904, when National Glass dissolved, the Cambridge plant continued in production and began introducing completely new patterns. About 1906 Cambridge brought out a new series of imitation cut-glass designs that it stamped with the trademark Near Cut.

Some patterns were made in shades of transparent blue, amber, and green, but a great deal of glass was clear or clear with amber or ruby staining.

One of its early imitation cut-glass patterns originally was named *Fern* but is today called *Fernland* or *Snowflake*.

Cambridge brought out several distinctive floral patterns with the Near Cut line. Each featured a bold, stylized botanical design. The most popular then, and now, are *Strawberry* or *Inverted Strawberry* (1912–1918), *Daisy* (circa 1910–1920), and *Thistle* or *Inverted Thistle*.

A good selection of imitation cut patterns with overall geometric designs was also part of the Nea[..] Cut line.

The *Strawberry* and *Thistle* patterns can b[..] found in dark emerald green as well as clear, an[..] nearly all of the Near Cut lines also were decorate[..] with the carnival glass treatment when that gla[..] was the rage.

Beginning about the 1920s, Cambridge deve[..] oped many more modernistic lines of glass and we[..] on to produce many interesting shapes and form[..] including the *Statuesque* line (with nude woma[..]

Fig. 11-3 A cruet and 8″ d. plate in Cambridge's *Inverted Stra[..]berry* pattern.

stems) and various figural animals. Lovely colors became a trademark of Cambridge wares, and today pieces made in distinctive lines like *Crown Tuscan* (a lovely, soft opaque pink) attract many collectors and bring hefty prices. To add to the collecting appeal, many pieces of Cambridge produced between 1925 and 1935 were pressed on the center of the bottom with a tiny "C" in a triangle trademark, while later examples carried its paper sticker label.

Duncan and Miller Glass Company, Washington, Pennsylvania (1893–1955)

This company evolved from the long-established George Duncan's Sons and Company, with its new Duncan and Miller name introduced in late 1900.

Duncan and Miller continued to produce many of the older Duncan patterns, and pieces trimmed with the popular ruby or amber staining were marketed widely until about 1920. Most of the turn-of-the-century patterns had busy geometric or imita-

Fig. 11-4 A wine glass in the early Duncan *Beaded Swirl* pattern. A nearly identical pattern was made by Westmoreland.

tion cut-glass designs, but a couple, like *Sunflower Patch* (circa 1913) and *Flowered Scroll* (circa 1894), featured stylized florals.

In the early twentieth century, Duncan and Miller began to produce a good variety of colonial-revival patterns, which remained popular for a number of years. Its *Sweet Sixty-One* (no. 61), circa 1906–1913, featured plain arched panels, while about the same time its *Thumbnail* (no. 73) also had plain panels. It also offered a *Puritan* pattern, a *Colonial* pattern, and a *Georgian* pattern (another take-off on old Honeycomb), as well as *Early American Sandwich*, an adaptation of 1830s lacy glass. Duncan and Miller also made a version of *Hobnail*, a pattern first popular in the 1880s. Various patterns appeared in milk glass and some were similar to Victorian lines, including reproductions of Crystal Wedding, not originally made in white.

Fenton Art Glass Company, Williamstown, West Virginia (1905–present)

Frank L. Fenton, after several years of working at various glass factories, decided to start his own company in 1905. With the help of his brother, John, a decorating shop was set up in Martins Ferry, Ohio. Later brother Charles H. joined the firm, and in 1906 they moved operations to Williamstown, West Virginia, where the factory remains.

When the move was made to Williamstown, the Fenton Art Glass Company expanded from simply decorating glassware for other factories to producing its own, original designs. It was fortunate to obtain the services of noted glass innovator Jacob Rosenthal.

Carnival glass was first introduced at the Fenton plant in the early years of the century, and this popular pressed ware with its bright iridescent finish became one of the major products of Fenton during its early years. However, as author Bill Heacock documented in his book *Fenton Glass: The First Twenty-Five Years,* the Fenton factory was also responsible for several other colorful pressed lines. A limited range of chocolate glass was produced, including pieces in the *Water Lily and Cattails* pattern, and this pattern (also made by the Northwood Glass Company) can be found in various colors of opalescent glass. Many pieces of mold-blown glass also were produced at Fenton, and many featured brightly enameled hand-painted decoration, a reminder of the firm's origins as a glass-decorating company.

Fenton, from its earliest days, focused on colored glassware and has been known for its wonderful designs and unique colors ever since. Adding to its rainbow spectrum of pressed glassware, Fenton introduced a pattern in the creamy ware called custard glass circa 1915. The design called *Cherry and Scale* by custard glass collectors features an overall diamond lattice motif, with alternating bands of the diamonds filled with small "cherries." This pattern also was produced in carnival glass by Fenton, but carnival collectors prefer to call it *Fentonia Fruit*.

By the 1920s Fenton was introducing new colors and more modern shapes. The bright carnival glass shine gave way to stretch glass, with its much lighter iridescent finish on pastel hues. A short-lived art glass line was brought out in the mid-1920s, but with their other well-established patterns and lovely colors Fenton was able to weather the 1930s.

Though most of America's pioneering glass companies have succumbed to economic vicissitudes in recent decades, all lovers of fine glass, pressed and mold-blown, can take pride in the fact that Fenton Art Glass continues its long tradition of excellence in producing colorful glassware today.

Fostoria Glass Company, Fostoria, Ohio and Moundsville, West Virginia (1887–1986)

For nearly a century the Fostoria Glass Company was a leader in the production of decorative, high-quality glassware. Sadly, the factory closed in 1986, and no more new Fostoria will be on the market, though a wonderful supply of old Fostoria remains for collectors to seek.

Established in Fostoria, Ohio, in 1887, the factory remained in that city for only three years before relocating to Moundsville, West Virginia, where it remained for the rest of its history. Fostoria is rather unusual among late-nineteenth-century American glass factories in that it never chose to join either of the large American glass combines, U.S. Glass or the National Glass Com-

pany. Instead Fostoria went its own way and produced a wide range of patterns over its long history.

Among collectors today the later pressed and blown stemware and tableware lines of Fostoria may be better known than its earliest products. However, throughout the 1890s and up to 1915 the factory did turn out many interesting patterns typical of the pressed glass of that era.

One of its earliest documented patterns, *Victoria* (no. 183), features a bold, swirled design on its simple, rounded shapes. Other abstract and geometric designs from Fostoria's early years include *Heavy Drape* (no. 1300, 1904–1906), *Long Buttress* (no. 1299, 1904–1913), *Louise* (no. 1121, circa 1901), *Rococo* (no. 234, 1891), a version of the *Shell and Jewel* pattern (no. 618) and *Wedding Bells* (no. 789, circa 1900).

Fostoria also picked up on the popular design

Fig. 11-5 A footed tumbler in Fostoria's *American*, a pattern introduced in 1915.

trends of the late 1890s and early 1900s by bringing out a number of imitation cut-glass pressed patterns as well as the contrasting simple colonial style lines.

Among its collectible cut imitation patterns are *Lorraine* (no. 301, aka *Flat Diamond Box,* circa 1893), *Brazilian* (no. 600, circa 1898), and *Sylvan* (no. 1119, circa 1902–1906). The *Rosby* pattern (no. 1704, circa 1910–1928) was another cut style line, and though most of the line was discontinued in the 1920s, the punch bowl and matching cups remained in production into the 1970s.

In the realm of simple colonial-revival pressed patterns, Fostoria had its *Bedford* line (no. 1000) from 1901 to 1904, and *Essex* (no. 1372), with its simple, broad flutes, from 1905 to 1925. *Puritan* (a name widely used by glass factories of that era) was Fostoria's no. 1432 line from 1906 to 1925, and it too featured long, plain panels.

The pattern most often associated with Fostoria pressed glass, however, is *American.* This handsome line first hit the market in 1915, right at the end of the period considered here.

American (no. 2056) is a simple and elegant design featuring an overall pattern of small cubes. From its introduction it must have been one of Fostoria's all-time best-sellers. For decades it was common to give a piece of American as a wedding gift, and many brides of the 1930s and 1940s still cherish these pieces today.

A. H. Heisey and Company, Newark, Ohio (1896–1957)

Founded as an independent glassmaker in 1896, Heisey, like Fostoria, never joined one of the large glass combines of the era. Also, as with Fostoria, the wares they produced from the 1920s onward are probably better known than many of its earlier lines to collectors today.

Fig. 11-6 A water set in Heisey's *Beaded Swag* pattern, each piece trimmed in gold.

Fig. 11-7 A handsome *Prince of Wales Plumes* tankard pitcher with gold trim.

In the early years some of Heisey's output was sold to the Oriental Glass Company of Pittsburgh, which was a decorating firm only. Oriental then turned around and sold the decorated wares itself. However, Heisey also began to sell its own Oriental-decorated wares, and these decorated patterns are very collectible today.

Most of Heisey's early patterns were typical of the geometric and imitation cut-glass lines being produced by many glasshouses. A large percentage of Heisey lines were made in clear glass and decorated with gold or ruby staining or enameled decoration. However, a couple like *Bead Swag* (or *Beaded Swag*; circa 1898–1900) and the ornate *Locket on Chain* (circa 1896), do show up in colors like green, vaseline, milk glass, or with overall ruby staining. The *Winged Scroll* pattern (circa 1898–1900) also was made in emerald green and canary yellow, and this pattern, and a few others, later were produced by Heisey in custard glass. The *Ring Band* pattern by Heisey was produced almost exclusively in custard.

There is quite a selection of early Heisey patterns in the imitation cut-glass vein, and some popular ones to look for are *Beaded Panel and Sunburst* (no. 1235, 1898), *Cut Block* (no. 1200, 1896), *Pineapple and Fan* (no. 1255, circa 1898), and *Prince of Wales Plumes* (no. 335, 1902).

A couple of very plain patterns from Heisey prefigure its switch, after about 1900, to a wide selection of simple, paneled colonial-style patterns. *Plain Band* (no. 1225, 1898) and *Touraine* (no. 337, circa 1902) are both very plain with rounded forms. Heisey became a major early producer of colonial-revival patterns before World War I. *Peerless* (no. 300 *Colonial*, 1898) and *Continential* (no. 339, 1903–1944) were early entries in this field, followed by numerous other lines.

Heisey also began bringing out some rather modernistic glass patterns just before World War I. A pattern today called *Quator* was its no. 355. Featuring heavy, diamond-shaped bodies with angled handles, it was made from 1913 to about 1935. *Yeoman* (no. 1184) was another simple, modern-looking line made by Heisey from 1913 to 1957.

In a few years, as pattern-glass collecting became an important hobby, Heisey also introduced some patterns based on or adapted from early American pressed glass. *Old Sandwich* (no. 1404) and *Ipswich* (no. 1405), both made for a few years in the early 1930s and again from 1951 to 1953, are examples of these popular revivals.

In the 1920s Heisey introduced a wide variety of new and modern lines and continued some of the popular older ones. That was also the decade when colored glass became a major emphasis of its production.

Heisey is also one of the few American glass firms that began to press a company trademark into many of its patterns. Beginning about 1900, the famous "H" in a diamond mark was pressed into many, but not all, Heisey pieces. Note, however, that a few years ago some modern imported wares, most often covered animal dishes of a type never made by Heisey, came out with a faked Heisey diamond mark. Whereas the original Heisey diamond is tall and fairly narrow with a capital *H*, this fake mark has the fat diamond running sideways with a rather squatty, poorly done capital *H*. After seeing the original mark, one should not be fooled by these faked marks. Today the diamond *H* mark is registered and can no longer be copied by fakers.

Fig. 11-8 Simple panels highlight Heisey's *Colonial* pattern. This pitcher and matching champagne tumblers feature engraved rims.

Fig. 11-9 A lovely covered butter dish in Heisey's *Continental* pattern.

Imperial Glass Company, Bellaire, Ohio (1901–1985)

Imperial was established in 1901 in Bellaire, Ohio, right across the Ohio River from Wheeling, West Virginia, and remained in that city for its entire life.

The company's earliest production was of general clear utilitarian ware, but soon it began producing a wide range of imitation cut-glass designs. About 1910 it began decorating its wares with the popular carnival glass iridescent finish.

In 1911 Imperial registered a pressed trademark, Nucut, which was surrounded by a banner and used to mark its large range of cut-style pressed patterns. Nucut wares were not given names but only numerical designations, so they pretty much are lumped together by collectors today. The company eventually produced a couple of simple, colonial-style lines today known as *Beaded Band and*

137

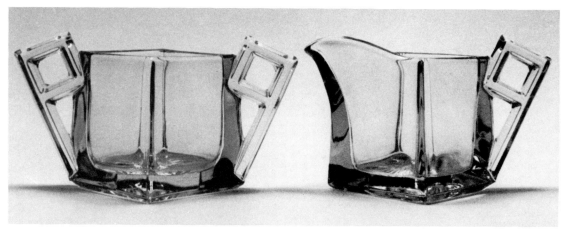

Fig. 11-10 The modernistic trend in glass design is highlighted by Heisey's *Quator* pattern, which came out in 1913.

Fig. 11-11 Heisey's "Diamond H" trademark in the bottom of the punch cup. One side of the diamond was not molded well, and the top of the *H* is very weak in this example.

Fig. 11-12 A cut imitation pattern nappy (handled dish) put out by Imperial. It is 5½" in diameter and marked in the center with its Nucut trademark.

Panel and *Colonial.* These and the Nucut patterns continued to be produced right through the 1920s.

Imperial really became better known for some of its innovative wares of the 1920s. Its *Free Hand* line of blown art glass was designed to rival the works of makers like Tiffany and Steuben, and it is scarce and quite costly today. After carnival glass faded in popularity, Imperial brought out its more lightly iridized *Imperial Jewels* line, and in 1921 it registered the Nuart trademark for a similar line of pastel, iridized glassware.

From the 1920s on Imperial became known for a wide range of modern tableware in pressed and mold-blown patterns and fine and delicate cuttings. It also revived and adapted early American glass with patterns like *Early American Hobnail* and *Cape Cod,* and it also did quite a bit with late-Victorian-style designs in colored and milk glass. One of its most popular and long-lived patterns, *Candlewick,* featuring a simple border of small knobs around the edges, was introduced in 1936 and was still being made when the factory closed in 1985.

In addition to its Nucut and Nuart markings, Imperial also introduced in 1914 another marking found on many pieces: a cross with the word "Imperial" divided into segments between the arms of the cross so it reads IM/PE/RI/AL. This marking was superceded in 1951 by the overlapped initials "IG" found on many pieces.

Imperial is another great American glasshouse, now gone, that left a rich heritage of collectible pressed and decorative glass.

McKee Glass Company, Jeannette, Pennsylvania (1903–1951)

The McKee Glass Company succeeded the M'Kee and Brothers Glass Company founded in Pittsburgh in the 1850s. It had moved to Jeannette, Pennsylvania, in 1889 and changed its name at the time. The company joined the National Glass Company in 1899 but went independent again in 1903, remaining a major glass producer until its closing in 1951.

After the turn of the century, McKee continued to produce a number of its older patterns, many of which featured geometric or imitation cut designs. Some of these patterns include *Rainbow, Aldine, Champion, Heart Band, Crescent, Eureka, Britannic, Prize, Sunbeam, Lenox,* and *Harvard.* Some new lines also were introduced after 1900. These include the unique *Gothic* line, circa 1904, more often called *Spearpoint Band,* which features bold, simple Gothic arches. Also new was *Virginia* (introduced in 1912), no relation to the U.S. Glass States series.

The major innovation in McKee ware came with the introduction of its extensive Pres-cut line beginning in 1901. The line consisted of twenty-two specific, named patterns that were available in a variety of pieces, although a few other patterns of bowls and punch sets also were included. This series is unique because each piece in each pattern carries the pressed Pres-cut trademark, usually found on the inside of the bottom. These prominent markings make it easy for today's collector to recognize an early McKee piece.

Most Pres-cut patterns were ornate imitation cut-glass designs, and most of these had a name ending in the suffix "tec." Thus, we have the 1890s *Aztec* pattern included in the Pres-cut line after 1901, followed by *Toltec* and *Nortec* (1903). The series was introduced over a period of years until the line was complete in 1915, but the patterns were not introduced in alphabetical order.

Other cut-style Pres-cut patterns include: *Bontec, Doltec, Fentec, Glentec, Martec, Plytec, Plutec, Quintec, Rotec, Sextec, Startec, Valtec,*

Fig. 11-13 A McKee *Fentec* oblong dish. It is marked in the center with McKee's early Pres-cut trademark.

Fig. 11-14 A footed sherbet in McKee's *Rock Crystal* pattern.

Wiltec, and *Yutec.* In addition to these, the *Sunburst* pattern was an ornate cut imitation design in the Pres-cut series.

Two Pres-cut patterns were designed to imitate finely engraved glass with floral motifs. *Puritan* features pairs of large daisylike flowers with leaf scrolls encircling the bodies of pieces, while the similar *Rock Crystal* pattern features more delicately defined pairs of blossoms terminating in fine leafy scrolls that run up the sides of pieces. At first glance, pieces of Rock Crystal resemble blown glass with hand-engraved designs, but it is a pressed pattern. Rock Crystal is also distinctive in that it is one of the few patterns of this era offered in a selection of solid colors in addition to clear. These colors included green, amber, rose pink, and ruby red. Colored examples of this line are greatly in demand today.

In sharp contrast to the cut imitation lines, McKee also followed the growing trend toward simple colonial designs and, in fact, had a series of patterns that it called Colonial. The company numbered these from no. 21 to no. 26 with additional no. 75 and no. 99 patterns also. Each of these Colonial patterns featured a simple, paneled design, although no. 75 also featured a honeycomb design of diamonds around the bases of pieces.

Nearly all Pres-cut patterns were produced right through the 1920s, and some even beyond, but after 1930 the items no longer carried the Pres-cut trademark. Rock Crystal and Fentec, in fact, were in the McKee line-up as late as 1942. Also, the Hocking Glass Company marketed a line of glass using the Pres-Cut trade name after McKee let the trademark lapse.

Fairly recently a number of Pres-cut pieces have been reproduced, but they do not carry the impressed markings. These newer pieces include an Aztec punch set and twenty-one-and-a-half-inch-diameter sandwich server; a Colonial eight-and-a-half-inch-diameter bowl and five-ounce punch cup; a Fentec six-quart punch bowl, undertray, and five-ounce cups; a *Sunburst* punch set with eight-and-a-half-inch-diameter bowl and five-ounce cups; a Rock Crystal ten-inch-diameter bowl; and several pieces of Fentec marketed as an early American party service or "chip" set. Seven various small bowls are in that group.

After McKee went out of business the Indiana Glass Company of Dunkirk, Indiana, acquired its Rock Crystal molds, but it is not believed to have reissued any pieces in this pattern.

Beginning in 1916 McKee introduced a new series of cut-glass patterns in a line it called *Innovation*. Each pattern was given a numerical code beginning with no. 410, and various numbers and specific pattern names were included until a total of twenty-four patterns was issued by 1920.

More modernistic patterns began to appear in McKee's line in the 1920s as new shapes and colors became popular. Delicate floral cutting decorated many of its products during this period.

The 1930s saw McKee continue to produce novelties, such as the famous *Bottoms-Up* beer

Fig. 11-15 Four goblets made by four different companies early in this century. Left to right are Heisey's *Colonial*, Duncan's *Button Arches*, McKee's colonial-style *Fern Garland*, and Westmoreland's *Wellington* with light gold trim.

stein, whisky jigger, and beverage cup, with their nude figure, and it even brought out an art line called *Louvre* ware in 1937, its version of the expensive Lalique and Verlys frosted glass pieces. Art Deco novelties also appeared during the 1930s, and its handsome *Dance Lumiere* lamp, featuring a semi-nude woman, is an expensive piece when found today.

As early as 1917 McKee started to produce a more durable type of kitchen glassware when it introduced its *Glasbake* line of heat-resistant glassware. A children's set was made in this line in 1924. Throughout the 1930s and 1940s McKee continued to be a leading producer of durable and attractive glassware for kitchen use. All of these wares, especially pieces marked with the company's "McK" in a circle mark, introduced in 1935, are collectible. Glasbake wares also carried this trademark pressed in the glass, and later a Range-tec line of stove-top ware was brought out in the 1940s and carried that trade name pressed in.

That many McKee patterns are so well marked certainly has added to their appeal among today's collectors. McKee was actually one of the first American glassmakers to permanently mark some of its pressed wares when it pressed a script McKee logo into some of its milk glass animal dishes in the third quarter of the nineteenth century. Only those few pieces were so marked, however, and none of its early tableware patterns carried a marking until the Pres-cut line appeared.

Because of its long and distinguished history in glass production, McKee offers unique opportunities for collectors of American pressed glass. Whether one prefers early flint glass patterns, glittering Victorian imitation cut-glass designs, or simple and sturdy kitchenware, there is a McKee glass to love.

New Martinsville Glass Manufacturing Company (Viking Glass Company/Dalzell-Viking), New Martinsville, West Virginia (circa 1901–present)

Incorporated in 1900, the glass factory first opened in 1901, producing a line of bar ware and some as yet unidentified pressed lines. In its early years it did introduce a unique line of mold-blown

art glass that it called *Muranese*. It was a cased (layered) glass with a gold inner layer and an outer layer of differing light hues. Some pieces resemble the earlier *Peach Blow* art glass, and some collectors started referring to it as *New Martinsville Peach Blow,* but the Muranese title is more appropriate.

Some of their interesting pressed lines include *Carnation* (no. 88), issued in 1906, which features a large flower and leaf design, and *Leaf and Star* (no. 711), which came out in 1909 and features a very stylized bold scrolled leaf and star design. A very charming pattern called *Heart in Sand* (no. 724, 1915, aka *Heart and Sand*), has a band of simple, large hearts around the body of pieces, raised against a finely stippled background resembling fine sand. This line is especially striking when the hearts have been ruby-stained, as they sometimes were. Another pattern featuring a finely stippled background is *Lorraine* (no. 722), which has plain stippled bodies with bands of a fret design around the top and base of each item.

New Martinsville also joined the flood of geometric and imitation cut-glass patterns hitting the market at the turn of the century. Its *Klear-Kut* pattern (no. 705) came out in 1906. Other cut-type patterns followed such as *Horseshoe Daisy* (no. 717, 1912), *Old Glory* (no. 719, 1913), *Royal* (no. 556), *Elite, Star in Bull's Eye, Floral Oval,* and others.

Simple colonial-revival patterns were also part of New Martinsville's production. Simple paneled patterns include *Lenior* (no. 75), sometimes misspelled "Lenoir." It was released in late 1910. Other patterns are *Colonial Line* (no. 728), *Placid* (no. 712), *Plain Colonial* (no. 725), *Monitor* (no. 149), *Chateau* (no. 714), *Florene* (no. 720), and *Old Colony* (no. 97), which was out by 1906.

Although production of some of these patterns continued for some time, by the 1920s New Martinsville was getting into more modern designs. New shapes and forms for the dining table, as well as for the boudoir dressing table, were produced in new pastel shades and sometimes with bright Art Deco color decoration.

After going through receivership in the late 1930s, new management took over in 1944 and renamed the factory the Viking Glass Company. This firm continued the fine tradition of New Martinsville glass, and this tradition continues to the present. The firm became the Dalzell-Viking Glass Company a few years ago.

The United States Glass Company (1891–1962)

A number of the important pressed patterns produced by this glass combine in the 1890s, most notably its States series, have been covered. In the late 1890s the company consolidated its holdings and closed some of its smaller, less-profitable factories. It continued producing its old stand-by lines but also introduced some interesting patterns, many of which feature cut imitation designs. *Manhattan*, with its band of bull's eyes above fine ribbing, came out in 1902, and *Rising Sun*, with its cut starburst design, arrived in 1908. Other related patterns include *Pattee Cross* (1909), *Bull's-eye and Fan* (1905, aka *Daisy in Oval Panels*), *Victoria* (1907, aka *Daisy and Scroll*), *Star-in-Bullseye* (1905), and *Newport* (1909, aka *Bull's-eye and Daisy*).

The colonials also became an important part of U.S. Glass production after 1900. Several patterns are simple paneled lines very similar to what Heisey, McKee, and other competitors were issuing. Its *Fort Pitt* pattern came out in 1910, while *Colonis* arrived in 1913, followed by *Georgian* (not a Honeycomb design) in 1915, and *Niagara* in 1919. The *Sheraton* pattern has a narrow band of Greek key design around the tops of the simple, paneled bodies. The unique *Reverse 44* pattern, which they called *Athenia*, came out about 1912 and featured a wide band of looping angular lines around the top above the paneled body. The loops in this upper band remind one somewhat of two numeral fours back to back, hence the Reverse 44 name. This pattern, by the way, is one of its few early lines to carry the pressed *USG* logo mark on some pieces.

After 1910 three new factories—in Tiffin, Ohio; Gas City, Indiana; and Glassport, Pennsylvania—were built by U.S. Glass. These, along with the Pittsburgh plant, carried on most of the company's output after that time. As with most other major glass factories of the time, U.S. Glass produced more modern styles beginning in the 1920s, including fine tableware and less-expensive kitchenware. In 1938 the main company offices moved to Tiffin, Ohio, and by 1951 only the Tiffin plant was left

Fig. 11-16 Four U.S. Glass Company goblets in early twentieth-century patterns. Left to right are decorated *Pattee Cross, Newport* (aka *Bull's-Eye and Daisy*) with stained "eyes," *Colonial* with enameled blossoms, and *Reverse 44* with shiny trim.

operating. Old Duncan and Miller Glass molds were acquired in 1955 and many of their patterns reissued. In 1962 the company became the Tiffin Art Glass Company, which pretty much marked the end of the U.S. Glass era. The plant went through various ownerships in the following years but was dismantled completely by 1985. This was a sad end to a proud and prolific glass-pressing heritage.

Westmoreland Specialty Company (Westmoreland Glass Company), Grapeville, Pennsylvania (1889–1985)

The Westmoreland Specialty Company opened in 1889 in East Liverpool, Ohio, and there produced some novelty items and tableware. In 1890 it relocated to a new plant in Grapeville, Pennsylvania, where it remained for the rest of its time.

In addition to producing milk glass pieces and a variety of glass whimsies, it made a number of tableware lines. Westmoreland made the *Shell and Jewel* pattern in the 1890s (they called it their *Victor* pattern), but the same design was made by Fostoria (its no. 618) and it also is attributed to glass factories in Canada. Apparently Westmoreland liked to copy other popular patterns by other makers, because in 1896 it introduced its *Sterling* pattern, a cut imitation design very similar to the *Shoshone* pattern (originally the U.S. Glass Company's Victor line). The *Westmoreland* no. 15 pattern (earlier *Pioneer's* no. 15) is a copy of the well-known *Cut Log* pattern, but the Westmoreland design does not have the fine serrations between each log found on Cut Log pieces. Another pattern, *Tweed,* today is referred to as *Late Rosette,* and it is a look-alike to the *Roman Rosette* pattern.

In addition to these copy-cat lines, Westmoreland introduced some popular patterns of its own. *Puritan,* circa 1895, is usually called *Beaded Swirl* (see Fig. 11-4) today, and *Elite* is most often listed as *Pillow and Sunburst* (circa 1897).

After the turn of the century Westmoreland continued to produce many of its earlier designs and introduced some new ones. Geometric and imitation cut-glass motifs were most common and included patterns like *Columned Thumbprints* (no. 185, circa 1903) *High Hob* (no. 2550, circa 1912) and *Wellington* (no. 300, circa 1903). In a plain colonial style Westmoreland had its *Paul Revere* pattern (1912) featuring wide, shaped panels, as well as two other simple colonial patterns, no. 1700 and no. 1776.

In the 1920s Westmoreland began producing more modernistic lines and introduced many with colors popular in that decade. In 1925 the company changed its name to the Westmoreland Glass Company and moved ahead with many new patterns. It was not long, however, before it began to look backward in time for pattern inspiration, and the *English Hobnail* pattern, somewhat resembling the early *Diamond Point* pattern, arrived in 1924 and became a popular Depression-era line. By the late 1920s it also had introduced reproduction dolphin-based candlesticks and bowls, and reproductions of early flint-era table lamps were part of its line from the late 1920s through the 1940s. *Princess Feather,* similar to other patterns by other companies, was based on early lacy glass designs, and this line stayed in production for several decades. Westmoreland also became a major producer of milk glass. Many of its pieces and patterns closely resemble Victorian glassware and can confuse the unwary. In its later years the firm began marking its glass with a "W" or "WG" logo, which will help alleviate some confusion, but a lot of unmarked Westmoreland milk glass is still out there. It is collectible in its own right, but do not mistake it for Victorian wares.

Like so many of America's great glasshouses, Westmoreland was forced to close; 1985 marked the demise of this nearly century-old concern. However, some of its molds apparently have gone to still-operating companies, so some pieces may be still in production.

Additional Collectible Patterns

Although the foregoing discussion covered the major American glass factories that operated early in this century, others produced pressed glass tableware. These are listed here. Some of these lesser-known plants also produced some very collectible lines of pattern glass listed and described here.

Fig. 11-17 A popular pattern from the early twentieth-century is *Bird and Strawberry*. On the left is a tumbler decorated with blue and red, while on the right is a plain, clear goblet in the same line.

Bird and Strawberry *Bird and Strawberry,* sometimes called *Blue Bird,* was made by the Indiana Glass Company of Dunkirk, Indiana, starting circa 1914. The body of each piece features large birds flying among strawberry vines, and there is a band of cane design around the top and bottom edges of many pieces. The pattern was made in clear but is most collectible when found with the birds stained blue and the strawberries stained red. These colored examples generally sell for twice as much as the plain pieces. A limited selection of pieces was made in this pattern, and some items, like the goblet, water pitcher, and covered compote, can bring $150 to $250 in clear and $200 to $350 in color. Many of the smaller, more common items will be in the $25 to $50 range in clear and $40 to $150 in color.

Thus far the flat-based celery vase and a high-pedestal covered compote have been reproduced.

Dew and Raindrop Another small company, Kokomo Glass Manufacturing Company (later the D. C. Jenkins Glass Company) of Kokomo, Indiana, produced a couple of collectible patterns.

Dew and Raindrop was its no. 50 line introduced about 1901. It features a band of large, raised ovals (raindrops) around the center of each piece with bands of tiny knobs (dew) above and below this band. A similar line also was brought out by the

Indiana Glass Company around the same period. Most pieces in *Dew and Raindrop* were clear, but rare examples may be found with ruby staining on the large ovals and rims.

This limited line was made in only about fifteen pieces, but it was popular enough with collectors to attract reproducers. A clear wine glass came out around the 1930s, and later a cordial glass (in amber, blue, or clear with a light ruby rim) and a sherbet cup and goblet also have been made. The new pieces are heavier than the old ones, and the dewdrop design is not as fine as on the originals. Still, one must take care when buying these pieces.

Paneled Grape *Paneled Grape* is another Kokomo pattern that is popular with collectors and that arrived on the scene circa 1904. The heavy paneled sides of pieces feature raised grapevines running up and down, and the paneled bowls of the goblets and wine glasses give them a distinctive appearance.

The line was produced in a range of only about thirty pieces, and sadly for collectors, some seventeen items have been widely reproduced. The original glass was made in clear only, but reproductions, beginning in the 1930s, came out in clear and several colors. The detailing on the leaves is not good on some of the reproductions, but it takes an experienced eye to sort the new from the old.

Paneled Thistle *Paneled Thistle* is a widely available pattern originally made by the short-lived J. B. Higbee Company of Bridgeville, Pennsylvania, as well as the Jefferson Glass Company of Toronto, Canada, which made a slight variant. The pattern first came out circa 1910 and must have been a good seller, judging by what still is available today. The body of each piece is divided into panels by heavy ribs, and each panel contains a stylized thistle sprig alternating with a panel featuring a starburst design. Most pieces were made in clear, and anything with color trim is rare.

Higbee was another early-twentieth-century glass company that began pressing its pieces with a trademark, and they used a small bee with the capital letters "H-I-G" spelled out across its back.

Sadly, the original popularity of the pattern and its appeal to glass collectors has lead to a plethora of reproductions since the early 1950s. Over thirty pieces have been reproduced or adapted from the original design, so collectors must use great caution

Fig. 11-18 Three popular patterns made after 1900. Left to right are goblets in the *Manhattan* pattern by U.S. Glass, and *Dew and Raindrop* and *Paneled Grape* by the Kokomo Glass Manufacturing Company.

Fig. 11-19 A *Paneled Thistle* wine glass with a flared rim. Another version of this pattern has pieces with straight edges.

when inspecting this pattern. To add to the problem, a look-alike bee trademark also has been put on some of the reproductions, so the marking is no guarantee of authenticity.

Higbee also continued production of the earlier Bryce, Higbee and Company *Fleur-de-Lis* or *Arched Fleur-de-Lis* pattern, but fortunately that pattern has not been reproduced.

S-Repeat *S-Repeat,* a unique pattern popular early in the century, is noteworthy because it was introduced by glassmaking great Harry Northwood. His Indiana, Pennsylvania, plant brought out S-Repeat about 1900, while he was associated with the National Glass Company (which he shortly left), and production probably was continued at that site when the Dugan glass firm took it over.

On this particular Northwood line, the pieces have long S scrolls in tight repeating formation, and it was made in several colors including light and dark purple, pale apple green, yellow green, light and sapphire blue, and, of course, clear. Sometimes the scrolls were highlighted with gilt trim.

S-Repeat was made in a nice range of pieces, with some items like the cruet set on matching tray (with cruet, salt and pepper shakers, and toothpick

145

holder) especially desirable. Unfortunately, this pattern has been reproduced. Watch out for the goblet, wine glass, cruet, and toothpick holder. They are not easy to distinguish from the old pieces and were remade in several colors, including some not used originally. This is a pattern worth collecting, but proceed with care.

As one can see, the pressed glass of the early twentieth century was quite often just a carry-over of patterns popular in previous years. There is a wide variety of styles to choose from, and the many colonial-style and cut imitation patterns offer myriad collecting opportunities for the beginning collector.

Other American Glass Companies Founded Circa 1900

Consolidated Lamp and Glass Company, Coraopolis, Pennsylvania (1894–1967)

Federal Glass Company, Columbus, Ohio (1901–1980)

Hazel-Atlas Glass Company, Wheeling, West Virginia (1902–present)

Hocking Glass Company (Anchor-Hocking Glass Corporation), Lancaster, Ohio (1905–present)

Indiana Glass Company, Dunkirk, Indiana (1907–present)

J. B. Higbee Glass Company, Bridgeville, Pennsylvania (1907–1918)

Jeannette Glass Company, Jeannette, Pennsylvania (circa 1900–present)

Kokomo Glass Manufacturing Company (D. C. Jenkins Glass Company), Kokomo, Indiana (1900–circa 1945)

L. E. Smith Company, Mount Pleasant, Pennsylvania (1907–present)

MacBeth-Evans Glass Company, Charleroi, Pennsylvania (1899–1936)

National Glass Company, Pittsburgh, Pennsylvania (1899–1904)

Paden City Glass Manufacturing Company, New Martinsville, West Virginia (circa 1901–present)

Tiffin Glass Company (formerly U.S. Glass, now part of Towle Sterling) Tiffin, Ohio (circa 1900–present)

Wheaton Glass Company, Millville, New Jersey (1888–present)

Desirability and Values

In nearly all cases patterns issued after 1900 and before 1915 fall into the same value ranges as the patterns of the preceding decade. There are so many patterns that look alike, especially the imitation cut and simple colonial types, that the values for most of them stay very close. Exceptions are some of the patterns marked by Heisey or with the McKee Pres-cut logo, which are a bit more in demand.

As with earlier pattern glass, rare pieces and unusual colors or colored trim raises the price, and patterns like Bird and Strawberry and S-Repeat are always in strong demand in color. Most pieces in a great many of the other patterns noted are available in clear for under $50, and even scarce pieces like pitchers, cruets, or syrup jugs often can be found for well under $100. For a piece in good condition in color or with color trim or ruby staining, values can jump from about 20 to 50 percent or more, depending on the popularity of the pattern and the relative rarity of the piece.

Fig. 11-20 Because of the very worn gold on its rim, this *Massachusetts* pattern mug might be a little less desirable to some collectors.

There are many, many good buys available in the look-alike patterns, since most people do not take the time to sort out exactly which company made which line. Even ruby-stained souvenir items, especially toothpick holders and small creamers, can be found for reasonable amounts and make a fascinating collection. Remember that pieces with worn or badly scratched ruby or amber staining should be priced accordingly and should not bring nearly as much as similar pieces in top condition.

Whether one prefers the busy cut-style patterns or the simple paneled colonial lines, one can have lots of fun collecting without spending a lot of money. Collectors can mix and match patterns or focus on one special favorite; the opportunities are endless. Remember, all these patterns will soon be true antiques.

Old Versus New

As mentioned earlier, the vast majority of pressed turn-of-the-century tableware patterns have not been reproduced. There are just too many to be bothered with.

However, a number of especially collectible designs have had one or more pieces reproduced in recent years. Some of these troublesome pieces were discussed earlier but the most copied lines and pieces are listed below for easy reference.

Atlanta (Fostoria's): Beware: a goblet.

Aztec: Beware: a punch set and twenty-one-and-a-half-inch-diameter sandwich server without the Pres-cut mark. Other unmarked items have been marketed as the *Whirling Star* line.

Beaded Swag: Beware: a toothpick holder in milk glass in the 1991 Mosser Glass Company catalog.

Bird and Strawberry: Beware: flat-bottomed celery vase in blue and a tall-pedestal covered compote in pale green.

Dew and Raindrop: Beware: a goblet, sherbet cup, and wine glass in clear and a cordial in several colors.

Fentec: Beware: six-quart punch bowl, undertray, and five-ounce cups and a "chip" set, which includes a pickle dish, bonbon dish, nappy, celery dish, olive dish, nut bowl, and eight-inch-diameter bowl.

Inverted Strawberry: Beware: cruet, water pitcher, plate, toothpick holder, and tumbler in a look-alike pattern made in clear, purple, emerald green with gold and clear with an iridescent carnival finish. Also, toy punch sets and cake stands are presently available in several colors.

Inverted Thistle: Beware: A look-alike pattern by Mosser Glass is offered currently with a pitcher, tumbler, open sugar bowl, creamer, and covered butter dish. They are available in clear, pink, ruby red, and emerald green with gold trim.

Manhattan: Beware: Look-alike patterns issued by Anchor-Hocking and Tiffin Glass in the early 1950s. Some pieces may be hard to distinguish from the old.

McKee's Colonial: Beware: eight-and-a-half-inch-diameter bowl and five-ounce punch cups.

Paneled Grape: Beware: Numerous reproductions by several companies since the 1930s. Pieces include: twelve-inch-diameter crimped bowl, butter dish, celery vase, cordial, four-inch-diameter tall-pedestal covered compote, larger tall-pedestal covered compote, creamer, goblet, plates in several sizes, water pitcher, flat sauce dish, spoon holder, sugar bowl with cover, two-handled open sugar bowl, footed sauce dish, sherbet dish, and wine glass. Most of these were made in various colors as well as clear. Remember: only clear pieces were made originally.

Paneled Thistle: Beware: five-and-a-half-inch-diameter flat shallow bowl; seven-and-a-half-inch diameter deep flat-bottomed bowl; master berry bowl; open-footed bowl; butter dish; tall-pedestal six-inch-diameter covered compote; tall-pedestal six-inch-diameter open compote; champagne glass; creamer; goblet (two styles); square, flattened, covered honey dish; eight-inch-long flat pickle dish; seven-inch-diameter, seven-and-a-half-inch-diameter, eight-inch-diameter, and ten-inch-diameter round plates; seven-inch-wide and seven-and-a-half-inch-wide square plates; master salt dip; flat sauce dish; eight-inch-long relish tray; tall salt shaker; handled spooner; small covered sugar bowl; open-handled sugar bowl; sugar shaker; toothpick holder; water pitcher; tumbler; and wine glass.

Rock Crystal: Beware: ten-inch-diameter bowl.

S-Repeat: Beware: goblet, wine glass, cruet, and toothpick holder.

Wedding Bells: Beware: a look-alike covered sugar bowl in a bluish purple color.

Part V
Some Special Pressed Glass and Glassmakers

CHAPTER 12

Commemorative, Novelty, and Souvenir Pressed Glass

The 1876 Centennial Exhibition

The 1876 Centennial Exhibition in Philadelphia is the first major American event commemorated with a wide range of pressed-glass pieces. In fact, this fair really marks the beginning of Victorian production of such souvenir and commemorative glassware. A few special events and noteworthy people were the subjects of earlier glass cup plates and flasks, but not until the centennial year of 1876 did America's glass industry have the technical skills and widespread markets to produce a large selection of such glass knickknacks.

Several Centennial tableware patterns brought out at the time of the centennial were already discussed; some important souvenir pieces still available to collect are mentioned below.

Today when we think of Centennial Exhibition glass souvenir items, the firm of Gillinder and Sons of Philadelphia first comes to mind. It actually had a glass furnace set up right on the fairgrounds and turned out a good selection of small pieces for sale there. Most of the pieces have the company's name impressed right on the base. A brief run-down of some of the pieces includes: a figural lion paperweight made in milk glass or frosted clear, with either a full-figure reclining lion or just a lion's head; an oval glass paperweight showing the Women's

Pavilion; a round paperweight with the bust of George Washington impressed in the base; a figural Memorial Hall paperweight showing that building in three dimensions; a figural toothpick holder, one of the earliest made in any material, with a figural chick standing beside an upturned half eggshell with the words ''Just Out'' impressed on the oval base in front; a frosted or clear glass hand-shaped vase with a hand holding a fanned-out sheaf of wheat; a model of a woman's high-heeled slipper with a bow on the front, made in clear or frosted glass and six inches in length. Various bust statuettes also were made of famous people such as George Washington. An oblong bread tray called the ''Constitution tray'' features an eagle in the center holding a long banner in its beak with the words ''Liberty And Freedom 1776.'' The eagle stands on a rectangular block impressed ''Constitution of the United States,'' and around the border is the motto ''Give Us This Day—Our Daily Bread.''

Although Gillinder pieces are the best known, several other glass companies also made interesting centennial items.

Atterbury and Company of Pittsburgh had several nice glass souvenirs of the centennial. It is best known for its figural milk glass animal dishes and a

Fig. 12-1 A notable Gillinder souvenir from 1876 is this clear woman's slipper. It also can be found with a frosted finish. It is marked "Gillinder—Centennial" inside the base.

Fig. 12-2 The *Centennial Drape* goblet with a band around the middle reading "Centennial 1876."

wide variety of lamps made some years later, but for the centennial it made the "Continental Hall" bread tray in clear. It features that building in the center and the "Give Us This Day . . ." motto around the edge. The distinctive handles are human hands clutching barbells.

The Atterbury "Three Graces" round platter also came out at the time of the centennial. Also known as the "Faith, Hope and Charity" plate, it features that wording around the rim and the figures of three graceful muses in the center. In its lamp line is a "Goddess of Liberty" lamp that features a portrait bust of Lady Liberty as the base below a rounded font.

The Central Glass Company of Wheeling, West Virginia, also made several interesting pieces for the centennial. A three-inch-high salt shaker in the shape of the Liberty Bell has "1776—Liberty—1876" impressed on the base. It also made a tall beer mug and ale glass in clear, each of which features a large star in the center of each side. One star has "1776" in the middle, the other "1876."

Fig. 12-3 A hanging match holder probably representing the Goddess of Liberty. It was referred to earlier as "Jenny Lind," which does not really seem appropriate today.

Bryce, Higbee and Company of Pittsburgh (later J. B. Higbee) joined in with its "Old State-house—Philadelphia" round tray, which features Independence Hall in the center.

Other noteworthy commemoratives were made by other firms and include the *Centennial Drape* goblet with "Centennial—1876" embossed in the swagged central band. A figural Independence Hall bank is in the shape of that building, made in clear and rare milk glass. Impressed on it is "Bank of Independence Hall—1776–1876." An unusual piece is a glass model of Plymouth Rock in clear, marked "Inkstand Co.—Prov. R.I.—Pilgrim Rock Trade Mrk. 1876" on the bottom.

A hanging match holder designed as the bust portrait of the Goddess of Liberty is marked on the back with an 1876 patent date. Also keep your eyes open for a small hand-shaped vase or toothpick holder that shows an arm holding a flaming torch, obviously based on the arm of the Statue of Liberty displayed at the exposition.

The so-called Bunker Hill oval platter features the Bunker Hill Monument in the center with the names of American Revolution heroes around the outer edge ("Prescott—1776—Stark" and "Warner—1876—Putney") on an inner border are the words "The Heroes of Bunker Hill—The Spirit of Seventy-Six."

Political Commemoratives

Even though some lacy glass cup plates were produced to commemorate the 1840 presidential election, no political items were made in pressed glass until nearly forty years later. By the 1870s a few such souvenirs were made, with many more to follow during later presidential campaigns. Some of these special pieces are mentioned here, arranged chronologically.

1872 A simple barrel-shaped goblet was made for this election, with one version featuring a bust portrait of Republican candidate Ulysses S. Grant on one side and his running mate, Henry Wilson, on the other. A matching goblet features the portraits of the Democratic candidates, Horace Greeley and B. G. Brown.

1880 Republican James A. Garfield was the winning candidate in this election, and there is a glass mug with his portrait on one side and a comical scene of a raccoon (the Republican emblem then) on the other. The names "Garfield" and "Arthur" (for Vice-President Chester Arthur) appear on the handle.

1881 Many more glass commemoratives came out in 1881 when President Garfield was shot by an assassin. He lingered for several months, but after his death numerous glass memorials were produced, including a reworked version of the above-described mug with Garfield's portrait on one side

and a drapery swag around his birth and death dates. A tumbler and cup plate were also produced with Garfield's likeness in the base.

A number of memorial plates were made, including one by Campbell, Jones and Company with the word "Memorial" in the border and Garfield's portrait in the center. The *Garfield Drape* tableware pattern also had a plate with a portrait of the slain president in the middle and "We Mourn Our Nation's Loss" around the border. An oval platter known as the "Three Presidents" platter features bust portraits of Garfield, Washington, and Lincoln in the middle below the words "In Remembrance." The "Martyr's" platter is also oval with loop end handles, and it features bust portraits of Lincoln and Garfield in the center above a spread-winged eagle and the words "Our Country's Martyrs." There is also a Martyr's glass mug with busts of Lincoln and Garfield on the sides.

1884 The beautiful *Classic* pattern plates that feature bust portraits of each of the four 1884 candidates were discussed earlier. In addition, there is a nicely produced rectangular handled tray that has a wide ivy leaf band around the central reserve, which features bust portraits of Democrats Grover Cleveland and Thomas A. Hendricks; a matching tray features their opponents James G. Blaine and John A. Logan. A round plate features a bust of Cleveland in the center and the word "REFORM" set off in the finely beaded wide border.

1885 This was not an election year, but the year former president and general Ulysses S. Grant died of cancer. He was mourned widely at the time, and several memorial pieces came out in glass to honor him.

Campbell, Jones and Company issued a "Memorial" plate similar in design to the one it made for Garfield in 1881. Another memorial plate has the general's bust in the center and a wide border of overlapping maple leaves overprinted with the wording "Let Us Have Peace—U. S. Grant." It was made in several colors. A square plate with cut corners made by Bryce, Higbee and Company is called the "Patriot and Soldier" plate, because it has the words "The Patriot and Soldier" above and "Gen. Ulysses S. Grant" below a profile portrait of Grant, all inside patterned borders.

1892 Not too many pressed items were made for this election. There is a model of a top hat called the "Cleveland Hat," which has the words "The Same Old Hat" on one side and "He's All Right" on the other.

1896 In contrast to 1892, quite a number of glass commemoratives promoted the candidates for this hotly contested election.

Republican William McKinley supported the gold standard and protective import tariffs, while the young and charismatic William Jennings Bryan, a populist Democrat, supported the free coinage of silver and relaxed tariffs.

A rectangular platter with rounded corners made for McKinley depicts him standing in the cen-ter of a plank marked "GOLD" and holding in his hand a scroll with "Sound Money Policy." A round plate by M'Kee and Brothers also has a bust of McKinley within a centered shield above the words "Protection and Plenty," one of his campaign slogans. The wide border of this piece features scattered five-point stars. A small milk glass plaque also was made with a portrait of McKinley.

Several pressed plates also were made honoring other presidential contenders. One pair in milk glass has an openwork border of rounded Gothic arches and the raised bust of either McKinley or Bryan in the center. Another pair of plates has an openwork border of a floral forget-me-nots twining around it and printed busts of the candidates in the center. These are in clear glass.

1900 McKinley won re-election to the presidency this year, but not too many glass items were released that include his picture and that of his dynamic running mate, Theodore Roosevelt, who had come to national prominence during his brief military career in the Spanish-American War. A few plates and tumblers do show either McKinley or both candidates.

President McKinley was assassinated in 1901 early in his second term while attending the Pan-American Exposition in Buffalo, New York. An attractive memorial platter in clear glass came out to honor him. It is oval with a wide leaf-band border, and in the center is an oval reserve with a standing portrait of McKinley and his birth and death dates. An inner border contains the phrase "It is God's Way—His Will Be Done," the president's dying words.

Fig. 12-4 Three commemorative pieces from the 1880s. On the left is a rectangular tray featuring bust portraits of the Republican presidential and vice-presidential candidates for 1888, Benjamin Harrison and Levi P. Morton. In the center is the "Knights of Labor" platter. On the right is the U. S. Grant "Patriot and Soldier" plate. Courtesy of the Gene Harris Antique Auction Center, Marshalltown, Iowa.

Fig. 12-5 On the left in this photo is the memorial platter honoring slain President William McKinley. In the center is a platter with the 1884 Republican presidential and vice-presidential candidates, James G. Blaine and John A. Logan. Teddy Roosevelt is featured on the tray on the far right. His portrait is framed by frolicking Teddy bears. Courtesy of the Gene Harris Antique Auction Center, Marshalltown, Iowa.

1904 After 1900 not as many political pieces in glass were made. When Theodore Roosevelt ran for his own full term as president in 1904, however, one unique piece was produced.

Readers may be aware that early in the century the famous Teddy bear toy came out; it was named for the popular president, even though he hated to be called Teddy. In 1904 an oval platter was made in clear glass with a profile portrait of Roosevelt in the center surrounded by a wide border of frolicking Teddy bears. At the top center is a spread-winged eagle and at the bottom a pair of crossed clubs (perhaps relating to his carry-a-big-stick policy), and with the clubs appears his slogan "A Square Deal."

1908 By this election, glass commemoratives were pretty scarce. A pair of milk glass plates feature the presidential candidates in the center. One has the smiling visage of Republican William Howard Taft, while the other shows William J. Bryan, the Democrat making his third and final run for the presidency. Each plate has a wide border composed of eagles, flags, and stars. There is also a pair of clear oval platters that have poorly defined bust portraits of the two parties' candidates.

A milk glass Uncle Sam top hat with a design of stars and stripes also was used during this campaign. There is no wording on the hat, which is painted bright red and blue, but it originally had a paper disc closure featuring either the portraits of Taft and Sherman or Bryan and Kern. It is seldom found today with the original paper closure intact.

Other Special People and Events

In addition to the political commemoratives discussed, many other people and special events were highlighted on unique pieces of pressed glass in the late nineteenth and early twentieth centuries.

Patriotism was always a popular theme for specialty pieces, and one of the loveliest of this type is a shield-shaped tray called the "Columbia" tray, since it features that lady's gracious portrait in the center. There is a wide band of Daisy and Button pattern across the top, and around the oval portrait are long stripes running up the sides. The stripes are alternately clear and patterned with small crosses. Appearing in the U.S. Glass catalog circa 1891, this piece apparently was made by Ripley and Company and may have first come out a few years before the catalog date. It may be found in clear as well as colored glass.

Similar is a covered dish in the form of the U.S. shield called the "Three Shields" dish. The base and cover are shield-shaped and have stripes, and there is a band of Daisy and Button pattern, all very similar to those features found on the Columbia tray. The third shield appears on this item as a small shield-shaped finial on the cover. A Bryce Brothers catalog circa mid-1880s shows this piece, which it called its "Banner Butter."

The stars and stripes are also commemorated on a rare rectangular tray called the "American Flag" platter. It features a plain flared and scalloped edge surrounding the American flag design in the center. Thirty-eight stars appear in the corner of the flag, and clear stripes and stripes patterned with small crosses alternate.

The Canton Glass Company of Canton, Ohio, released its "Railroad" platter circa 1882. It is a rectangular piece with notched corners featuring a large steam engine and train in the center. Bryce, Higbee and Company also brought out a couple of rather unusual portrait plates, one showing the likeness of Pope Leo XIII and another the portrait of Kaiser Wilhelm I of Germany.

Fig. 12-6 The Canton Glass Company brought out its "Railroad" platter in the early 1880s.

American agriculture is remembered on an oval "Reaper" platter, which shows a farm scene with the McCormick reaper being pulled by a team of horses. The early labor movement is also highlighted on an oval platter. The "Knights of Labor," a labor organization originally founded in 1869, had this piece made, probably in the 1880s. The platter features a center scene of a standing laborer shaking hands with a knight in armor below the words "Knights of Labor" (See Fig. 12-4.) There is an inner border printed with "United We Stand—Divided We Fall," and another border features a farmer holding a sickle at the top and a horse at the bottom, with a sailing ship on one side and a train on the other.

Lest we today believe that all Victorian men were male chauvinists, we should remember that one noteworthy working woman was commemorated on her own glass tray in 1890. Pioneer newspaperwoman Elizabeth Cochrane Seaman, using the pen name Nellie Bly, took up the challenge put forward in Jules Verne's popular novel and traveled around the world in eighty days. This would have been an ordeal for any man, but in 1890 Seaman accomplished it in seventy-two days, six hours, and eleven minutes. The Thompson Glass Company of Uniontown, Pennsylvania, made this unique piece showing in the center the standing figure of Nellie Bly dressed in an overcoat and carrying a small valise. Above her and around the ribbed border are the impressed names and dates of her epic journey.

A popular religious theme is portrayed on the Model Flint Glass Company's "Lord's Supper" bread tray. The Findlay, Ohio, firm released this piece in 1891, and it remained popular for many years and has been reproduced in more recent times. The border of the rectangular tray has a scalloped edge around a border of meandering grapevines. The center scene of Christ and His disciples sharing the Last Supper is based on Leonardo da Vinci's famous painting. It is most commonly found with a solid border, but a rare version with the grapevines cut out in a relief is known.

America played host to several world's fairs in the late nineteenth and early twentieth centuries, and all of these had pressed glass souvenirs widely produced and offered to the thousands who attended them.

Chicago was the site of the famous World's

Fig. 12-7 This ruby-stained *Dakota* pattern tumbler has an engraved souvenir inscription for the Chicago Columbian Exposition of 1893.

Columbian Exposition of 1893. Originally planned for 1892 to celebrate the four-hundredth anniversary of Columbus's arrival in the New World, it did not make that date, but it was held and tremendously successful in 1893.

Many, many souvenirs of all types still abound from this event, and numerous pressed-glass pieces, including plates and paperweights, still can be found. The Libbey Glass Company of Toledo, Ohio, famous for beautiful cut glass, had a plant right on the fairgrounds and offered a variety of glass mementos. At this event ruby-stained pressed glass really caught the attention of the buying public. A variety of pattern glass pieces, especially toothpick holders, tumblers, and small creamers decorated with ruby staining were offered for sale. These souvenirs generally were engraved with the name and dates of the fair and often personalized with the purchaser's name. All these glass artifacts are very collectible today and should continue to appreciate as the fair's centennial approaches.

In 1901, Buffalo, New York, held the Pan-American Exposition to promote increased trade among the nations of the Western Hemisphere. Various glass pieces came from this event, including a figural buffalo paperweight made in clear, frosted clear, and milk white glass by the Indiana Tumbler and Goblet Company of Greentown, Indiana. It carries the date 1901. Unfortunately, this event was marred by the assassination of President McKinley, who was shot while visiting the fair.

Another extremely popular and successful fair was presented in St. Louis, Missouri, in 1904 and was officially titled the Louisiana Purchase Exposition, although it is known generally as the St. Louis World's Fair. It commemorated the one-hundredth anniversary of the Louisiana Purchase and the growth and glory of the United States in that one hundred years, especially marvels like electricity and the ice cream cone. Again, numerous pressed-glass souvenirs were made for this event, and a variety of glass plates and ruby-stained and engraved items are to be found today.

In addition to the various fairs and expositions of the era, one other historic event was celebrated widely with numerous pressed-glass memorials— the Spanish-American War of 1898.

The war lasted only a few months, but the American public was stirred to a fever pitch of enthusiasm for the war with great official hoopla and jingoism. One of the purported causes of the war against Spain was the sinking of the American battleship *Maine* in Havana Harbor, which, at the time, was blamed on Spanish agents. The slogan "Remember the *Maine*" became the motto of the war, and numerous pressed-glass pieces, including small milk glass models of battleships, were produced immediately. Clear and milk glass plates and engraved tumblers also memorialized the tragic vessel.

A major hero of this war was Admiral George Dewey, whose major triumph was the decimation of the pitiful Spanish naval fleet at Manila Harbor in the Philippines. At the time it was looked upon as a tremendous victory, and Dewey was lionized by all America. Glassmakers did not miss a beat and began issuing numerous pieces featuring his likeness including bust statuettes, boat-shaped dishes with his bust as the finial on the cover, and several plates and tumblers. The Beatty-Brady Glass Company of Dunkirk, Indiana, produced a commemorative pitcher and tumblers. Two versions of the pitcher are known, and the most common features Dewey's bust portrait on one side with military arms around

Fig. 12-8 This is the more common version of the "Dewey" commemorative pitcher produced by the Beatty-Brady Glass Company.

the top and stacks of cannon balls below. The opposite side features a view of his flagship, the *Olympia*. The second version, called the "Gridley" pitcher, features the Dewey portrait on one side and a roster of many of the American ships participating in the battle of Manila Harbor on the other. Around the base are rows of pointed artillery shells, and under the spout, with other patriotic symbols, is the inscription "Gridley—You May Fire When Ready," Dewey's order starting the battle.

In addition, the Indiana Tumbler and Goblet Company brought out its very popular *Dewey* pattern in the admiral's honor, and it is still known by that name today. Greentown purportedly brought out a pattern called *Sampson* at the same time to honor another American naval hero of the war, Rear-Admiral William T. Sampson. Current research, however, does not show that any pattern by that name was ever released.

These are just a few of the noteworthy souvenir and commemorative pieces made between the

1870s and World War I. Numerous other people of note, both American and foreign, were immortalized on glass pieces, as were fraternal organizations, lesser-known politicians, and interesting sites like Niagara Falls. They are all unique pieces of Americana.

Pressed-Glass Novelties

In addition to the numerous souvenirs and commemoratives just covered, there was an immense array of whimsical or novelty items produced in pressed glass during the same period. Nearly every glass company of any size probably had at least one such item in its line, but some companies offered quite a diversity of charming pieces.

To give a better idea of what was produced, the brief list below describes some of the most popular novelties available to collect. Items are grouped according to the company that produced them, with a focus on companies in the Pittsburgh-Wheeling or Ohio region.

Pittsburgh-Wheeling Factories

Adams and Company, Pittsburgh

Famous for many noteworthy patterns of pressed tableware, Adams also made some interesting novelties beginning in the 1880s. It had a "Shoe Brush" figural match safe, a "Tomato" figural covered dish, and a "Grape Cluster" match safe.

It also made one of the popular "Gypsy Ket-tle" toothpick or match holders in the Daisy and Button pattern. Its version originally was meant to have a cover, so it has an inside rim lip where the lid rested. The lids, of course, often are missing today. This kettle also was raised on three small feet. It was made in several colors and has been reproduced. Another Daisy and Button piece, modeled after a coal hod, also was made by Adams around 1886 but so far has not been reproduced.

Bryce, McKee and Company (later Bryce Brothers), Pittsburgh and Mount Pleasant, Pennsylvania

This firm produced a very collectible woman's shoe using a new patent issued in 1886. The new process formed the shoe by folding the front top over the sides, leaving a center seam on the top. The result was a low-heeled slipper in the Daisy and Button pattern. A similar patent for making shoes also was assigned to George Duncan and Sons at the same time, and they made quite similar pieces. Various Daisy and Button shoes have been reproduced, but not those made with the frontal seam technique.

Bryce, McKee and Company also apparently

Fig. 12-9 Mugs were popular novelties with the Victorians. Here we see a graduated group of four in different patterns. The tiny opaque blue piece on the far left is in the *Gooseberry* pattern. Next to it is a blue *Three-Panel* pattern mug followed by an amber *Medallion* (aka *Ceres* or *Cameo*) piece made by Atterbury about 1870. On the far right is a blue example of the *Robin and Nest* mug that was Bryce Brothers' no. 1203 mug of about 1890.

made a long, nearly flat-heeled shoe with very low sides in the Daisy and Button pattern, which is sometimes found on its original silver-plated roller skate holder.

Bryce, Higbee and Company (later J. B. Higbee Glass Company), Pittsburgh

Although somewhat similar in name to the glass firm above, Bryce, Higbee was a totally different company with a different range of novelties.

It manufactured a unique group of novelty plates for Victorian children. One featuring the bust portrait of a young girl in the center with the alphabet around the border is called the "Emma" plate. Unfortunately, it has been reproduced in several colors. A similar plate with an alphabet border features the head of a large dog and is called the "Rover" plate.

A unique child's table set also was made by this company. Called the "Menagerie" set, each piece is made in the shape of a different animal. There is a bear sugar bowl, fish spooner, turtle butter dish, owl creamer, and bear horseradish dish. These pieces are especially rare in color.

Campbell, Jones and Company, Pittsburgh

One of the notable novelties produced by this firm is a flat dish in the shape of a whisk broom. It features a bold band of Daisy and Button at the top with reeded broom below and was patented in 1886. George Duncan and Sons also made this same design, and it has been copied in recent years. However, the originals had a faceted handle at the top, while the copies have handles rounded on one side and flat on the other.

A dish shaped like a sleigh was patented in 1886 by Campbell, Jones, and it features on its sides a floral design based on the *Rose Sprig* tableware line. There is also a boat-shaped relish dish in that line. Neither has been reproduced.

Central Glass Company, Wheeling, West Virginia

This company, which was responsible for such famous pattern glass designs as Log Cabin and U.S. Coin, also made a nice selection of novelty pieces.

For children it had a mug featuring a rabbit on one side and an elephant on the other.

It also introduced two types of women's shoes with molded-on roller wheels. One is a high-topped shoe with finely ribbed sides (it has been repro-

Fig. 12-10 The *Rose Sprig* pattern of tableware included this unusual boat-shaped relish dish.

Fig. 12-11 The Duncan-made version of the *Daisy and Button* slipper in amber.

duced), and the other is a low-sided shoe in the Daisy and Button pattern that apparently has not been copied. It also made a hanging match holder in the form of a "scuff slipper" in the Daisy and Button pattern.

George Duncan and Sons, Pittsburgh

In sharp contrast to some other glass firms, George Duncan and Sons was one of the most prolific producers of Victorian glass novelties. Its production, well documented by writers Thomas and Neila Bredehoft, offers a wide selection of charming and unique pieces.

Already mentioned is a low-heeled woman's shoe or slipper in the Daisy and Button design, similar to one made by Bryce, McKee. Usually each company's shoe carries the impressed patent date information inside: the Duncan shoe has this information arranged parallel to the sides of the shoe, while the Bryce version includes it at right angles to the sides. Again, although similar shoes have been reproduced, they do not have the front-seam construction of these types.

A smaller shoe, originally called the "no. 3 slipper," also was made by Duncan in the daisy and square design. It has been reproduced but the copies dip down in the back of the shoe, while the old ones have a high, rounded back.

A "Baby Bootie" figural in the Daisy and Button pattern also came from Duncan and has been reproduced, but by looking at the bottom one can tell the old from the new. The original bootie has a wide, pointed cavity on the inside front (as seen from below), while on the copies this cavity is round and narrow at the toe end.

Another piece of Duncan glass footwear is a piece called a "Boot," which is a high-topped piece in the Daisy and Button pattern. It, too, has been reproduced in many colors.

Probably the most abundantly produced (and prolifically reproduced) Duncan novelty is the "Top Hat" in the Daisy and Button pattern. Duncan made it in four sizes—a very large celery vase, a spooner, a toothpick holder, and an individual salt dip. The three smaller sizes have been reproduced with the toothpick holder size especially common. It is very difficult to tell the old from the new, so finding an authentic old piece will be a challenge.

As mentioned, Duncan made a version of the "Whisk Broom" dish and the "Gypsy Kettle." However, the Duncan kettle features the daisy and square motif instead of Daisy and Button. Its version also has a wire bail handle but no feet to rest upon, and it never was meant to have a lid.

A unique clothing accessory produced by Duncan was the "Umbrella" vase or match holder in the Daisy and Button pattern. It was made to look like a nearly closed umbrella and came complete with a wire hook handle. Two versions of this little piece, issued around 1886, are known. On one the umbrella rests point down on a small conical foot, and on the other there is no base and the piece has to be hung up by its handle. The overall length with the wire handle is about six and three-quarters inches, and this item has not been reproduced.

A piece that appears to have no purpose but shelf ornamentation is a high-back armchair in the Daisy and Button pattern. The chair has a solid seat and a deep base enclosed by panels of Daisy and Button design. It was available about 1887 and was made in several colors. A second chair also appears to have been issued by Duncan, but no old catalog illustrations are known of this "no. 2 Chair Toothpick." Some experts believe it may be the piece called "Bathing Tub" by collectors. The Duncan armchair has a high rounded back and arms and should not be confused with another armchair novelty. The other armchair also has a high back but features a cylindrical container opening in the seat that the Duncan piece does not have.

Any of these Duncan novelties would be a fun addition to a collection of pressed glass.

King, Son and Company, Pittsburgh

This glassmaker, responsible for a wide variety of pressed tableware, also came out with some distinctive novelty pieces in the 1880s and early 1890s.

It reportedly issued in 1885 its own shoe, which it called a "Cinderella Slipper." It may be the one shown in a catalog of circa 1890 that features a crosshatched diamond design with a large bow at the instep. This piece was reproduced by the Crystal Art Glass firm beginning in 1947. It was more recently in production by Kanawaha Glass of Dunbar, West Virginia.

Shown in the same ad were several other novelties, most notably a large hanging figural "Elephant Head" match holder probably made to represent the head of P. T. Barnum's famous show elephant,

Fig. 12-12 The King company brought out this impressive "Helmet" butter dish in the 1880s.

158

Jumbo, which was the talk of the country in the 1880s. Several other small figurals were in its line then, including a "Scuff Slipper" hanging match holder similar to the one put out by the Central Glass Company.

A unique piece attributed to this firm is the covered "Helmet" butter dish in the Daisy and Button pattern. Designed to resemble a Greek or Roman warrior's helmet, complete with top plume, it is a wonderfully designed piece and quite a rarity to find intact today, especially in color.

M'Kee and Brothers, Pittsburgh

M'Kee and Brothers and its successor, the McKee Glass Company, did its part in introducing in-

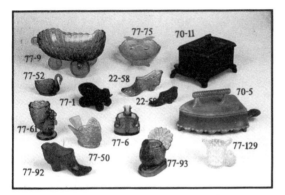

Fig. 12-13 A photograph of currently available Victorian-style whimseys from the L. G. Wright Glass Company catalog. Note the McKee "Coach" bowl in the upper right and the "Cookstove" and "Sad Iron" dishes. Several new slippers and figural toothpick holders also are included in this grouping. Courtesy of the L. G. Wright Glass Company.

teresting glass novelties in the last decades of the nineteenth century and in the early years of this century.

Around 1886 M'Kee introduced its "Coach Bowl," which is in the shape of an antique three-wheeled baby carriage. The sides feature vertical bands of hexagonal hobs and crossbanding alternating with clear narrow stripes. There are large wheels at the back and a small wheel at the front below the hook-shaped rudder bar at the prow. The front hook is sometimes broken off this piece and the damage ground down, so make sure the piece is complete if you find one. Unfortunately, it has been reproduced in several colors and is still available.

A couple of novelty banks were made by M'Kee, the most notable a rectangular building with a coin slot at the top of the hip roof.

Around the turn of the century, McKee became well known for its production of milk glass dishes, often decorative pieces for the dressing table or for wall hanging, as well as a range of covered animal dishes. Some of these carried the McKee name spelled out in script, a rare case of a company marking at that time. Only the animal dishes, however, ever carried that form of their logo mark.

United States Glass Company, Pittsburgh

When U.S. Glass was organized in 1891 the member glass firms continued to produce many of the patterns and pieces they had introduced previously. This would have held true for the novelties as well.

U.S. Glass catalogs from around the turn of the

Fig. 12-14 The two glass slippers in this photo are old examples probably made by U.S. Glass. The one on the left was available in 1915 or later, and the *Cane* pattern one on the right was probably a bit earlier. In the middle is a little green opaque mug in the *Oriental* line made by the Westmoreland Specialty Company circa 1900.

century show a large range of novelties. Examples of figural pieces include a hatchet, a ball peen hammer, a tomahawk (reproduced), a coal hod, a tiny bucket, plain canoe, fedora hat, toy spade, plain and Daisy and Button slippers, and a wash tub and matching washboard, all pressed from glass in various hues. In addition it offered a wide selection of children's toy table sets, which are highly collectible today.

Ohio Region Glasshouses

Canton Glass Company, Canton, Ohio

This glasshouse was reponsible for a couple of famous tableware patterns such as *Jumbo* and *Swan*, and it also had some novelty items of note.

In 1882 it patented what it called an "Imperial Crown" jelly dish, which was a drum-shaped dish with small raised crowns on the sides and a small figural crown finial.

Findlay, Ohio, Factories

Several glass factories opened in this Ohio town in the 1880s to take advantage of the abundant supplies of cheap natural gas. Many of them introduced unique glass novelties. The most famous firms and pieces are noted here.

Bellaire Goblet Company

Several pieces featuring animal figures came from this firm, including the "Standing Pig" on an oval base paperweight and the large "Pig on a Flatcar," the animal seated at one end of an eight-wheeled railroad car with a barrel for toothpicks at the other end. There was also the small figural "Turtle" salt dish.

It had a couple of shoe novelties, one featuring three high-top women's shoes back-to-back on a three-part base. The shoes feature a fine-cut design. Another tall single shoe featuring a similar fine-cut design has a wide band of smooth glass around the top and a scalloped band of buttons running down one side.

Another piece of personal apparel was modeled into a toothpick holder. The "Corset" toothpick holder with its overall diamond-point design must have been considered quite risqué when offered in the 1880s.

Columbia Glass Company

Columbia also produced several charming novelties, including its "Puss-in-Slipper" (or boot) woman's shoe. It features a Daisy and Button design on the sides with a little cat's head peeking out at the top. A unique feature of this piece is the alligator skin design in the toe section. This piece was reproduced by the Degenhart's of Crystal Art Glass beginning in 1947, but the copies lack a protruding lip around the sole at the toe that is on the old pieces.

A little bushy-tailed dog forms the base of a small Columbia-made vase. Called "Dog Vase," this cornucopia-form vase with a fine-cut design shows a dog on a small round base in a seated begging position holding up its paws.

Family pets also appear on a group of children's dishes by this firm. A pair of six-inch- diameter "Pet" plates feature the head of a spaniel-like dog on one and a tabby cat on the other. Accompanying these is a pair of rounded, footed cups, one with the embossed face of a small boy, the other with a small girl's face. The cups were meant to sit on a saucer decorated with a vining acorn branch.

Dalzell, Gilmore and Leighton Company

This Findlay company was responsible for quite a range of novelty wares, especially some interesting figural decanters.

A couple of figural dishes are sought after today. One is the "Connecticut Skillet" in the shape of an old cast-iron frying pan, the other a "Hairbrush" dish. Both pieces also were produced by the Indiana Tumbler and Goblet Company of Greentown, Indiana, about that same time.

Several figural pieces made by Dalzell feature a caricature likeness of African-Americans. The "Snowball" wine set features a standing black man wearing a straw hat and work clothes and holding a tray with three wine glasses. Accompanying this is the "Mrs. Snowball," decanter on which the head forms the stopper. A couple of small cologne bottles also match the Snowball pieces, one in the form of a kneeling black boy and the other a standing black boy wearing a sombrerolike straw hat. With the strong interest in black Americana today, these pieces should be choice collectibles.

Other figural decanters from this firm include a standing stocky man wearing a top hat and tails and

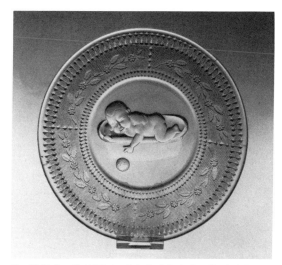

Fig. 12-16 The 7" d. "Crying Baby" plate in the *Stippled Forget-Me-Not* pattern. The center scene apparently was based on a Pears Soap Company advertisement of the same era that shows a crying baby in a sitz-type bathtub reaching for a bar of soap. Above the scene in the ad is the slogan "He won't be happy until he gets it." The same might be said for today's collector searching for this elusive piece of glass.

Dalzell, Gilmore & Leighton Co.
FINDLAY, OHIO.

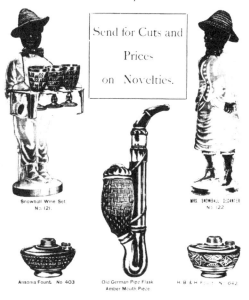

Snowball Wine Set
No. 121.

MRS. SNOWBALL DECANTER
No. 122

Ansonia Fount. No 403

Old German Pipe Flask
Amber Mouth Piece

H. B. & H. FONT No. 042

Fig. 12-15 Some unique Dalzell, Gilmore and Leighton Company novelties are shown in this early trade journal advertisement. The "Snowball Wine Set" on the left features a black man holding a tray with goblets, while his mate, the "Mrs. Snowball Decanter," is shown on the right. Below them are the "Old German Pipe Flask" and two small lamp fonts. Courtesy of James Measell.

carrying a walking stick. The company called this piece the "German Gentleman Decanter." A clown in a baggy outfit and wearing a pointed hat is another Dalzell decanter. Still another is one called "Parrot," which shows the bird on two front feet and balanced by a long tail. The head, which has a comb more like a cockatoo than a parrot, forms the stopper.

In addition to these figural pieces, several water pitchers feature humans or animals.

Findlay Flint Glass Company

Around 1890 this glass firm issued its *Stippled Forget-Me-Not* pattern of tableware, which included three unusual pieces. The tiny flowers on a stippled background form the border of each, but each has a different design in the center. The seven-inch-diameter plate has at its center the scene of a crying baby in a tub reaching for a ball. The nine-inch-diameter handled plate shows a cat in its center, and the eleven-inch-diameter plate features a stork and palm-like rushes in the middle.

A figural toothpick holder called "Elephant's Head" is smaller than the King, Son and Company piece and less carefully designed. This piece was reproduced by the Crystal Art Glass company, but each piece has one decorative cord around the head rather than the two cords on old pieces. The new pieces are also slightly larger than the old.

Another unusual piece of clothing was modeled into a toothpick holder by this firm. The "Drawers" toothpick holder is made in the shape of the lower half of knee-length underwear, and from the shapely form it must have represented a woman's set. This must have been considered naughty at the time.

Many other novelties from the end of the Victorian era can be found with diligent searching. A covered dish in the shape of an early kitchen range

CROCKERY AND GLASS JOURNAL

Send for Cuts and Prices on Novelties.

161

was made, as was a patterned covered dish in the shape of an old sad iron (see Fig. 12-13). Another covered butter dish in Daisy and Button had a tall bell-shaped top. All three of these pieces have been reproduced and are still available.

Memories of the old blacksmith's shop are evoked by a couple of figural blacksmith's anvils. On one the small anvil sits atop a round tree stump and has impressed on the sides "K of L" for "Knights of Labor," the early labor organization. The patent for this piece was assigned to the Hemingray Glass Company of Cincinnati, Ohio, and Covington, Kentucky. The firm later became well known for its production of glass insulators. The second anvil is a figural piece, with the anvil sides decorated with a cubed block design, and it is hollow and deep enough to hold matches or toothpicks. The Windsor Glass Company of Pittsburgh had this piece in its line-up circa 1887.

Although there is no space here to touch on every sort of whimsey and novelty made in glass for our Victorian ancestors, the pieces covered in this section give a good idea of the wide range made. Many are still available at reasonable prices, and once one becomes familiar with the few bad apples, one can confidently collect the many other gems.

Desirability and Values

Considering their age and quality, a great many Victorian novelty and commemorative pieces are available today for modest cost. Value often depends on the current appeal of a subject or theme. When the U.S. bicentennial was celebrated in 1976, pieces from the 1876 centennial surged in value, but prices seem to have leveled off a bit again. There probably will be a similar price surge as 1993 approaches and pieces made for the Columbian Exposition of 1893 reach official antique status.

In the political realm, presidents who are still well remembered and appreciated today, like Abraham Lincoln and Theodore Roosevelt, have collectors avidly looking for pieces with their likeness. Hence, such pieces retain a good value. Lesser-known presidents like Garfield and McKinley inspire less enthusiasm, and their commemorative pieces command lower prices on the market.

For most of the commemorative trays described, values for good, clear examples seem to hold in the $100 to $200 range, with many in the $50 to $100 range. Color, of course, increases the cost somewhat. A piece like the Nellie Bly platter, with its special appeal to today's working women, has a value of around $200 and may continue to appreciate. The McKinley memorial platter, on the other hand, can be found for $50 or sometimes less.

Prices for most World's Fair souvenirs are still quite reasonable, including many pieces from the Philadelphia 1876 Centennial Exhibition. Many of the small vases and the figural slipper in clear are offered in the $50 to $75 range. More unusual or larger figurals command more, and a rarity like the Shakespeare bust may push $200 while the Lincoln bust in frosted glass may be close to $400.

Many of the smaller novelty figurals, especially the various women's shoes, can be found for reasonable amounts, sometimes under $50. The plethora of reproductions may be part of the reason. However, with some study one can sort out what has been copied and what has not. The strongest prices probably are for the larger figural covered dishes, like the Helmet dish, especially in color. Even in clear such pieces can be in the $200 range in top condition, with colored examples bringing quite a bit more. Platters with a patriotic motif also are in much demand, and pieces like the Three-Shield dish can sell in the $200 to $300 range.

There is a Victorian commemorative or novelty certain to appeal to each collector, and prices are generally reasonable. Collectors who study and buy with care can help preserve some of these charming objects and celebrate the country's history and growth.

CHAPTER 13

Special Colored Glassware

In addition to the many patterns of glassware covered so far in this book, several very special categories of colored pressed glass need to be discussed briefly. These colored and color treated pieces often were produced in the same patterns in clear, but some were used to produce specific limited lines or distinctive pieces with a special appeal all their own. This special glassware is covered in a chronological survey beginning with milk glass (or milk white glass), first produced widely in the 1870s, and ending with carnival glass, which was introduced early in the twentieth century and remained in production into the 1920s.

Milk White and Slag Glass

As far back as the 1830s, some pieces of lacy glass were made in a milky white opaque glass color. Even earlier, in the eighteenth and early nineteenth centuries, English and continental European glasshouses produced blown glass in a white meant to imitate the rare procelain wares of that era. A few patterns of pressed glass from the 1840s and 1850s also were produced in a milky white color, including the scarce pattern known as *California,* which apparently came out circa 1849 at the time of the California Gold Rush. It was made only in a creamer and sugar bowl, however.

By the 1860s the Birch Leaf and Blackberry patterns saw extensive production in milk glass, and about that time many candlesticks and kerosene lamp bases also were made in white.

However, in the 1870s the production of milk glass wares really took off. One of the major companies responsible for its production during that period was Atterbury and Company of Pittsburgh. Today Atterbury is most noted for its large line of figural animal dishes. The line came out in the 1880s and often carries the impressed patent date on the base. Its most famous animal dishes include "Rabbit," patented in 1886; "Duck," circa 1887; and "Boar's Head" (cover on a ribbed dish base), circa 1888. The "Bull's Head" (circa 1880s) dish is a full-figured head in which the top half forms the cover and the hooked end of a ladle forms the tongue sticking out of the mouth. Today this tongue ladle often is missing from this rare piece.

Later Atterbury added other animals to its menagerie, including dish covers called "Chick and Eggs," "Hen on Nest," "Reclining Lion," "Entwined Fish," "Reclining Fox," "Reclining Cat," "Swan" (one with raised wings and another with a square block design on the wings), and "Hand Holding a Bird."

All the pieces above are seen most often in all-white, but the hen and duck dishes sometimes are found with the heads in contrasting colors of blue or purple, which adds to their market value considerably.

Another noteworthy late-nineteenth-century glassmaker that turned out a great deal of milk glass was Challinor, Taylor and Company of Tarentum, Pennsylvania, in business only from 1884 to 1891. This company made many milk glass items, including another dish with a figural duck cover referred to as the "Wavy Base Duck" because of the undulating rim on the top edge of the base.

Other noteworthy figurals from Challinor include an "Owl" pitcher and creamer, "Indian Head" match safe, "Bull's Head" cover on a ribbed base, "Fish" pickle dish, and "Rooster" "Hen," and "Swan" covers on basketweave bases.

By the turn of the century many American

Fig. 13-1 This is an original "Hen on Nest" milk glass dish made by Challinor, Taylor and Company. The eyes on this piece, however, have been replaced.

Fig. 13-3 This handsome milk glass "Owl" jar was made by Atterbury. This piece has been reproduced, but this is an original, complete with its red glass eyes.

Fig. 13-2 This "Reclining Cat" milk glass animal dish, based on the Atterbury original, is a quality reproduction made by the Westmoreland Glass Company. Fortunately, it is marked with the "WG" trademark inside the cover.

glassmakers were producing a wide spectrum of milk glass novelties, which include decorative plates with animal and scenic designs, covered animal dishes of all sorts (Hen on Nest is the most popular and abundant), commemorative dishes (especially from the Spanish-American War era), and all sorts of toothpick and match holders.

McKee Glass Company led the production of these later milk glass wares, and in addition to the many small decorative dishes and trays meant for a woman's dressing table, it turned out several animal dishes. These animals included "Squirrel," "Horse on a Split Rib Base," "Lion on a Split Rib Base" and "Turkey."

The Westmoreland Specialty Company also made several animal covered dishes around the turn of the century that were sold filled with mustard. Its line included "Hen on Nest," "Hen on a Sleigh" base, and "Chick on a Sleigh." There was even "Santa Claus on a Sleigh," which is highly desirable when found in old glass. Another animal covered dish from this firm is "Closed Neck Swan," given that name because the loop formed by the swan's neck is filled with glass rather than hollow, as on some other similar dishes by other companies.

So many old Westmoreland pieces were reproduced or reissued by the company from the 1940s on that it is very difficult to sort out the old from the new. After 1967 the firm did begin marking most of its reproductions with a small entwined "WG" logo mark, which will be of some help.

In addition to the major American makers of

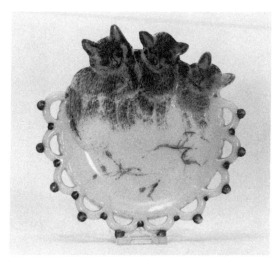

Fig. 13-4 This "Three Kittens" milk glass plate is 7" in diameter and is an original from the turn of the century. It features its original painted trim. Unfortunately this piece has been heavily reproduced, but not with the painted trim.

Fig. 13-5 A plate is known as the "Good Luck Rabbit" or "Rabbit and Horseshoe" design and was patented in 1902. Although reproduced, this is an original piece carrying its original heavy gold and dark green paint and with a floral sprig below the rabbit. It measures 7½" d.

Fig. 13-6 Sometimes called the "Marine Border" plate, this milk glass piece features an anchor and ship's wheel design. This example is heavily painted in blue-green over the milk glass and has a worn souvenir inscription in the center. This 7¼" d. piece was reportedly made by the Westmoreland Specialty Company and patented in 1901.

milk glass, one also may run across some pieces from the noted Vallerysthal glass factory of France, which operated until 1939 when the factory was destroyed. Some of its wares were marked with its name, and probably the best-known piece from its factory is the figural robin on a pedestal-based nest dish. It has been reproduced widely, however. English firms also made milk glass, and their wares also often carried a pressed-in logo mark and a diamond-shaped English registry mark (equivalent to U.S. patent markings).

A glass closely related to milk white glass is sometimes referred to today as blue milk glass, a strange term. It is more properly called blue opaque glass and is most often a turquoise blue opaque ware made in many of the same shapes as plain milk glass. Many small novelties like toothpick holders and salt shakers also were made using this color, and a few animal covered dishes also can be found in this blue. Related colors of opaque green and pink also were used in the late nineteenth and early twentieth centuries, and all these colors are very collectible and will sell for more than the same items in milk glass.

Since milk glass has been so widely reproduced for so many years, it is a very tricky business learning to separate the old from the new. Some companies did begin to mark some of their reproductions: "WG" for Westmoreland, entwined "IG" for Imperial, and "K" for the Kemple Glass Company.

Fig. 13-7 A cluster of cherries is featured on the sides of the blue opaque covered creamer on the left, while the one on the right features swan handles. The "Swan and Cattails" design was made by the Westmoreland Specialty Company. Both of these patterns were reproduced later by Westmoreland in milk glass.

Other companies like L. G. Wright sold unmarked pieces. Imported wares also have been on the market, but they had only an easily removed paper sticker attached as a marker.

A few tips will help in differentiating early milk glass from later copies. Design detailing is one point, since copies seldom have the sharpness and clarity of detail of the old pieces. Old pieces usually are heavier than the new, and new pieces sometimes have a slick or oily feel. According to glass author Dorothy Hammond, many older pieces have, up in the foot, a small C-shaped mark left from the molding process; this mark is missing on new milk glass. Some pieces of new milk glass have a denser, brighter white color than the old, which one can learn to recognize. Some collectors talk about old milk glass as having a "fire," or fiery orange opalescence visible around the edges when a piece is held to a strong light. This fire often is found on old pieces, but new glass also can have it as one can see on a milk glass Noxema face cream jar.

Closely related to plain white milk glass is the decorative glassware called today *slag, marble,* or *agate* glass. White milk glass is mixed with a contrasting color, most often deep purple, giving objects a distinctive marbleized effect. It was a diffi-

Fig. 13-8 Two pieces of purple slag glass. On the left is a *Spool* pattern vase made by Northwood. On the right is a *Bird in Nest with Flowers* mug made by Challinor, Taylor and Company.

cult glassmaking technique to master, and slag glass is much scarcer than milk glass, although it was used to make many of the same pieces.

Challinor, Taylor and Company was the leading U.S. maker of slag glass, which it patented in 1886. It was described as a variegated glassware and was sold under the descriptive name *mosaic glass.* Slag glass generally was not made in full table services but most often in miscellaneous pitchers, vases, creamer and sugar sets, cake stands, bowls, toothpick holders, and mugs. The *Fluted* pattern, which features narrow panels on the flat, flaring bodies of pieces, is one of the few lines made in more than a few pieces. Only rarely was slag glass used to produce animal covered dishes, but many reproductions using this type of glass have been made in recent years, so beware!

In addition to the purple and white mixture, one can also find slag in white mixed with red, butterscotch, turquoise blue, dark blue, orange, and green, and the very rare pink and white known as *pink slag*. All these color combinations are scarce, but pink slag is especially rare. It was made for a very short time shortly after the turn of the century using the Inverted Fan and Feather pattern. The National Glass Company produced it using the Northwood pattern mold after Harry Northwood severed connections with National.

The Imperial Glass Company made quite a few reproductions of purple slag but, fortunately, many of these items carry its "IG" mark. Pink slag was reproduced in a toothpick holder and tumbler, but new pieces have very poor coloring compared to the old.

In addition to American slag glass, much slag glass also was made by English glass firms, especially in the more unusual colors. Again, many English pieces are marked with the glassmaker's logo.

In general, the current market values for slag in purple, as well as its sister colors, are fairly modest. Many interesting old pieces in purple slag can be found in the $50 to $100 range, with rarer items in the $100 to $200 range. Only pink slag glass falls outside this range, and most pieces in this color sell in the range of $400 to $800.

Fig. 13-9 An early opalescent *Hobnail* piece. This blue spooner in the "square-footed" version of *Hobnail* was made by the La Belle Glass Company circa 1886.

Milk glass pieces also can be found quite often in the $50 to $100 range, with some common decorative milk glass plates for well under $50. Generally the rare, large covered animal dishes bring the best money, and scarce old examples can sell in the $150 to $200 range and a few in the $200 to $400 realm.

Opalescent Glass

Various formulas for decorative art glass were being developed in the mid-1880s as the demand and market for novelty and color in glassware boomed. Heat-reactive glassware emerged, including the famous Amberina and Burmese lines. At the same time it was discovered that adding bone ash to the glass batch would cause a color-changing reaction. In this instance the reheated portions of a piece turned a pearly white color, and such glassware is called *opalescent glass*. Pressed, mold-blown, and free-blown glass articles could be colored using this technique, which remained widely popular through the turn of the century.

Several glass companies produced opalescent wares over the years, but the popularity was spread by the early wares of Hobbs, Brockunier and Company of Wheeling, West Virginia, and the La Belle Glass Company of Bridgeport, Ohio. Mold-blown lamp fonts in various hues, especially in the Coin Spot pattern, were early favorites, and many items of tableware were produced in the Hobnail and Daisy and Button patterns. These two leading glassmakers also were challenged by wares from the Consolidated Lamp and Glass Company of Fostoria, Ohio, and the Beaumont Glass Company of Martins Ferry, Ohio.

A leading proponent of mold-blown opalescent glass during its early years was famous glassmaker Harry Northwood, who was responsible for many popular patterns and designs in opalescent glass featuring rich shades of ruby and blue contrasting with pearly white highlights. By the late 1890s Northwood also was introducing a lovely selection of pressed-glass patterns in opalescent glass in complete table settings. One of the most famous of these lines is *Alaska*, an ornate design with squared tapering pieces featuring knobby feet at the bottom corners and ruffled rims around the tops. Closely related to Alaska is Northwood's *Klondyke* pattern. Both paid tribute to the fame of the Alaska Gold Rush of the late 1890s. Today Klondyke is also known as *Fluted Scrolls* to help avoid confusion with other Klondyke-named patterns. *Drapery* and *Argonaut Shell* (originally called *Nautilus* by the glassmaker) are two other Northwood patterns often made in opalescent glass and available in several colors.

Between 1885 and circa 1910 some sixty pressed-glass patterns were made that can be found with an opalescent treatment, and some thirty-nine mold-blown patterns were made. In addition, various novelties and one-of-a-kind pieces like vases, bowls, and compotes, which were manipulated while hot into varied shapes, also add to the diversity in opalescent glassware.

All opalescent items are collectible, but the Northwood pieces are especially desirable, particularly since by 1906 he had begun marking most pieces leaving his factory with his famous mark—the underlined "N" in a circle.

Considering the vast array of opalescent glass made during its heyday, it is remarkable that not too many pieces have been reproduced in recent years.

A couple of Northwood pieces to watch out for are the figural "Town Pump" and matching "Trough" dish, resembling a bumpy log with the upright pump meant to stand beside the trough. These pieces can be confusing, but less of a problem is the Northwood "Corn" vase, also made by the Dugan Glass Company, which took over Northwood's factory in Indiana, Pennsylvania. The top sides of the old corn vase are pulled up into points, while the reproductions have a flat-top rim.

Another piece to beware is the "Dolphin" compote, first made by Northwood about 1902.

Fig. 13-10 The famous Northwood "Town Pump and Trough" set in blue opalescent. Watch out for reproductions.

Fig. 13-11 On the left is the Northwood company's *Opal Open* pattern rose bowl in clear opalescent. This piece has been reproduced, but the copies have the open loops in the pedestal filled in with glass. On the right is a *Beaded Fan* rose bowl made by the Jefferson Glass Company. It is also in clear opalescent.

This piece has a figural dolphin pedestal on a domed foot, and one side of the ruffled bowl is curled up. It is a difficult piece to distinguish, so buy with caution. Another piece probably made by Northwood that has been reproduced is the "Opal Open" rose bowl.

Of the opalescent patterns made in table sets, not too many have been reproduced. Be careful of Northwood's *Argonaut Shell*, since the tumbler, berry set, toothpick holder, and salt and pepper shakers have been copied. The *Jewelled Heart* pattern by Dugan has been reproduced in a toothpick holder, creamer, sugar bowl, and goblet. A non-Northwood pattern, *Wreathed Cherry,* was reproduced in several pieces as far back as the 1950s.

Collectors of American opalescent glass need to be aware that a good deal of similar glass also was made in England and, in fact, the English apparently introduced the opalescent technique about ten years before American glassmakers did.

Values for pressed and mold-blown opalescent glass have skyrocketed since the publication of William Heacock's book on the subject, but many one-of-a-kind novelty bowls, especially in clear with opalescent edging, still can be found for modest amounts ($15 to $30). In colors, especially blue, prices often will be more. Prices for patterns made in tableware are generally on a par with the values of other popular pressed-glass patterns in comparable colors. Clear pieces with opalescent edging are generally the least expensive, and green and yellow opalescent somewhat more. Again, blue opalescent pieces command the highest prices. Overall, more common pieces like spooners, bowls, and tumblers can be found in the $25 to $50 range. Scarcer pieces like sugar bowls, creamers, and butter dishes may be in the $50 to $125 range, and rare pieces like large pitchers and cruets can be $150 to $300, especially in desirable colors.

Although the lovely mold-blown patterns in opalescent glass like *Spanish Lace* and *Daisy and Fern* have not been discussed much here, suffice to

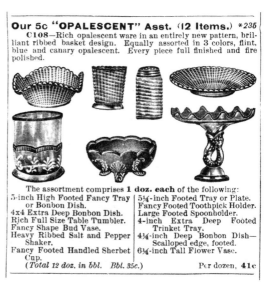

Our 5c "OPALESCENT" Asst. (12 Items.) *235

C108—Rich opalescent ware in an entirely new pattern, brilliant ribbed basket design. Equally assorted in 3 colors, flint, blue and canary opalescent. Every piece full finished and fire polished.

The assortment comprises **1 doz. each** of the following:

5-inch High Footed Fancy Tray or Bonbon Dish.	5¼-inch Footed Tray or Plate.
4x4 Extra Deep Bonbon Dish.	Fancy Footed Toothpick Holder.
Rich Full Size Table Tumbler.	Large Footed Spoonholder.
Fancy Shape Bud Vase.	4-inch Extra Deep Footed Trinket Tray.
Heavy Ribbed Salt and Pepper Shaker.	4¼-inch Deep Bonbon Dish—
Fancy Footed Handled Sherbet Cup.	Scalloped edge, footed.
	6¼-inch Tall Flower Vase.

(Total 12 doz. in bbl. Bbl. 35c.)   Per dozen, **41c**

Fig. 13-12 This advertisement from the spring 1902 Butler Brothers catalog shows a selection of pressed opalescent pieces that are known to have been made by the Model Flint Glass Company of Albany, Indiana. Courtesy of the Corning Museum of Glass.

say that pieces in colored opalescent in these and related designs often will bring considerably more than their pressed counterparts, and the range of items in mold-blown opalescent patterns is generally more restricted than in the pressed lines.

Custard Glass

This distinctive form of pressed glass has been given its collector's name because it resembles, at least in some eyes, creamy dessert custard. It is simply a name descriptive of the color and has nothing to do with what the glass was used for or how it was made. In fact, a major producer of custard glass, Harry Northwood, first advertised this new ware as ivory glass, which is just as accurate a description of the color. Today custard glass almost falls into the realm of art glass and generally commands prices quite a bit higher than average patterns in clear pattern glass.

Although custard glass became especially popular around the turn of the century, the color had been used as early as 1880 in England and Europe,

though most such pieces were made from free-blown glass and made into decorative mantel vases.

In 1898 Northwood took the glass retailing market by storm with the introduction of his first ivory glass pattern, which he named *Louis XV.* The deep rounded shapes feature ornate raised rococo scrolls with a single blossom sprig in the centers, and most pieces are raised on short scroll feet. The feet and blossom sprigs also were trimmed with a bright gold, which added to the object's flashiness. It must have been exactly what consumers wanted at the time, because it was an immediate success. Soon Northwood became the major producer of this ivory ware, and over the next few years he introduced several additional patterns in this line including *Wild Bouquet, Fluted Scrolls with Flower Band* (also known as *Jackson,* and similar to Northwood's earlier Klondyke pattern), *Chrysanthemum Sprig* (which he called *Pagoda*), *Inverted Fan and Feather, Maple Leaf, Argonaut Shell* (*Nautilus*), *Intaglio,* and *Everglades* (called *Carnelian* by Northwood). The grape patterns include *Grape and Cable, Grape and Thumbprint, Grape and Gothic Arches,* and the less well known *Grape Arbor.* Rounding out his custard lines are *Peacock and Urn, Beaded Circle,* and *Geneva.* Readers may recognize a couple of these as patterns Northwood produced also in opalescent glass.

As the commerical success of custard glass continued into the early twentieth century, several other American glass firms also began to make pressed patterns in this color. Already mentioned is that Heisey made the Winged Scroll and Ring Band patterns, and Fenton Art Glass offered its Cherry and Scale line.

Although the early custard patterns had pretty well died out in popularity by World War I, some pieces in this color were made during the following decades, and the McKee Glass Company even had a similar color it called French ivory, used to produce inexpensive kitchenware during the 1930s.

One Northwood pattern used for custard glass, *Chrysanthemum Sprig* (*Pagoda*) also was made in a blue opaque color, which collectors started called blue custard glass. Like the term blue milk glass, this is a misnomer since the glass formula for the two types of glass is the same and both should be referred to simply as *blue opaque* glass. Whatever you call it, this pattern in this color is rare and very expensive, costing as much or more than the most expensive pieces of custard glass.

The blue Chrysanthemum Sprig, as well as several other Northwood custard patterns, sometimes carries the unique early Northwood mark on the underside. This mark consists of Northwood spelled out in script, superceded in a few years by the Northwood "N" in a circle mark, which also

Fig. 13-14 A sauce dish in custard glass in Heisey's *Winged Scroll* pattern. The scrolls are highlighted by gold trim.

Fig. 13-15 A novelty dish in Fenton's *Prayer Rug* pattern. The custard glass body is trimmed with bright silver and red paint.

Fig. 13-13 A creamer in Northwood's *Pagoda* pattern that is today most commonly known as *Chrysanthemum Sprig.* This piece has its original painted decorative trim in excellent condition.

appears on some opalescent and much carnival glass made by Northwood. Some of the Heisey custard pieces also may be marked with the "H" in diamond Heisey mark.

The small, commoner pieces of custard such as tumblers, spooners, sauce dishes, and some goblets may be found in the $50 to $100 range, while large pieces such as covered sugar bowls, butter dishes, and large berry bowls most often will be in the $100 to $200 range. Scarce pieces such as large pitchers, cruets, and syrup jugs very often run from $200 to $300. Values vary from pattern to pattern because common items in one line may be rare in another. In blue opaque Chrysanthemum Sprig, even the common sauce dish sells in the $100 to $125 range, while most pieces are from $400 to $500. Rarities like the butter dish or celery vase push $1,000.

Since much early custard glass from every glassmaker also was decorated at the factory with gold trim or colored highlights, the condition of this decoration also can affect the sale price, with the best pieces having the best decoration selling for a bit more than undecorated items or items with badly worn trim color. Also, some custard patterns, especially Northwood's *Grape and Cable* and *Grape and Thumbprint,* have backgrounds dusted with a light brown staining referred to today as nutmeg. This brown trim was meant to highlight the raised portions of the design and should not be confused with plain old dirt and grime. An old piece may be coated with dirt, too, but do not scrub it too hard as some of that brown may be original color.

Fortunately for collectors, not too many patterns and pieces in custard glass have been reproduced. A few years ago some reproductions marked with the Northwood *N* came out, but since the American Carnival Glass Association holds the rights to the Northwood mark and molds, it put a stop to these marked copies. The fake mark was reworked to resemble a crooked *W*, and this mark will be found on the custard and other colored reproductions.

The new custard should not be too hard to tell from the old, as it is generally much thinner and lighter in weight than the old and does not have its soft, rich color. One of the main custard lines reproduced is *Argonaut Shell,* and some eight pieces in that pattern have been copied.

The major reference on custard glass is William Heacock's *Encyclopedia of Victorian Colored Pattern Glass Book 4: Custard Glass from A to Z. Harry Northwood: The Early Years, 1881–1900,* a new book by William Heacock, James Measell, and Barry Wiggins, also has excellent coverage of Northwood's custard production. A helpful series of six booklets by James H. Gaddis, *Keys to Custard Glass Identification,* was published by the Wallace-Homestead Book Company of Des Moines, and the Early America Company of Pontiac, Illinois, between 1969 and 1971.

Chocolate Glass

If custard does not happen to appeal to one's culinary and collecting tastes, one might prefer chocolate glass. Yes, chocoholics of the world have their very own glass to collect and, unlike custard, it has gone by that name since it was introduced to the market about 1900.

An innovative glassmaker named Jacob Rosenthal was the genius who developed the formula for this deep caramel or cafe-au-lait colored glass, which has shadings of creamy tan or lighter swirls in darker brown. Sometimes this type of glass is also called *caramel slag.*

Chocolate glass was introduced by the Indiana Tumbler and Goblet Company of Greentown, Indiana in late 1900 and was extensively produced there, especially in the patterns called *Cactus* and *Leaf Brackets.* Several other Greentown patterns and animal covered dishes and novelty pieces also can be found in chocolate.

In 1902 Rosenthal sold his formula for chocolate glass to the National Glass Company, of which Greentown was a member, and shortly other members of National also were making pieces in this color. Until National was disbanded in 1904, some twenty-two glass patterns and about a dozen individual pieces like bowls and pitchers were made in chocolate by member factories.

About 1907 or 1908 Rosenthal, who was then with the Fenton Art Glass Company, introduced chocolate glass production at that factory. It was

Fig. 13-16 One of the most famous pieces made in chocolate glass is the "Dolphin" covered dish made by the Indiana Tumbler and Goblet Company of Greentown, Indiana. Courtesy of James Measell.

made by Fenton in its *Water Lily and Cattails* and *Orange Tree* patterns, as well as a few other pieces. Its production of chocolate glass seems to have ended by about 1912, and this dark, rich glassware faded from the marketplace.

All pieces in chocolate glass are collectible, but some show up quite frequently while others are extremely rare. Common smaller pieces like sauce dishes can be found in the $35 to $50 range. Most bowls, tumblers, and other abundant items fall into the $75 to $100 range. Rarities like some cruets, large pitchers, syrup jugs, large covered compotes, and covered animal dishes cost in the $200 to $400 realm, with some close to $500 or more.

As with custard glass, some pieces in chocolate have been reproduced, but generally the color, when compared to the old, is poor—either very pale or very dark. The St. Clair Glass Works reproduced the salt dip and salt and pepper shakers in the

Cactus pattern, but the beading around the leaves on these copies is blurry and runs together. Today Mosser Glass makes several pieces in a chocolate color.

St. Clair also reproduced the famous Greentown *Dolphin* covered dish. The reproduction has a pleated or sawtooth band between the sides of the dolphin's jaws. To distinguish these copies from the originals look at the little fish finials on the covers: these are much fatter or thicker on the new pieces. Also, count the number of teeth on the sawtooth bands: the old pieces have ten on each side, but the St. Clair copy has nine on one side and ten on the other. Fortunately, too, most of the St. Clair pieces are marked clearly with the name "Joe St. Clair."

The *Robin with Berry* covered dish, which Greentown made in colors and chocolate, was reproduced in colors by the L. G. Wright Glass Company, and the Crystal Art Glass Company also made it in colors and in chocolate. Their copy has the bird on a vertically split-rib base different from the original base, and the berry in the bird's mouth is too smooth.

St. Clair also made this dish on the split-rib base, and the detailing on the bird's feathers is very poor when compared to the original. "Lamb" and "Turkey" covered dishes were made by Crystal Art Glass in chocolate also.

The Greentown "Sheaf of Wheat" and "Witch Head" figural toothpick holders also were repro-

duced by St. Clair, and these pieces are harder to tell from the old ones, so caution is necessary.

Probably the best discussion of chocolate glass is in James Measell's book *Greentown Glass: The Indian Tumbler and Goblet Company* published in 1979 by Grand Rapids, Michigan, Public Museum and the Grand Rapids Museum Association. Also very helpful is *A Guide to Reproductions of Greentown Glass* by Brenda and James Measell, published by the Homestead Press of Tulsa, Oklahoma, in 1974.

Carnival Glass

Book after book has been written on this specialized decorative glass since its rebirth of popularity in the 1960s, so only highlights can be given in these pages.

Most carnival glass seen today was produced in the first two decades of this century. It was manufactured by spraying metallic salts on hot, just-pressed pieces of glass and reheating them to produce the characteristic shiny metallic finish. The

idea was to imitate, in a cheaper line of glass, the lovely iridescent finishes developed by Louis Comfort Tiffany in his Favrile art glass. Carnival, in fact, is sometimes referred to as the "poor man's Tiffany." Originally carnival was marketed by descriptions like golden iridescent glassware or Venetian art iridescent ware.

The name "carnival" came from the belief that when carnival glass dropped in popularity, boxcar

Fig. 13-17 On the left is a milk pitcher in marigold carnival glass in Imperial's *Windmill* or *Windmill Medallion* pattern. On the right is a blue individual-size creamer in Fenton's *Orange Tree* pattern.

loads of stock were sold off cheaply and used as give-aways at traveling carnivals and amusement parks. So far there is no hard evidence to prove that this was the case, but the name remains in common use.

Produced in dozens and dozens of pressed patterns, carnival glass was made in many different colors, especially blues, greens, purples, and a flash-on-clear golden orange hue called *marigold,* which is the most common color. One of these base colors was sprayed with the finish, which gave the piece a metallic silvery or golden shine with the base color showing through. The color of a carnival glass piece refers to the base color of the glass itself, not the finish. The earliest patterns in carnival usually were produced in deep, dark colors, but later, soft pastel shades with a lighter coating of iridescence were made, and these pastel shades are especially desirable in today's market.

Nearly every major American glasshouse of the early twentieth century made carnival, but it was introduced by the Fenton Art Glass Company of Williamstown, West Virginia, in late 1907.

Northwood, famous for so many lines of glass, in 1909 brought out his carnival lines, which he called Parisian art ware, and a huge volume in a wide range of patterns was made at his factory until it closed in 1925.

In 1910 the Imperial Glass Company added a

Fig. 13-19 Another Northwood carnival design, this is a nut bowl in green in the *Leaf and Beads* pattern.

carnival finish to many of its Nucut pressed patterns, a great many with imitation cut-glass designs, and carnival was in its line-up into the 1920s. In fact, in 1925 it produced one of its most famous carnival pieces, the ''Homestead'' plate, which features a landscape scene in the center.

Other companies that made some patterns or a variety of novelty pieces in carnival glass include the Westmoreland Specialty Company of Grapeville, Pennsylvania, which had some carnival glass in its line as early as 1908 but phased it out about 1912. It made approxmately thirty items in carnival.

The short-lived Millersburg Glass Company of Millersburg, Ohio, also made some noteworthy contributions to carnival glass. It made a very fine quality of carnival glass and produced some handsome pattern lines as well as such rarities as the ''People's'' vase (featuring raised figures of dancing peasants), the ''Millersburg Courthouse'' bowl (a souvenir piece), and the ''Morning Glory'' pattern pitcher. The company apparently became overextended and had to file for bankruptcy in 1911, which ended all production at that factory.

Thomas Dugan, who had worked with Northwood at his Indiana, Pennsylvania, plant while it was part of the National Glass Company, finally bought that plant after National disbanded in 1904 and Northwood had gone off to start another glass factory. It became the Dugan Glass Company and introduced carnival glass in 1910. In 1913, after Dugan was no longer involved there, the firm became the Diamond Glass-Ware Company, and Dia-

Fig. 13-18 On the left is a blue dish in Fenton's carnival *Pine Cone* pattern, and beside it stands Northwood's "Beauty Bud" vase in amethyst.

Fig. 13-20 There were several grape patterns in carnival glass. This 8" d. marigold colored bowl is in Imperial's *Grape* pattern.

Fig. 13-21 The Dugan factory produced this *Leaf Rays* pattern nappy in a marigold opalescent hue of carnival glass.

mond also apparently continued production of carnival.

The many patterns of carnival glass feature varied design motifs, including geometric, imitation cut glass, flower, fruit, bird, animal, and even fish patterns. Most carnival patterns were produced in shapes such as bowls, small compotes, vases, punch sets, and water sets, and such pieces are still abundant. Pieces such as plates, mugs, cruets, wine decanters, and wine glasses are much scarcer.

Some patterns were made in only one or two forms, such as a vase, compote, or water set. Clusters of grapes and peacocks in garden settings are featured on a variety of commoner carnival patterns. Remember that patterns decorated in carnival were also produced in plain colors and clear, as well as some in custard glass, which was popular at the same time.

By the 1920s many of the early, ornate carnival patterns were fading out, and the pastel hues became more popular, along with the more lightly iridized glass today called *stretch glass*. The orangy and amber marigold color continued in production for the longest time, and it shows up on patterns of the late 1920s and 1930s like *Iris* (also known as *Iris and Herringbone*), which saw production as late as the 1950s and 1970s. The *Floragold* line with its shiny marigold finish also was produced in the 1950s, but production of the handsome deeply molded patterns in shades of blue, green, and purple had long since ceased.

Carnival glass became popular worldwide, and a limited number of pieces and patterns were made in England and elsewhere in Europe. In addition, some distinctive designs were produced in far-off Australia, many of which feature birds and animals native to that continent. They are especially unusual and desirable pieces for collections.

Carnival reproductions have abounded for years. In fact, the Imperial Glass Company first remade some carnival in the early 1960s, just about the time glass collectors were rediscovering the old wares. Imperial continued to manufacture some fine-quality reproductions (or reissues) during the rest of its operation but, fortunately, began to mark most pieces with its "IG" logo mark. The Westmoreland Glass Company also reproduced old carnival patterns, but these also often carry its "WG" logo mark. A number of unmarked carnival items was made by Fenton Art Glass for distributors such as the L. G. Wright Glass Company and the Levay Company. Several other smaller firms also reissued carnival pieces, but these items usually are marked clearly.

One appealing aspect of carnival glass collecting is that there is a huge variety of pieces to choose from in a wide range of prices. Common smaller pieces, especially in marigold, can be found in the $20 to $40 range, and a great many attractive bowls and vases in various colors are available in the $50 to $100 range. Better and scarcer patterns and colors may fall in the realm of $100 to $200, and super-rarities may bring from $1,000 to $6,000 or more. Certain colors may be rare in a pattern that is otherwise common. For instance, in the *Butterfly and Berry* pattern by Fenton, a marigold creamer may run about $40, but that same piece in other colors will cost about $100. In addition to base color quality, the quality of the iridescent finish is an important factor that sophisticated carnival collectors consider.

Carnival glass offers a wonderful world of opportunity for glass collectors. It is a field full of enthusiastic collectors eager to share their knowledge and expertise.

CHAPTER 14

Special Glass Companies

Although there were dozens of noteworthy American glass manufacturers in the late nineteenth century, three special firms are deserving of some extra coverage, since their products offer singular collecting opportunities. Each has a cadre of dedicated collectors seeking examples of their diverse glass products.

Iowa City Flint Glass Manufacturing Company

This small glass factory is noteworthy not only for the brevity of its existence; Iowa City Flint Glass Manufacturing Company was one of the most westerly nineteenth-century glass plants that produced pattern glass tableware.

The company was organized in the small eastern Iowa town of Iowa City in 1880, but production there did not commence until spring 1881. By summer 1882 the plant was closed down, and glass production ceased. Even in that very short span of time, Iowa City turned out an interesting and varied selection of pressed-glass patterns and pieces.

Even though a boxcar full of glass reportedly was produced at the plant each day, the glassware that can be attributed to Iowa City is quite scarce and relatively expensive today. Thanks to an early hand-drawn pattern book, possibly used by a factory salesperson, and the research of Miriam Righter, we do have a good idea of exactly what patterns and pieces can be attributed with certainty to Iowa City.

Iowa City is justly famous for the pieces featuring animals and birds. Probably best known in this range is a series of motto plates, each with a different scene at its center. These include: "Be Gentle," with a lamb in the center; "Be Affectionate," with a cow and calf scene; "Be True," with a dog; "Be Playful," with a kitten; and "Be Industrious," with

a beehive. The last of this group, often called the "Elaine" plate, shows a young girl in the center. According to the sketchbook, this piece was to carry the motto "Be Virtuous," but the wording was never added to the mold.

Plates, platters, and bowls featuring *Frosted Stork* and *Frosted Crane* scenes in their centers are also well-known Iowa City pieces. Several types were made with different border designs. Some have plain, unpatterned borders, others feature swimming swan or standing deer vignettes and still others have a border sometimes called oval and bar or "one-o-one."

A rare group of goblets also was made at Iowa City. Several feature figures of animals, including *Deer, Elephant,* and the especially rare *Cat—Rabbit—Horse* goblet with three animals. The related *Sage* pattern features a leafy bush.

Only a couple of tableware patterns with a wide range of pieces can be attributed to Iowa City. One features a band of tall triangles somewhat resembling teepees, so early glass researchers called it *Teepee* or *Wigwam*. The name used by the company is *Alhambra*. The second pattern, *Melon and Leaf,* has pieces with plain, rounded bodies raised on a low, domed foot. The foot is molded with four broad, scrolled, stippled leaves, and the covers on pieces feature a figural melon finial.

Iowa City glass was made only in clear and clear with frosted details, and although the glass quality is not comparable to the best pieces from larger factories, its scarcity has insured a ready market. Most pieces will be priced in the $50 to $100 range, and rare pieces like the animal goblets can sell for several hundred dollars. It is a challenge to find pieces of Iowa City glass, but there is always the chance of turning up a sleeper.

The only reference book on this factory is the short *Iowa City Glass* by Miriam Righter, which gives a thorough history of the company and illus-

Fig. 14-1 The Iowa City "Elaine" 10" d. plate with an oval and bar or one-o-one pattern border.

trates its various products. It was published in 1981 by J. W. Carberry of Iowa City.

Indiana Tumbler and Goblet Company

The discovery of abundant local natural gas brought glassmaking to this little Indiana town. Between 1894 and 1903, when the factory was destroyed by fire, a remarkable variety of Greentown glass was made there, with a couple of distinctive lines approaching art glass quality.

Today Greentown products are collected widely because of the interesting variety of patterns, pieces, and colors issued, many produced only at that plant. In 1899 the owners decided to join the new National Glass Company, and after the factory fire some of their patterns were continued at other National factories.

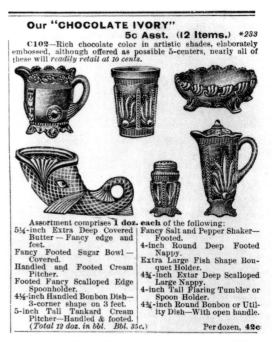

Fig. 14-3 This Butler Brothers catalog ad from spring 1902 shows a grouping of Greentown chocolate glass pieces. In the top row, left to right, are a *Dewey* pattern creamer, a *Cactus* tumbler, and a *Leaf Brackets* sauce dish. In the bottom row, left to right, are the famous "Dolphin" dish, a shaker and covered pitcher in the *Cactus* pattern. Courtesy of the Rakow Library of the Corning Museum of Glass.

Fig. 14-2 A goblet in Iowa City's *Alhambra* pattern of tableware.

Among the most famous and collectible of Greentown tableware lines are *Shuttle* (no. 29), *Austrian* (no. 200), *Dewey* (named for Admiral Dewey), *Herringbone Buttress* (no. 140), *Teardrop and Tassel* (supposedly its *Sampson* pattern), *Cord Drapery* (no. 350), *Beaded Panel,* and *Cactus* (no. 375). Recent research indicates a no. 11 pattern was a simple Diamond and Double Fan, and there are a few pieces very similar to *Champion* by McKee. Several others exist, but these are the best known and most widely available. All were made in clear and may also be found in lovely shades of amber, teal blue, cobalt blue, emerald green, or canary. Another special color made only at Greentown and used on only a limited number of pieces is called *Nile green.* It is a milky pale chartreuse that often is marbleized with an effect similar to slag glass. It is very rare and pieces bring premium prices.

Chocolate glass, as discussed, was another major innovation from the Greentown factory, and several of the above-mentioned patterns and other novelties were made in this line.

Greentown is also well known for a group of interesting novelty items and figural dishes it alone manufactured. Several oval-based dishes with figural animal covers came from Greentown and include the "Hen," "Rabbit," "Bird with Berry" and "Fighting Cocks," while the "Cat on Hamper" can be found with tall or low square, flared basket bases with a cat head cover finial. The most famous animal dish, the "Dolphin," is in the form of a wide-mouthed dolphin with a small figural fish finial on the domed cover. The company's line included some mugs and steins as well as several figural novelties including the "Connecticut Skillet," "Mitted Hand" dish, "Scotch Thistle," and "Hairbrush."

One scarce covered dish with a ribbed base comes with a figural cover featuring the bust portrait of Admiral Dewey. A figural "Buffalo" paperweight, mentioned earlier, was issued at the time of the 1901 Pan-American Exposition in Buffalo, New York. Greentown also had a figural "Corn" vase, with an ear of corn raised on a slender pedestaled base, and with leaves flared outward around the rim. It is completely different from and less realistic looking than the better-known Northwood Corn vase.

Greentown also came out with a group of interesting pitchers featuring animal portraits. Its "Squirrel" pitcher shows a running squirrel on a tree branch on one side, and a squirrel sitting up and eating a nut on the other. The "Racing Deer and Doe" pitcher shows a standing doe on one side and a running stag on the other. Finally, the "Heron" pitcher features a long-necked bird reaching up to a leafy branch on one side, while on the other the bird reaches down to the water in which it stands. All three of these pieces are known to exist in clear and chocolate glass.

Greentown's greatest glory probably stems from the production of a lovely art glass line developed for it by Jacob Rosenthal, the man also responsible for chocolate glass. In 1902 Rosenthal originated the formula for his *Golden Agate* glass, which is today more commonly known as *Holly Amber.* Introduced in late 1902, the line was produced only for a few months in 1903 before the Greentown factory burned. This helps explain its great rarity today.

Pattern pieces feature a band of holly leaves and berries around the center, with bands of small beads trimming the rounded border bands at the top and base of pieces. The base glass is deep amber, with the raised areas in a milky white swirled color. The process for making the glass still is not known, and after the factory burned it was never made again.

Since it was made for such a limited period, the forty or so different pieces in this line are all rare

Fig. 14-4 The scarce *Fighting Cocks* covered dish by Greentown. Courtesy of James Measell.

Fig. 14-5 On the left is a reproduction *Holly Amber* tall mug in a reddish glass totally unlike the old piece, as can be seen in the authentic *Holly Amber* mug on the right.

and expensive, and most examples sell in the $400 to $800 each. The *Holly* pattern also was made in plain clear glass, and though it is scarce it is not nearly as expensive as Holly Amber. A few unusual pieces of Holly are known in other colors, but clear and amber pieces are most common today.

Not many pieces in the various Greentown tableware patterns have been reproduced. Already discussed was the Dewey pattern butter dish made by Imperial. The Cactus pattern also has been reproduced by Fenton in opalescent colors, but it never was made in these at Greentown. Also, some pieces of Cactus in chocolate glass, which were discussed with that glass, have been made. A Fleur-de-Lis pattern tumbler in chocolate glass also has been copied, and several pieces of Holly Amber have been reproduced in various colors and in chocolate glass. With a little study one should be able to distinguish these from the old pieces.

Many of the Greentown novelties have been copied in recent years, including the ''Trunk,'' the ''Dustpan,'' and the ''Connecticut Skillet.'' The authentic skillet has been found only in clear, choco-

late, and Nile green, but it has been copied in several colors. The major Greentown animal dishes have been reproduced including ''Rabbit,'' ''Bird with Berry,'' and ''Dolphin,'' but, again, a little study soon will reveal what to watch for in copies. ''Witch Head,'' ''Dog Head,'' and ''Sheaf of Wheat'' toothpick holders also have been copied, and some of the copies are marked by the glassmaker.

Several books on Greentown and its products, have been issued recently. The late Ruth Herrick wrote and published *Greentown Glass: The Indiana Tumbler and Goblet Company and Allied Manufacturers* in 1959. This pioneering book was followed by updated and expanded works by James Measell. His *Greentown Glass: The Indiana Tumbler and Goblet Company* was published in 1979 by the Grand Rapids, Michigan, Public Museum and the Grand Rapids Museum Association. *A Guide to Reproductions of Greentown Glass* by Brenda and James Measell was published in 1974 by the Homestead Press of Tulsa, Oklahoma. All are worthwhile additions to the collector's reference library.

Northwood Glass Companies

The last group of American glass factories to be discussed here was operated by the noteworthy glassmaker Harry Northwood, already mentioned numerous times. From the late 1880s through the opening decades of this century, Northwood had important factories in Ohio, Pennsylvania, and West Virginia. Each factory produced special and lovely glassware that is much sought today.

Northwood was born in England in 1860, the son of John Northwood I, a leading English glass artisan especially noted for his exquisite cameo glass work. Young Harry was, then, brought up in the glass business, and it is not surprising that he decided to follow glassmaking as a career.

At age 21 Northwood immigrated to the fertile fields of American glassmaking. He arrived in the United States in 1881 and began his career with Hobbs, Brockunier and Company of Wheeling, West Virginia, as a glass etcher. He soon garnered reknown in glassmaking circles as a skilled artisan. In early 1884 Northwood moved on to the La Belle Glass Company of Bridgeport, Ohio, and he worked there, and briefly for a couple of other glass firms, until 1887. By 1887 he became manager of the La Belle company, and when fire completely destroyed the plant that year, he struck out on his own.

In late 1887 he founded his first glass company in a building in Martins Ferry, Ohio, formerly owned by the Union Flint Glass Works. Production at this factory began in 1888, launching Northwood's career as a great innovator in American glass production. Many patterns of decorative mold-blown colored and opalescent glass were made by the Northwood company, including patterns for tableware and lamps. Among the best-known colored lines from Martins Ferry are *Coin Spot, Ribbed Opal Lattice, Chrysanthemum Swirl, Ribbed Pillar (Northwood Pleat), Jewel (Threaded Swirl), Parian Swirl, Royal Ivy, Royal Oak,* and *Leaf Umbrella.*

For various reasons Northwood left Martins Ferry in early 1892 and set up his next glassworks in Ellwood City, Pennsylvania, where he built a new glass plant.

His new works in Ellwood City produced some of the same patterns that had been made in Ohio, especially his opalescent lines, to which he added the popular *Daisy and Fern* pattern in 1895. He also made a variety of opalescent novelties and colored opaque pieces such as salt shakers and syrup jugs. However, financial troubles at the factory led to Northwood's departure in 1895, and shortly thereafter the Ellwood City factory closed.

Moving to Indiana, Pennsylvania, Northwood set up shop at the former site of the Indiana Glass Company (1892–1893) and formed his next company, the Northwood Glass Manufacturing Company. This operation was his most financially successful and produced some of his most famous glassware.

New lines of mold-blown opal (milk white) glass became leading products at the Indiana, Pennsylvania, factory, and patterns including *Apple Blossom, Panelled Sprig,* and *Netted Oak* were introduced. In the late 1890s Northwood introduced his Gold Rush patterns, *Klondyke* and *Alaska,* made in opalescent glass. Many other opalescent novelties also were produced then. Cased (layered) glass lines like *Quilted Phlox* and *Grape and Leaf* also were brought out by Northwood, and, of course, his famous ivory (custard) glass took the market by storm in the late 1890s.

In November 1899 Northwood Glass joined the new National Glass Company. Harry Northwood did not feel he could stay with the factory under the combine's control, so he decided to take his family and return to England where he managed the National Glass Company's London showroom and office.

Fig. 14-6 This water set is in the *Cherry and Lattice* pattern, one of Northwood's early-twentieth-century designs. The pieces feature cranberry-stained cherries and gold leaves and trim.

Finally, in 1902 Northwood and his family returned for good to the United States where Northwood started his last glassworks. This time he took over the old Hobbs, Brockunier and Company factory in Wheeling, West Virginia, and this plant continued to produce quality glassware under his supervision until his death in 1919. At this factory, circa 1906, Northwood introduced his famous *N* in a circle trademark found on so many of his pressed patterns. Colorful patterns like *Regent, Leaf Medallion, Peach, Jewel and Flower, Panelled Holly, Sunburst on Shield, Cherry and Lattice,* and *Cherry and Cable* came from this factory in rich, dark shades or with bright gilt or color trim. Also in Wheeling, Northwood in 1908 began producing carnival glass, which became for several years a major portion of the factory's output.

Northwood is also known to have produced, along with several other companies, a decorated glassware today called *Goofus glass*. In this glass the relief designs are painted, usually on the back, with bright paint, most often gold shading to red, or red and green on gold.

After Northwood's death the factory carried on for some years, but finally the end came in late 1925. With the closing of the last Northwood factory, an important era in pressed and mold-blown glass production came to the end. The era probably will never be rivalled in the quality, innovation, and beauty of its glassware for the American table.

CHAPTER 15

Collecting and Caring for Pressed Glass

Collecting

There are many ways to collect pressed glass, or any other antique for that matter. Very often a collection begins with a family heirloom or two. This personal connection with the past can make seeking out other pieces very gratifying.

Many times, while collecting one special pattern, collectors discover others that they also like, thus broadening their collecting interests. For those who must be more selective many options exist, including collecting only specific pieces (such as goblets or toothpick holders), collecting by color, or collecting by theme (such as goblets with birds or flowers). Other options are to look for pieces from a certain era, such as the 1850s or 1870s, or even narrowing a collection to pieces made by a single

Fig. 15-1 A *Dakota* pattern tumbler engraved with the name "Jack." I bought this piece because my grandfather's nickname was Jack and his family settled in North Dakota—a nice family tie-in.

Fig. 15-2 An early mold-blown scroll flask and fragments of a similar flask found during my house excavation work.

glass manufacturer. Most modern collectors try to collect all the pieces they can in a single pattern, but remember there is no solid evidence that Victorian families ever owned such large sets. An average Victorian family probably owned only a few pieces in any one pattern, such as a table set or water set, and most likely patterns were mixed and matched according to what was available locally.

Anyone fortunate enough to live in an old house might try to discover what pieces or patterns were used typically at the time the house was built. Sometimes this involves work in historical archaeology, something even an amateur can enjoy. This collecting option presented itself to me while I was restoring an 1828 stone miner's cottage. It was necessary to take up the flooring on the ground floor and excavate the debris. During this task I discovered a wealth of glass and pottery shards, buttons, thimbles, and other little mementos of the early residents of this humble cottage. I screened every shovelful of dirt I removed and soon had a fascinating collection of bits and pieces representing the life-styles of the home's owners during the past 150 years. Many of the chinaware and glass shards were large enough that I could identify the original patterns, and so I started searching for matching pieces. Among the glass fragments were pieces of an early mold-blown scroll flask and, even more exciting, several pieces of an early Heart pattern lacy cup plate. Today I have complete examples of these objects to display with the old fragments. Over the years the search for pieces and patterns to match my tray of shards has provided me with a new way of tying the past to the present.

Very often shards and debris turn up in and around older homes during restoration, and all these little pieces should be preserved and studied for the clues they provide as to how the past owners lived. There are, of course, very sophisticated methods of excavation used by trained historical archaeologists, but even the backyard gardener can help preserve the past by salvaging and cleaning up the little bits of detritus turned up during his labors. Who knows, it may lead to a whole new collecting interest!

Care and Display

Glass, although seemingly fragile, is surprisingly resilient and sturdy, as is proven by the survival of objects from ancient Rome, which have come down to us in relatively undamaged condition.

A great deal of American pressed glass from the past 160 years is still around. This is really quite remarkable considering the hard use it probably underwent in its early life, and it proves that with a little care the glass can survive intact for another one hundred years or more.

All that pressed glass requires is some gentle cleaning once in a while. The biggest danger to its survival is exposure to extremes of heat or cold. In the average display case this is not a problem, but when washing pieces make sure the water temperature is lukewarm, not steamy hot. Of course, it is never wise to wash early glass in an automatic dishwasher. The extremely hot water certainly could cause it to crack or shatter, and the shaking and rattling may lead to chipping. Just use a mild soap or detergent and add a bit of vinegar to the washing solution, as it adds sparkle when the pieces are dried.

Although some people like to display glass pieces on a window sill or window shelves, there is some danger in this. Old pressed glass left in a sunny window for years very likely may start to discolor and develop a slight purple hue due to the chemical reaction of the magnesium in the glass and the unscreened sunlight. The sun-colored effect is not desirable for those seeking crystal clear examples, as most people do. Today there are materials that can be applied to window glass to screen out damaging ultraviolet rays. This is an especially good idea if you have many antique furnishings in your home, since sunlight is very damaging to all textiles and furniture.

The other danger of displaying glass in a window is exposing it to extreme temperatures. Remember that the window pane will amplify the heat of the sun, and a piece of glass may suddenly develop a crack, even though it was carefully annealed when first produced. Pieces of free-blown and mold-blown glass are especially susceptible to this danger, a blown piece may shatter suddenly while sitting in a hot, sunny spot.

Glass sitting in a very cold window during the winter can also be in danger, especially if it suddenly is warmed when the furnace kicks on or as the sunlight pours in on a frigid winter morning. A piece of glass packed up and left in a very cold area, like the trunk of a car, should not be unpacked for several hours if it is taken into a heated home. Wait until the packaging heats up to room temperature. Again, cold pieces of glass suddenly exposed to warm air have been known to crack or shatter right before the owner's eyes.

Glass of any type looks wonderful in a lighted cabinet. The heat from the bulbs should not be a problem as long as pieces are not placed too close to them. Plate glass shelving usually is preferred in such cabinets so that the light can diffuse through all the pieces. Keep in mind, of course, that this shelving must be well supported and sturdy enough to hold all the weight of the glassware displayed on it. A row of goblets can be surprisingly heavy, and, of course, early flint glass is especially weighty. Make sure your glass shelves will hold up under the strain. Quarter-inch or thicker shelving is appropriate, especially for longer spans of shelving.

Sometimes a collector comes across a piece of antique glass, most often a decanter or vase, that appears to be very discolored inside the base. Occasionally this is just accumulated dirt and can be washed or scrubbed off. Some people even suggest filling the piece with water and dropping in a foaming denture tablet or two. Leave this mixture in a piece for at least twenty-four hours; in some instances, this helps remove sediment.

However, quite often the glass will be "sick"—that is, having discoloration caused by an actual chemical degeneration in the surface—and little can be done to correct this. Most often this "sickness" is caused by water or liquor left standing in a piece month after month and year after year. Remember: always clean out a bowl, vase, or de-

canter as soon as possible after use and let it dry completely.

This is especially crucial with old decanters, because moisture left inside can cause *vapor lock* should the stopper be replaced. This happens because the moisture inside continues to evaporate and tries to escape around the tight stopper, causing a vapor seal to form, not unlike what happens in a pressure cooker. Unfortunately, breaking this lock can be very difficult if not impossible without damaging the pieces. Try warming the neck of such a sealed decanter with your hands, since this little change of temperature sometimes loosens the bond. Running lukewarm water on the neck also may work sometimes. It is probably best to let a washed decanter dry for a few days before replacing the stopper. Try dropping a facial tissue inside to act as a moisture absorber, but make sure it can be retrieved with ease. Remember: if there is any dampness in a decanter after cleaning, do not replace the stopper. If a piece is "sick" its appearance can sometimes be improved by applying a thin coating of mineral oil inside. It is not a permanent cure, but it may make the piece look better for display.

Recently another factor regarding the use of old decanters has come to light. Scientific research confirms that old flint glass and lead crystal decanters can leach small traces of lead when left filled with liquor for a long period of time. Although it probably would take many years for this leaching to produce dangerous lead levels in the liquid, it is best not to leave one's stock of bourbon or sherry in a lovely old decanter, even though it makes a handsome display. It should be perfectly safe to use the decanter for a dinner party and to serve drinks in old flint glass goblets or wines, but avoid leaving liquor in the decanter for months at a time.

Whatever type of glass one collects, there are many ways to use and display it. With a little care a collection will survive to inspire another generation of glass lovers.

Selected Reading

These listings cover major references on various types of early American glass and glass companies. Some titles may be out of print, but probably are available through larger area libraries.

General Information

Batty, Bob H. *A Complete Guide to Pressed Glass.* Gretna, La.: Pelican Publishing Co., 1978.

Brothers, J. Stanley, Jr. *Thumbnail Sketches.* Kalamazoo, Mich.: Self-published, 1940.

Gores, Stan. *1876 Centennial Collectibles and Price Guide.* Fond du Lac, Wisc.: The Haber Printing Co., 1974.

Heacock, William. *Encyclopedia of Victorian Colored Pattern Glass.* 9 vols. Marietta, Ohio: Antique Publications, 1976–1987.

Lechler, Doris Anderson. *Toy Glass.* Marietta, Ohio: Antique Publications, 1989.

McCain, Mollie Helen. *The Collector's Encyclopedia of Pattern Glass.* Paducah, Ky.: Collector Books, 1982, 1990.

Oliver, Elizabeth. *American Antique Glass: A Golden Guide.* New York: Golden Press, 1977.

Peterson, Arthur G. *Four Hundred Trademarks on Glass.* Stamford, Conn.: Jo-D Books, 1968, 1985.

———. *Glass Patents and Patterns.* Self-published, 1973.

Pullin, Anne Geffken. *Glass Signatures, Trademarks, and Trade Names, from the Seventeenth to the Twentieth Century.* Radnor, Pa.: Wallace-Homestead Book Co., 1986.

Shuman, John A., and Susan W. Shuman III. *"Lion" Pattern Glass.* Boston: Branden Press, 1977.

Spillman, Jane Shadel. *American and European Pressed Glass in the Corning Museum of Glass.* Corning, N.Y.: Corning Museum of Glass, 1981.

Unitt, Doris, and Peter Unitt. *American and Canadian Goblets.* Petersborough, Ontario: Clock House, 1970, 1974.

Welker, John, and Elizabeth Welker. *Pressed Glass in America, Encyclopedia of the First Hundred Years, 1825–1925.* Doylestown, Pa.: Antique Acres Press, 1985.

Types of Glass

Carnival Glass

Cosentino, Geraldine and Regina Steward. *Carnival Glass: A Guide for the Beginning Collector (A Golden Handbook of Collectibles).* New York: Golden Press, 1976.

Edwards, Bill. *Millersburg: The Queen of Carnival Glass.* Paducah, Ky.: Collector Books, 1975.

———. *The Standard Encyclopedia of Carnival Glass,* rev. 2d ed. Paducah, Ky.: Collector Books, 1988.

Greguire, Helen. *Carnival in Lights.* Self-published, 1975.

Hand, Sherman. *The Collectors' Encyclopedia of Carnival Glass.* Paducah, Ky.: Collector Books, 1978.

———. *Colors in Carnival.* 4 vols. Des Moines, Iowa: Wallace-Homestead Book Company, 1968–1974.

Hartung, Marion T. *Book of Carnival Glass.* 10 vols. Emporia, Kans.: Self-published, 1960–1973.

Klamkin, Marian. *The Collectors' Guide to Carnival Glass.* New York: Hawthorn Books, 1976.

Moore, Donald E. *The Shape of Things in Carnival Glass.* Self-published, 1974.

Notley, Raymond. *Carnival Glass.* Shire Album 104. London: Shire Publications, Ltd., 1983.

Olson, O. Joe. *God and Home: Carnival Glass Superstar.* Self-published, 1976.

Owens, Richard E. *Carnival Glass Tumblers.* Des

Moines, Iowa: Wallace-Homestead Book Co., 1978.

Presznick, Rose. *Carnival Glass.* 4 vols. Self-published, various years.

Reichel, Lloyd. *Modern Carnival Glass Collectors' Book I: 1971.* Self-published, 1971.

Taylor, Dorothy. *Encore by Dorothy.* 2 vols. Self-published, 1979.

Flint Pattern Glass

Barlow, Raymond E. and Joan E. Kaiser. *The Glass Industry in Sandwich.* Vol. 2. West Chester, Pa.: Schiffer Publishing Ltd. and Windham, N.H.: Barlow-Kaiser Publishing Co., 1989.

———. *The Glass Industry in Sandwich* Vol. 3. West Chester, Pa.: Schiffer Publishing Ltd. and Windham, N.H.: Barlow-Kaiser Publishing Co., 1987.

———. *The Glass Industry in Sandwich.* Vol. 4. Windham, N.H.: Barlow-Kaiser Publishing Co., 1983.

Barret, Richard Carter. *A Collector's Handbook of Blown and Pressed American Glass.* Manchester, Vt.: Forward's Color Productions, 1971.

Fauster, Carl U. *Libbey Glass Since 1818: Pictorial History and Collector's Guide.* Toledo, Ohio: Len Beach Press, 1979.

Florence, Gene. *The Collector's Encyclopedia of Depression Glass.* 9th rev. ed. Paducah, Ky.: Collector Books, 1990.

———. *Elegant Glassware of the Depression Era.* 4th rev. ed. Paducah, Ky.: Collector Books, 1991.

Hammond, Dorothy. *Confusing Collectibles: A Guide to the Identification of Contemporary Objects.* Des Moines, Iowa: Wallace-Homestead Book Co., 1969.

———. *More Confusing Collectibles.* Wichita, Kans.: C. B. P. Publishing Co., 1972.

Heacock, William. *Fenton Glass: The First Twenty-Five Years.* Marietta, Ohio: Antique Publications, 1978.

Jenks, Bill, and Jerry Luna. *Early American Pattern Glass, 1850–1910: Major Collectible Table Settings.* Radnor, Pa.: Wallace-Homestead Book Co., 1990.

Kamm, Minnie Watson. *Pattern Glass Pitchers.* 8 vols. Grosse Pointe, Mich.: Kamm Publications, 1939–1954.

Lee, Ruth Webb. *Antique Fakes and Reproduc-tions.* Wellesley Hills, Mass.: Lee Publications, 1938, 1950.

Metz, Alice Hulett. *Early American Pattern Glass.* Self-published, 1958.

———. *Much More Early American Pattern Glass.* Self-published, 1971.

M'Kee Victorian Glass: Five Complete Glass Catalogs from 1859/60 to 1871. Mineola, N.Y.: Dover Publications, Inc., 1981. Introductions by Lowell Innes and Jane Shadel Spillman.

Pappert, Emma. *The Illustrated Guide to American Glass.* New York: Hawthorn Books, 1972.

Pepper, Adeline. *The Glass Gaffers of New Jersey and Their Creations from 1739 to the Present.* New York: Charles Scribner's Sons, 1971.

Revi, Albert Christian. *American Pressed Glass and Figure Bottles.* New York and Nashville: Thomas Nelson, Inc., 1964, 1972.

Stout, Sandra McPhee. *The Complete Book of Mc-Kee Glass.* North Kansas City, Mo.: Trojan Press, 1972.

Van Tassel, Valentine. *American Glass.* New York: Gramercy Publishing Co., 1950.

Weatherman, Hazel Marie. *Colored Glassware of the Depression Era.* Vol. 1. Springfield, Mo.: Weatherman Glassbooks, 1974.

———. *Colored Glassware of the Depression Era.* Vol. 2. Springfield, Mo.: Weatherman Glassbooks, 1974.

———. *Fostoria: Its First Fifty Years.* Springfield, Mo.: Weatherman Glassbooks, 1972.

Lacy Glass

American Glass from the Pages of ANTIQUES. New York: Weathervane Books, 1974.

Innes, Lowell. *Pittsburgh Glass, 1797–1891: A History and Guide for Collectors.* Boston: Houghton Mifflin Co., 1976.

Lee, Ruth Webb. *Early American Pressed Glass.* Wellesley Hills, Mass.: Lee Publications, 1931, 1960; Rutland, Vt.: Charles E. Tuttle Co., Inc., 1985.

———. *Sandwich Glass: The History of the Boston and Sandwich Glass Company.* Wellesley Hills, Mass.: Lee Publications, 1939, 1947, 1966.

Lee, Ruth Webb, and James H. Rose. *American Glass Cup Plates.* Wellesley Hills, Mass.: Lee Publications, 1948, 1971; Rutland, Vt.: Charles E. Tuttle Co., Inc., 1985.

McKearin, George S., and Helen McKearin. *Amer-*

ican Glass. New York: Crown Publishers, 1941, 1948.

Neal, L. W., and Dorothy B. Neal. *Pressed Glass Salt Dishes of the Lacy Period, 1825–1850*. Philadelphia: Privately published, 1962.

Spillman, Jane Shadel. *The Knopf Collectors' Guide to American Antiques: Glass, Vols. 1 and 2*. New York: Alfred A. Knopf, Inc., 1982.

Watkins, Lura W. *Cambridge Glass, 1818–1888*. Boston: Marshall, Jones, and Co., 1930.

Wilson, Kenneth M. *New England Glass and Glassmaking*. New York: Thomas Y. Crowell Co., 1972.

Milk Glass

Belknap, E. McCamly. *Milk Glass*. New York: Crown Publishers, 1949.

Ferson, Regis F., and Mary F. Ferson. *Yesterday's Milk Glass Today*. Greenburg, Pa.: Chas. H. Henry Printing Co., 1981.

Grist, Everett. *Covered Animal Dishes*. Paducah, Ky.: Collector Books, 1988.

Heacock, William. *Fenton Glass: The First Twenty-Five Years*. Marietta, Ohio: O-Val Advertising Corp., 1978.

———. *Fenton Glass: The Second Twenty-Five Years*. Marietta, Ohio: O-Val Advertising Corp., 1980.

———. *Fenton Glass: The Third Twenty-Five Years*. Marietta, Ohio: O-Val Advertising Corp., 1989.

Kaye, Barbara Joyce. *White Gold: A Primer for Previously Unlisted Milk Glass*. Self-published, 1990.

Millard, S. T. *Opaque Glass*. Des Moines, Iowa: Wallace-Homestead Book Co., 1975.

Revi, Albert Christian. *American Pressed Glass and Figure Bottles*. New York: Thomas Nelson Inc., 1964.

Opalescent Glass

Godden, Geoffrey. *Antique Glass and China: A Guide for the Beginning Collector*. South Brunswick, N.J.: A. S. Barnes, 1967.

Hartung, Marion T. *Opalescent Pattern Glass*. Des Moines, Iowa: Wallace-Homestead Book Co., 1971.

Heacock, William. *Encyclopedia of Victorian Colored Pattern Glass*. Vol. 2. Marietta, Ohio: Antique Publications, 1976–1979.

Heacock, William, James Measell, and Berry Wiggins. *Harry Northwood: The Early Years, 1881–1900*. Marietta, Ohio: Antique Publications, 1990.

Manley, Cyril. *Decorative Victorian Glass*. New York: Van Nostrand Reinhold Co., 1981.

Specific Glass Companies

Cambridge Glass Company

Bennett, Arnold, and Judy Bennett. *The Cambridge Glass Book*. Des Moines, Iowa, Wallace-Homestead Book Co., 1970.

National Cambridge Glass Collectors, Inc. *Colors in Cambridge Glass*. Paducah, Ky.: Collector Books, 1984.

George Duncan and Sons—Duncan and Miller

Bones, Frances. *The Book of Duncan Glass*. Des Moines, Iowa: Wallace-Homestead Book Co., 1973.

Bredehoft, Neila M., George A. Fogg, and Francis C. Maloney. *Early Duncan Glassware: Geo. Duncan and Sons, 1876–1892*. Self-published, 1987.

Bredehoft, Neila, and Tom Bredehoft. *Victorian Novelties and Figurals: Geo. Duncan and Sons*. St. Louisville, Ohio: Cherry Hill Publications, 1989.

Krause, Gail. *The Encyclopedia of Duncan Glass*. Hicksville, N.Y.: Exposition Press, 1976.

Fenton Art Glass Company

Heacock, William. *Fenton Glass: The First Twenty-Five Years*. Marietta, Ohio: O-Val Advertising Corp., 1978.

———. *Fenton Glass: The Second Twenty-Five Years*. Marietta, Ohio: O-Val Advertising Corp., 1980.

———. *Fenton Glass: The Third Twenty-Five Years*. Marietta, Ohio: O-Val Advertising Corp., 1989.

Fostoria Glass Company

Fostoria Glass Company: Full Line Catalog (1901 Reprint). Paducah, Ky.: Collector Books, n.d.

Weatherman, Hazel Marie. *Fostoria: Its First Fifty Years*. Springfield, Mo.: Weatherman Glassbooks, 1972.

Heisey Glass Company

Bradley, Stephen H., Constance S. Ryan, and Robert R. Ryan. *Heisey Stemware*. Newark, Ohio: Spencer Walker Press, 1976.

Bredehoft, Neila. *The Collector's Encyclopedia of Heisey Glass, 1925–1938*. Paducah, Ky.: Collector Books, 1986.

Bredehoft, Neila, and Tom Bredehoft. *Handbook of Heisey Production Cuttings*. St. Louisville, Ohio: Cherry Hill Publications, 1991.

Conder, Lyle, ed. *Collector's Guide to Heisey's Glassware for Your Table*. Gas City, Ind.: L-W Book Sales, 1991.

Felt, Tom, and Bob O'Grady. *Heisey Candlesticks, Candelabra and Lamps*. Newark, Ohio: Heisey Collectors of America, 1984.

Heisey's Glassware: Catalogue No. 76. 1915. Reprint with added pages. Newark, Ohio: Heisey Collectors of America, 1982.

Heisey's Glassware: Pressed Ware Catalogue No. 109. Reprint. Gas City, Ind.: L-W Promotions, 1974.

Ream, Louise W., Neila Bredehoft, and Thomas Bredehoft. *Encyclopedia of Heisey Glassware*. Vol. 1, Etchings and Carvings. Newark, Ohio: Heisey Collectors of America, 1977.

Imperial Glass Company

Archer, Margaret, and Douglas Archer. *Imperial Glass Company: 1904–1938 Catalogs*. Reprints. Paducah, Ky.: Collector Books, 1978, 1990. Reprinted with the cooperation of the Imperial Glass Corporation, Belaire, Ohio.

Ross, Richard, and Wilma Ross. *Imperial Glass*. Des Moines, Iowa: Wallace-Homestead Book Co., 1971.

McKee Glass Company

Gross, Vicki, and Mike Gross. *That Collectible McKee in Color*. Self-published, 1973.

Stout, Sandra McPhee. *The Complete Book of McKee Glass*. North Kansas City, Mo.: Trojan Press, 1972.

Miscellaneous Glass Companies

Barnett, Jerry. *Paden City: The Color Company*. Self-published, 1978.

D. C. Jenkins Glass Co.: Pressed and Blown Glassware Catalog. Ca. 1930. Reprint. Greentown, Ind.: National Greentown Glass Association, 1984.

Heacock, William, and Fred Bickenheuser. *Encyclopedia of Victorian Colored Pattern Glass*. Vol. 5, U. S. Glass from A to Z. Marietta, Ohio: Antique Publications, 1978.

Heacock, William, James Measell, and Barry Wiggins. *Harry Northwood: The Early Years, 1881–1900*. Marietta, Ohio: Antique Publications, 1990.

———. *Harry Northwood: The Wheeling Years, 1900–1925*. Marietta, Ohio: Antique Publications, 1991.

Measell, James, and Don E. Smith. *Findlay Glass: The Glass Tableware Manufacturers, 1886–1902*. Marietta, Ohio: Antique Publications, 1986.

Miller, Everett R., and Addie R. Miller. *The New Martinsville Glass Story*. Vols. 1 and 2, 1920–1950. Marietta, Ohio: Richardson Publishing Co., 1972, 1975.

Pears, Thomas C. *Bakewell: Pears and Company Glass Catalogue*. Ca. 1875. Reprint. Pittsburgh, Pa.: Davis and Warde, 1977.

Pressed Glass Commemoratives and Novelties

Bredehoft, Neila, and Thomas Bredehoft. *Victorian Novelties and Figurals: Geo. Duncan and Sons*. St. Louisville, Ohio: Cherry Hill Publications, 1989.

Bredehoft, Neila, George A. Fogg, and Francis C. Maloney. *Early Duncan Glassware: Geo. Duncan and Sons, Pittsburgh, 1874–1892*. Self-published, 1987.

Florence, Gene. *Degenhart Glass and Paperweights: A Collector's Guide to Colors and Values*. Cambridge, Ohio: Degenhart Paperweight and Glass Museum, Inc., 1982.

Gores, Stan. *1876 Centennial Collectibles and Price Guide*. Fond du Lac, Wisc.: Haber Printing Co., 1974.

Heacock, William. *One Thousand Toothpick Holders: A Collector's Guide*. Marietta, Ohio: Antique Publications, 1977.

Lee, Ruth Webb. *Victorian Glass*. Rutland, Vt.: Charles E. Tuttle Co., Inc., 1944, 1985.

Lindsey, Bessie M. *American Historical Glass*. Rutland, Vt.: Charles E. Tuttle Co., Inc., 1967.

Measell, James, and Don E. Smith. *Findlay Glass: The Tableware Manufacturers, 1886–1902.* (Marietta, Ohio: Antique Publications, 1986).

Revi, Albert Christian. *American Pressed Glass and Figure Bottles.* New York: Thomas Nelson Inc., 1964.

Yalom, Libby. *Shoes of Glass.* Marietta, Ohio: Antique Publications, 1988.

Publications of Interest to Collectors

Antique Monthly, 2100 Powers Ferry Rd., Atlanta, GA 30339

Antique Review, 12 East Stafford Ave., Worthington, OH 43085

The Antique Trader Weekly, P.O. Box 1050, Dubuque, IA 52004

Antique Week, 27 N. Jefferson, Knightstown, IN 46148

Antiques and Collecting Hobbies, 1006 S. Michigan Ave., Chicago, IL 60605

Antiques and the Arts Weekly, 5 Church Hill Rd., Newtown, CT 06470

Collectors Journal, P.O. Box 601, Vinton, IA 52349

Collectors News, P.O. Box 156, Grundy Center, IA 50638

The Daze, Box 57, Otisville, MI 48463

Glass Collector's Digest, P.O. Box 553, Marietta, OH 45750

The Magazine Antiques, 575 Broadway, New York, NY 10012

Maine Antique Digest, P.O. Box 1429, Waldoboro, ME 04572

Mass Bay Antiques, P.O. Box 293, Danvers, MA 01923

New England Antiques Journal, 4 Church St., Ware, MA 01082

New York-Pennsylvania Collector, Drawer C, Fishers, NY 14453

Glass Collectors' Clubs

Types of Glass

Akro Agate

Akro Agate Art Association
Joseph Bourque
Box 758
Salem, NH 03079

Aladdin

Mystic Light of the Aladdin Knights
℅ J. W. Courter
Route 1
Simpson, IL 62985

Cambridge

National Cambridge Collectors
P.O. Box 416
Cambridge, OH 43725

Candlewick

National Candlewick Collector's Club
℅ Virginia R. Scott
275 Milledge Terrace
Athens, GA 30606

Carnival

American Carnival Glass Association
℅ Dennis Runk
P.O. Box 235
Littlestown, PA 17340

Collectible Carnival Glass Association
℅ Wilma Thurston
2360 N. Old S.R. 9
Columbus, IN 47203

Heart of America Carnival Glass Association
℅ C. Lucile Britt
3048 Tamarak Dr.
Manhattan, KS 66502

International Carnival Glass Association
℅ Lee Markley, Secretary
R.R. 1, Box 14
Mentone, IN 46539

New England Carnival Glass Club
℅ Eva Backer, Membership
12 Sherwood Rd.
West Hartford, CT 06117

Cut

American Cut Glass Association
1603 S.E. 19th, Suite 112
Edmond, OK 73013

Depression

National Depression Glass Association
P.O. Box 69843
Odessa, TX 79769

Duncan

National Duncan Glass Society
P.O. Box 965
Washington, PA 15301

Fenton

Fenton Art Glass Collectors
P.O. Box 384
Williamstown, WV 26187

National Fenton Glass Society
P.O. Box 4008
Marietta, OH 45750

Fostoria

The Fostoria Glass Society
P.O. Box 826
Moundsville, WV 26041

Fry

H. C. Fry Glass Society
P.O. Box 41
Beaver, PA 15009

Greentown

National Greentown Glass Association
℅ Jerry D. Garrett, Planner
1807 West Madison St.
Kokomo, IN 46901

Heisey
  Heisey Collectors of America
  P.O. Box 4367
  Newark, OH 43055

Imperial
  National Imperial Glass Collector's Society
  P.O. Box 534
  Bellaire, OH 43906

Milk Glass
  National Milk Glass Collectors
  % Kathy Mroz, Treasurer
  P.O. Box 402
  Northfield, MN 55057

Morgantown
  Old Morgantown Glass Collectors' Guild
  P.O. Box 894
  Morgantown, WV 26507

Stretch Glass
  Stretch Glass Society
  % Joanne Rodgers, President
  P.O. Box 770643
  Lakewood, OH 44107

Tiffin
  Tiffin Glass Collectors' Club
  P.O. Box 554
  Tiffin, OH 44883

Westmoreland
  National Westmoreland Glass Collectors' Club
  P.O. Box 372
  Export, PA 15632

Special Glass Items

Antique and Art Glass Salt Shaker Collectors'
Society
2832 Rapidan Trail
Maitland, FL 32751

Glass Knife Collectors' Club
P.O. Box 342
Los Alamitos, CA 90720

Marble Collectors' Society
P.O. Box 222
Trumbull, CT 06611

National Reamer Collectors
% Larry Branstad
Rt. 1, Box 200
Grantsburg, WI 54840

National Toothpick Holder Collectors' Society
% Joyce Ender, Membership
Red Arrow Hwy., P.O. Box 246
Sawyer, MI 49125

Pairpoint Cup Plate Collectors
P.O. Box 52D
East Weymouth, MA 02189

Paperweight Collectors Association
P.O. Box 468
Garden City Park, NY 11010

Perfume and Scent Bottle Collectors
% Jeanne Parris
2022 E. Charleston Blvd.
Las Vegas, NV 89104

General Glass Clubs

Glass Collectors Club of Toledo
2727 Middlesex Dr.
Toledo, OH 43606

Glass Museum Foundation
1157 N. Orange, Box 921
Redlands, CA 92373

Glass Research Society of New Jersey
Wheaton Village
Millville, NJ 08332

National Early American Glass Club
P.O. Box 8489
Silver Spring, MD 20907

Companies that Produced or Distributed Reproduction Pressed Glass

Most of the following firms have permanently marked at least a portion of the output that they have produced or distributed during the past fifty years.

A. A. Importing Company, St. Louis, Missouri

Boyd's Crystal Art Glass, Cambridge, Ohio

Crystal Art Glass Company, Cambridge, Ohio

Dalzell-Viking Glass Company (formerly Viking Glass), New Martinsville, West Virginia

Fenton Art Glass Company, Williamstown, West Virginia

Guernsey Glass Company, Cambridge, Ohio

Imperial Glass Company, Bellaire, Ohio

John E. Kemple Glass Works, Kenova, West Virginia

Kanawaha Glass, Dunbar, West Virginia

L.E. Smith Glass Company, Mount Pleasant, Pennsylvania

L. G. Wright Glass Company, New Martinsville, West Virginia

Levay Distributing Company, Edwardsville, Illinois

Mosser Glass, Cambridge, Ohio

Plum Glass Company, Pittsburgh, Pennsylvania

St. Clair Glass Works, Elwood, Indiana

Summit Art Glass Company, Mogadore, Ohio

Weisher Enterprises, Wheeling, West Virginia

Westmoreland Glass Company, Grapeville, Pennsylvania

Permanent Collections of American Glass

Many local and regional museums around the country have displays with some pressed glass included, but the following are especially noteworthy.

New England

Connecticut: Wadsworth Atheneum, Hartford.

Maine: Jones Gallery of Glass and Ceramics (June–October), Sebago; Portland Museum of Art, Portland.

Massachusetts: Old Sturbridge Village, Sturbridge; Sandwich Glass Museum (April–November), Sandwich.

New Hampshire: The Currier Gallery of Art, Manchester.

Vermont: Bennington Museum (March–November), Bennington.

Mid-Atlantic

Delaware: Henry Francis du Pont Winterthur Museum, Winterthur.

New Jersey: Museum of American Glass, Wheaton Village, Millville.

New York: Corning Museum of Glass, Corning; Cooper-Hewitt Museum, the Smithsonian Institution's National Museum of Design (by appointment), New York; Metropolitan Museum of Art, New York; New-York Historical Society, New York.

Pennsylvania: Historical Society of Western Pennsylvania, Pittsburgh; Philadelphia Museum of Art, Philadelphia; Westmoreland Glass Museum, Port Vue.

West Virginia: Huntington Galleries, Huntington; Oglebay Institute—Mansion Museum, Wheeling.

Southeast

Florida: Morse Gallery of Art (Tiffany glass), Winter Park.

Louisiana: New Orleans Museum of Art, New Orleans.

Tennessee: Houston Antique Museum, Chattanooga.

Virginia: Chrysler Museum at Norfolk, Norfolk.

Washington, D.C.: National Museum of American History, Smithsonian Institution.

Midwest

Indiana: Greentown Glass Museum, Greentown; Indiana Glass Museum, Dunkirk.

Michigan: Henry Ford Museum, Dearborn.

Minnesota: A. M. Chisholm Museum, Duluth.

Ohio: Cambridge Glass Museum, Cambridge; Milan Historical Museum, Milan; National Heisey Glass Museum, Newark; Toledo Museum of Art, Toledo.

Wisconsin: John Nelson Bergstrom Art Center and Mahler Glass Museum, Neenah.

Southwest and West

California: Los Angeles County Museum of Art, Los Angeles; Wine Museum of San Francisco and M. H. de Young Museum, San Francisco.

Texas: Mills Collection, Texas Christian University, Fort Worth.

Index